AI Marketing

AI Marketing

The Magic That Unites the World

Eliane Karsaklian

BEP

BUSINESS EXPERT PRESS

Leader in applied, concise business books

AI Marketing: The Magic That Unites the World

First published in 2025 by
Business Expert Press, LLC
222 East 46th Street, New York, NY 10017
www.businessexpertpress.com

ISBN-13: 978-1-63742-780-4 (paperback)
ISBN-13: 978-1-63742-781-1 (e-book)

Business Expert Press Marketing Collection

First edition: 2025

10 9 8 7 6 5 4 3 2 1

EU SAFETY REPRESENTATIVE
Mare Nostrum Group B.V.
Mauritskade 21D
1091 GC Amsterdam
The Netherlands
gpsr@mare-nostrum.co.uk

Description

Did you know that investors at Wall Street wait for the Groundhog Day's forecast to make their financial decisions? Did you know that your favorite **influencer** is not a real person? Did you know that your **smartphone** works like a magic wand? Don't you feel cursed without it? You will know all about it in this book.

Consumers just like you are looking for an effortless life, and technology is making it possible with self-driving and self-parking cars, smart houses, beds automatically adjusting to one's sleeping needs, and robot vacuuming homes all without human intervention while we share our personal **QR codes**.

Brands bring you magical solutions: Mr. Clean Magic Eraser, L'Oreal Magic Roots. And you can customize your life by magically creating your own world with the **metaverse** and the products you want with a 3D printer.

Technology and magic enclose mysteries that we cannot assess; we see the **input and the output**, but no one knows exactly what happens within the process.

Whether you are curious and confused about technology or a marketer without IT background expected to incorporate artificial intelligence (AI) in your **marketing strategies**, this book is for you.

Extensively documented with publications and empirical research, this book demonstrates **how brands use AI to entice customers**. It also discusses the use of AI as a competitive advantage for marketers and its deployment around the world.

Put some magic in your life!

Contents

Foreword

Foreword—"Do You Believe in Magic?"

So says the song in the Campbell's Soup advertisement, which shows how easy it is to prepare a great meal in little time and with little effort, just like with magic. Lucky Charms is *magically delicious*, Cirkul *adds some magic to your water*, L'Oréal's *Magic Roots* covers your grey roots in a few minutes, and Popeye's from Louisiana has *Ghost Pepper Wings*. These are just a few examples of countless brand names and tag lines evoking magic and mystery.

In a recent advertisement, IKEA portrays a family moving to a new house with their child picking items, including furniture, out of a blue IKEA plastic bag referencing the magic of Mary Poppins, while Sthil's tools clean your garden with *Fantasia Sorcerer's Apprentice's* song in the background. Meanwhile, Coca-Cola launched a brand new logo with the *Real Magic* advertising campaign featuring real, virtual, and international worlds by using video games as a tool to bring peace to the world thanks to the beverage's magical power of bringing people together (*one Coke away from each other*).

Marketers have used the word magic across industries to promote all product categories with the goal of showing how easy and effortless it is to get immediate benefits when using their products. Indeed, magic is the art of getting results[1], and from Mr. Clean Magic Eraser to Disney's Magic Kingdom, there is a broad array of products promising magical experiences and results, such as the new Google Pixel smartphone that can fix reality or Hyundai's Smaht Pahk remote self-parking car; "this is a ghost car" as stated in the advertisement. What was science fiction yesterday becomes a reality today as, for example, the first flying car (Alef Aeronautics), like James Bond's one, that has recently obtained approval from the Federal Aviation Administration and will be available for purchase in 2025.

We were raised with fairy tales, futuristic fiction, and magic, and it keeps fascinating and attracting adults, who still seek for magical solutions to solve their daily issues. We wish we could travel across time and space just with the power of our minds. As we can't do so physically, we use technology. Technology gives magical powers to products and by extension to consumers by immersing them in a virtual world.

We are drawn to magic mainly when life gets tough and when the scientific options don't seem to be powerful enough to come up with immediate solutions. Indeed, the use of magic has increased in several countries during the COVID-19 pandemic—Voodoo is back in Africa, and animal sacrifice has been practiced in Latin America. Still today, children with clear skin and Albinus are offered in sacrifice rituals in some African countries or are exterminated because they are believed to be the work of sorcery. We are also attracted to magic because of the mystery: we like what is unexplained and adventurous. We enjoy feeling fear when the threat is not close to us or is not real. Otherwise, the entertainment industry with its movies, TV series, and video games would be already dead. Everything is possible in entertainment as is in the magic world, and technology is making it look real. As technology becomes exponentially more powerful, and in an era where human attention span is limited to six seconds, where people don't read anything longer than one minute and never give their undivided attention to anything, only magical solutions with immediate results can grab their interest.

Indeed, according to one estimate, an average American is exposed to 34 gigabytes (around 12 hours) of information daily. With near constant stream of images, words, and sounds coming through smartphones, the internet, books, radio, television, email, and social media (Ranganath, 2024).

A Customized Life for Me

The search for a tailor-made life with customized clothes, shoes, cars, drinks, phones, and bodies rules customers' choices. While Botox is the magic of time traveling by making you look younger, with virtual reality (VR), you can visit the Roman Empire as well as travel to the future or other planets and, thanks to the immersive experience, feel as if you were really there. An immersive experience is all about illusion based on the human senses such as optical illusions. The human mind is shaped by its experiences, and right now, these are all immersive thanks to VR.

Companies promise to make the world a better place to live in by creating devices and services, which, just like magic, could solve all of consumers' problems with the goal of making them happy. Desires are emotional and propel us toward our goals and because happiness is transient, there is a constant need to add something new in our lives to renew the happiness that is often materialized by new purchases. It is an association between magic and illusion. Soon enough VR environments may overtake our physical world as the primary locus of our experience, which means that every aspect of our environment, and by extension of ourselves, will have been designed by someone else.

Magic gives power. When you do magic or use technology, you are in control. Technology enables TV on demand for you to pick what you want to watch when you want to watch it. You also need your phone to count your daily steps and work out and to regulate your bed in the right position. You need a Skyline smart house to open and close the windows, a MyQ to operate the garage door and a Townew trash can to replace the used trash bag with a new one without you. Moreover, under your remote command with a Ring doorbell with integrated camera, you can check outside when you are in and inside when you are away. Thanks to new devices, you can measure your own level of diabetes, which triggers an alarm on your phone, or your blood pressure, and your heartbeat at home even if your Oura connected ring monitors your health 24/7. Meanwhile, if you need to write a report, you have ChatGPT to come up with one fantastic write-up in a few seconds, while GoDaddy creates a website for you with artificial intelligence (AI), and LinkedIn rewrites your post with AI for you. If you are traveling, no need to carry your suitcase; your CowaRobot suitcase follows you around the airport.

We create a tailor-made reality where we want to live which is pretty much based on our own beliefs than in factual reality. In doing so, we refuse to adapt ourselves to reality while creating a world all to ourselves, which we only populate with people who think like us, and thanks to eugenics, we can also shape our future children's appearance. This is how we create a magical society based on beliefs and desires—a perfect world for ourselves. Thanks to this magical thinking, each individual has the power to create their own world, which multiplies the number of coexisting worlds on the same planet. These worlds are called communities (Karsaklian 2023)[2].

There are more similarities between magic and technology that one would imagine. You might not think that technology involves mystery, because you can't dissociate it from your life and yourself, and because it looks so rational and tangible. Nevertheless, technology, especially AI, is still a black box. Both magic and AI enclose mysteries that we cannot assess. In both cases, we see the input and the output, but no one knows exactly how the input is processed to be turned into that specific output.

But is AI intelligence? AI is attention and attention is needed for people to learn and memorize. AI is meant to work like a human brain. Better yet, because the machine/bot only critiques itself in views of improvement; there are no excuses, guilt, or shame. ChatGPT already knows more than humans do. However, memory is not intelligence, it is learning, and as stated by Rapaille,[3] learning involves emotions, and thus, people should be emotionally involved with the topic to learn about it. Now we say that machines can learn from data, which seems to be more assimilated with reasoning than with learning, which, by the way, is just a statistical model.

With the advancement of AI tools and technology, businesses can now automate content writing, creation, and curation, which are vital to any successful digital marketing campaign. AI content generation tools use algorithms and natural language processing techniques to create content. The algorithms can generate articles, product descriptions, and even the news. AI content creation tools aim to provide the same high-quality, unique, and engaging content that a human would.

One of the most significant advantages of using AI-generated content is the speed of content creation, whether it is long- or short-form content. With AI, businesses can generate hundreds of articles in minutes, which is impossible to achieve with human writers. Additionally, AI content generation can help companies save money and time they would otherwise spend on writing content ideas or hiring a team of content writers.

This book was thoroughly written without any use of AI! It is a pleasure to spend time thinking and writing about marketing. To supplement the literature and research findings, I had the privilege of interviewing three experts in AI.

The Magic of Expertise

I met **Professor Pinnaree Tea-makorn** when I was a visiting professor at Sasin School of Management in Bangkok, Thailand, in 2023. She teaches AI and reminded me that AI has been around for more than 40 years and that different people had different ideas about AI when it started. Before anything else, the main question we should ask ourselves *is what we'll do with AI?* Is it about cost cutting? Better and faster performance? Therefore, rather than jumping into it, it is necessary to perform a cost-benefit analysis to know if it is worth the investment.

She stressed the fact that to implement AI you need to have the right people to work on it. Human resources should hire those who can use AI to leverage the competitive advantage of the company. This will create the need for new positions and jobs in the company. However, AI is still a black box and you never know if the model will work, she argues. And if you bring the uncertainty from customer behavior to it, there will be a lack of accuracy. In addition, as a learning machine, it will learn from past experience or past data and might perpetuate some biases in the algorithms. For example, it might see that the company has hired more men for engineering positions in the past and continue eliminating female candidates.

Dr. Yele Adelakun is an associate professor of information systems at DePaul University in Chicago, Illinois, and had very kindly invited me to attend his DePaul Innovation Development Lab's annual conference in 2023: ODi'23 (Optimizing Digital Innovation) for which the theme was *Revolutionizing the Future with AI.*

During our conversation, Professor Adelakun stated that robots have several big advantages. For example, the police could fight criminality as needed without the risks of wounds or death to which humans are exposed (a kind of Robocop). Machines can also summarize a large amount of data, analyze them, and provide expert recommendations for decision making, for example, financial analytics. Yet, robots should not replace humans, but together they can be very powerful. For example, in Japan, pet robots are used as companions for seniors and isolated people.

AI today is like internet in the 2000s, he says: few people had access and today we are just useless without it. Tracking systems are better with AI, which can follow the whole supply chain from the beginning to the end. However, for a while, AI will increase the gap between developed and underdeveloped countries just as it happened with internet.

Some jobs and markets will perish, while others will emerge. For example, with self-driving cars, there will be no need for driver's licenses. Yet, *civilian developers* (anyone can create anything with AI) may be able to reach less sophisticated creations with AI with the basic access everyone can have to it, but when it comes to data accuracy leading to strategic decisions, qualified professionals are needed to avoid AI hallucination (when AI perceives patterns or objects that are nonexistent). This topic is more thoroughly discussed in Chapter 3.

Professor Adelakun states that generative AI is performant for descriptive analysis but not for prescriptive. Basically, it is all about data because AI is useless without data. AI should not take over humans because humans should always be in control and safety nets are needed. But, AI can provide a more structured and organized life. This can be easily done, thanks to eye, facial, voice, and fingerprint recognition.

I met **John Burkey** at the ID'23 conference in which he was a keynote speaker. He is CEO, CTO, and founder of Brighten.ai. I was surprised when he mentioned that machines could be culturally sensitive. During our interview, he stated that machines can have cultural sensitivity if humans provide the needed inputs for them to gather the data, analyze it, describe it, and make recommendations about the best use of culture in given situations. Humans need to feed the machine with accurate information. For instance, providing some personality traits and preferences in order to create customized offers to the clients.

By using the appropriate segmentation criteria (demographic, psychographic, geographic, etc.) the machine can perform a hyper segmentation of the markets and create a sharper targeted offer to one specific profile, which would give the idea of unicity to consumers by creating micro channels.

It would be fair to assume that a new trend is emerging. After decades of mass media and mass consumption, we are looking at micro channels to reach micro segments who certainly follow micro-influencers.

We went from turning a real person into a star (actors, singers, etc.) and using them as brands' celebrity endorsers, to creating personas with whom consumers would identify, to influencers with millions of followers to micro-influencers. In this context, the creation of digital influencers can reach even more targeted consumers by looking more like them and increasing the likelihood of personal identification. At the personal level, consumers can tailor-make the films, songs, or games they fancy rather than purchasing products created by others, states Burkey.

AI assumes that we are in a state of entropy and will give our lives some structure. At least to the data. AI organizes chaos by creating a more structured world and thus increases productivity by circumventing cognitive and social loads. In doing so, it accelerates the decision-making and creative processes because it is all based on data and statistical analysis rather than on personal opinions, which often lead to argumentations and counter-argumentations in a team. The amount of information processed in a very little time contributes to upscaling, with more work done in less time, less cost, and more accuracy. Thanks to AI, the innovation cycle will be shorter and better.

John Burkey illustrated our discussion with the following bot, which he kept updating as our conversation unfolded:

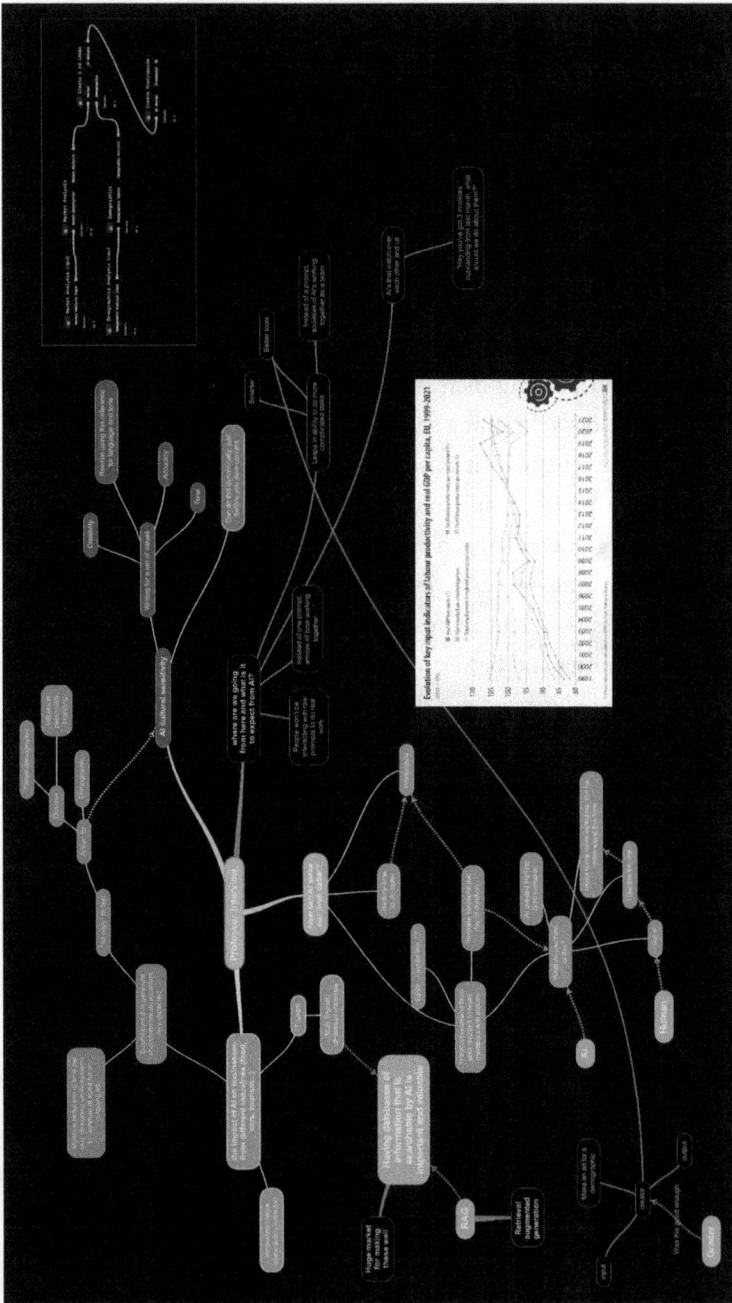

Acknowledgments

This book would not have been possible without the guidance of Professor Naresh Malhotra, to whom I am deeply grateful.

The quality of this book was enhanced thanks to the expertise of Professor Tea-makorn from Sasin School of Management, Professor Yele Adelakun, Director of the iD Lab at DePaul University, and the reputed AI professional John Burkey.

I can't thank you all enough for having shared your knowledge with me and, by extension, with our readers.

It has been magical getting to know you!

Introduction

One's real life is so often the life that one does not lead
———The Picture of Dorian Gray

The desire to change and improve our situation has been around forever. Magic and spell working have always been a part of the aim of improvement and still are. There are multicultural magical practices with their own rituals, symbols, and words of power. Indeed, magic exists around the world, but the practices differ depending on the culture. Anyone working in international business knows that culture matters. In addition, cultures are different because they rest on different deep-rooted beliefs. Whether the markets are globalized or not, we think, believe, and act differently because of our different historical and geographical roots. As our values differ, so do our beliefs and rituals.

Yet, technology and AI are bringing us together not in changing our cultural habits and practices, but in satisfying the same kind of needs: easiness and immediacy. For instance, consumer empowerment inspired the new communication campaign for Away. The brand of suitcases attracted interest with a campaign based on the fascinating intersection of travel, imagination, and cutting-edge technology facilitated by AI as the power to change experiences. The company wanted to put the power of discovery back in the hands of its consumers, pushing their imaginations beyond their limits. In the words of the brand's Chief Marketing Officer (CMO), Carla Dunham,

> while many brands have experimented with AI in various ways, at Away, we felt it was important to share our perspective on AI in a way that reinforces our core belief—that the more you travel, the better we all become. AI possesses the power to create dreamscapes you'd think are unimaginable. In this case, Away has deliberately disrupted AI as we know it—blurring the lines between AI and reality to show our audience that extraordinary is out there, in the real world (https://www.adweek.com).

Interestingly, the statement from the company's CMO confronts virtual and real worlds. By using virtual reality (VR), the company aims at inviting consumers to visit the real world. As enticing as this concept seems to be, the big risk in asking people to confront ideals with reality is that it can lead to big disappointments when there is a gap between the experience and the promise. It seems important to recognize that the more we believe in the perfection of VR, the further it takes us from the flaws of the real-world's reality. As stated by Feyerabend (2010, 15), "we need a dream-world in order to discover the features of the real world we think we inhabit."

Thus, comparing both and deepening the gap between expectations and customer experience can lead to dramatic consequences depending on the degree of disappointment, peoples' psychological stability, and the strength of brand loyalty. As pointed out by Nobel-Winning Psychologist Daniel Kahneman[1], satisfaction comes from the experiences we remember.

Yet, as customer engagement is a top priority for marketers, generative AI offers exciting opportunities to create interactive and immersive experiences that captivate audiences. For example, chatbots powered by generative AI can simulate human-like conversations, providing instant customer support and personalized recommendations. VR and augmented reality (AR) experiences powered by generative AI can transport customers into virtual worlds where they can engage with products and services on a completely new level. These interactive experiences leave a lasting impression, drive customer engagement, and brand advocacy. It is just a matter of balance between what customers experience in real and virtual realities.

A study from Salesforce Generative AI Snapshot Series demonstrates how marketers use generative AI today: basic content creation—76 percent, copywriting—76 percent, improving creative thinking—71 percent, analyzing market data—63 percent, generating image assets—62 percent. (www.salesforce.com/news/stories/generative-ai-statistics/).

Generative AI is also changing marketers' jobs because 58 percent use it to analyze performance data, 57 percent to create groups and segments for marketing campaigns, 55 percent to create marketing campaigns and journey plans, 54 percent to personalize messaging content, and 53 percent to conduct copy testing and experimentation to build and optimize search engine optimization strategy.

Consumer experience and power have an undeniable impact on customer relationship management (CRM) whose role is to increase revenue by optimizing business practices based on understanding and improving customer relationships. In CRM, a marketing effort aims at moving customers from awareness to consideration and then on to purchase, loyalty, and advocacy[2].

Therefore, AI can be used to drive customer acquisition, customer retention, and customer profitability, three major objectives of successful CRM. Marketers can input questions into AI software like ChatGPT, which will provide detailed answers that can serve as a useful starting place for bettering business practices, developing targeted strategies, or optimizing marketing campaigns. ChatGPT crossed over 100 million users in about two months, and it seems like the momentum is just starting. ChatGPT has instantly made AI mainstream and is educating users on how to use natural language prompts to get human-like responses, which represents a new paradigm in technology. Its core technology—generative AI—is transforming all industries mainly through customer service as a variety of software vendors have retooled their systems with generative AI functions (https://arstechnica.com).

The use of AI resulted in the widespread adoption of chatbots and businesses certainly realized benefits from these technologies. It was easier to track service, it was cost-effective, and customer service levels improved. Despite all this, these technologies were not particularly smart. They were essentially hard-wired solutions for predefined scenarios and resulted in clients' frustrations. This meant that it was difficult to handle more complex calls. After all, a common action for callers has been to keep pressing the "0" button to get the attention of a human agent. Nevertheless, generative AI represents a quantum leap in capability. There is now real intelligence. A bot can understand open-ended prompts and create engaging responses. In terms of the benefits. While interactive voice response and chatbots may have seen 5 to 10 percent improvements, generative AI is poised to show levels of 50X or more. Indeed, generative AI represents a generational change in technology. Unlike traditional systems, the responses from the models are meant to simulate the communication with a human with the benefits of processing large amounts of complex data in little time (www.forbes.com/).

Many of the fastest-growing new technologies use AI , which refers to having machines operate like humans with respect to learning and decision making. An intelligent agent, a device that observes an environment and acts to achieve a goal, implements AI. AI and intelligent agents can be added to products as in the driverless car—the intelligent agent takes over part or all of driving. Intelligent agents are not new. Since 1927, thermostats have been able to sense a room's temperature and activate heating or cooling to maintain a consistent temperature. These days, thermostats are smarter and deliver more value. The Nest thermostat automatically learns a customer's schedule and preferences—its sensors observe when you go to sleep, wake up, and go to work. It also learns your preferred temperature for each of these times of the day. Customers save money (and the environment) by using heat and air-conditioning only when they need it. Intelligent agents are already used to perform many marketing tasks: when you go to a website and text with an *agent*—many times, you are actually texting with a computer trained to answer the basic questions a customer might ask[3].

Indeed, advances in AI have caused a seismic shift from a world in which answers were crucial to one in which questions became more critical. The big differentiator is the ability to craft smart prompts. For example, Ford's AI team questions how to prompt AI to do what you want, as the company's marketing team had a hard time seeing the simple word MOVE misspelled several times.

A recent research reveals that strategic questions can be grouped into five domains: *investigative, speculative, productive, interpretive,* and *subjective* . Each one unlocks a different aspect of the decision-making process. Together, they can help you tackle key issues that are all too easy to miss: investigative: What's known?; speculative: What if?; productive: Now what?; interpretive: So, what...?; and subjective: What's unsaid?[4]

At the beginning, the essential function of the Web was to help create, connect, and discover. Anyone with a keyboard and Wi-Fi could have an impact on others. Today, digital natives are immersed in the metaverse, playing, shopping, and working from the comfort of their couches. From there, they can hold team-building activities, interact with 3D objects, enjoy concerts, and will shortly be able to touch and smell things virtually. People can create the desired image of themselves with their avatars and speak in any language, which is automatically translated, to others—no effort needed. Isn't it magical?

Content Creation and Curation

Content creation is the process of producing original, high-quality, and engaging material, such as blog posts, videos, podcasts, and social media posts, to promote a brand, product, or service. Content curation, on the other hand, is the process of collecting and organizing existing content from various sources and presenting it meaningfully to a specific audience to provide them with relevant and valuable information on a particular topic or industry.

However, one of the biggest challenges of an AI content generator is the lack of human touch. While the content generated by AI is unique, it may lack the emotional and creative elements often present in content produced by human writers. Additionally, AI content generation can sometimes produce low-quality content, harming a business's reputation.

AI content curation seeks to provide curated content that is relevant and useful for the target audiences and uses algorithms to collect and organize existing content from different sources. These algorithms can analyze and categorize content based on the audience's preferences and interests. With AI, businesses can curate content specific to the audience's interests, which can help increase engagement and build brand loyalty. Additionally, AI content curation can help businesses save the time and resources typically associated with manual content curation.

A considerable disadvantage of some AI content curation tools is the lack of human judgment. While the algorithms can analyze and categorize content quite well, they may have trouble understanding the context and nuances of the content. AI content curation has also been known to sometimes result in the presentation of biased or inaccurate information. A recent incident with Gemini (Google) illustrates this issue and is discussed later in the book.

In marketing, AI copywriting refers to the process of creating marketing and advertising content using AI algorithms. AI copywriting systems are generally used to generate copy for emails, social media content, and product descriptions, providing persuasive and engaging content to drive and optimize conversions and sales. With AI, a business can generate copy based on data and analytics, helping to improve the effectiveness of their marketing campaigns. Additionally, AI copywriting saves time and resources by eliminating the need to hire a copywriter. While the copy generated by AI is optimized for conversions, it often lacks the emotional and creative features present in copy written by humans. So again, it is not uncommon for an AI copywriting tool to produce copy that is too formulaic or lacks authenticity, which can scare your customers away. For example, recently, some TV channels in the United States have been testing audio description with AI, and viewers complained about the robotic, monotone narration, which was in total discrepancy with the shows' tone and pace. Very annoyed customers were looking for other ways to watch their favorite shows and complaining about those channels on social media.

Finally, generative AI has the potential to enhance the overall customer experience by providing intelligent solutions and seamless interactions. For example, voice assistants powered by generative AI can offer personalized recommendations, answer customer queries, and provide real-time support. Virtual shopping assistants can guide customers through personalized product selections based on their preferences and needs. These AI-powered solutions create a more convenient and efficient customer experience, fostering loyalty and satisfaction.

For example, while most insurance companies rely on intermediaries (agents and brokers) to sell their products, Lemonade Insurance sells directly to end users. This low-cost, direct-to-consumer model uses an AI chatbot/salesperson to guide customers through the purchase process. AI answers customers' questions and asks questions the insurer needs to know to provide a quote. AI works fast, delivering insurance quotes in less than 90 seconds after the start of the conversation. When a Lemonade policyholder has a loss, making a claim is quick and easy. They open the Lemonade app on their smartphone and start messaging with AI. It walks them through a series of questions that vary depending on their loss. About one-third of the time, AI pays a claim on the spot, but when a claim needs more human interpretation, AI passes it to Lemonade's claims experience team who are trained to be empathetic, transparent, on the customers' side, and make quick decisions (https://www.lemonade.com/).

Intuitions and Algorithms

Intuition is one of the best talents humans have. It helps identify challenges and opportunities, but we don't instinctively see our intuitions as *intuitions*, we just see them as the real world. Today, we are told that algorithms rule our lives, intuitions, as well as decisions. We have mental flowcharts made of *yes* and *no*, which lead to a series of branches of yesses and nos. Some decisions might be more rational than others, but they might all follow an algorithmic pattern. Before you can question your intuitions, you have to realize what your mind's eye is looking at *is* an intuition—some cognitive algorithm, as seen from the inside—rather than a direct perception of the way things really are, and that your own well-established habits are a behavioral algorithm.

Our intuitions are not bias-free. They are shaped by both internal—past experience and knowledge—and external influences—information, others' opinions, reviews, and advertising. Most of our choices are led by implicit and explicit biases. We are not conscious of our implicit biases, but they help us to make some choices based on our preferences, while the explicit biases are conscious and we know what our preferences lay on and eliminate the options that are incompatible with them.

As algorithms are created by people, they carry their creators' biases. A recent example of biased algorithms having created a global controversy about AI was the Gemini image-generating service from Google, which depicted inaccurate historical facts through the lenses of modern diversity and inclusiveness values and policies, falsifying the appearance and reality faced by people having lived in the past centuries. Other than being historically and genetically inaccurate, it suggests the biased idea of a world where diversity, equity, and inclusion (DEI) has always existed. The images of black Founding Fathers, black and Asian Nazi fighters, black Vikings, a female Pope, and only gay couples were portrayed by Gemini, which we all know are way farther from reality.

Facing global criticisms about its program and after having lost $90 billion in market value, the company stated that they have been struggling to solve a known problem in AI, which is that without some guidance, tools will naturally generate stereotypical images based on the data they are trained on. What the company doesn't say is that the data come from humans, and humans have prejudices, and the examples described previously are not only stereotypical but also mainly representative of explicit biases toward DEI.

With all the comfort that AI promises to provide us, the risks of alienation are very high. For example, today there are multiple options to read from all the books that have been published in the world about any topic and you make your choice as per your own criteria. But, when you inquire about the same topics online, AI will deliver information limited by the sources chosen by someone else who decides what kind of contents you should read and be aware of.

As stated by Valenzuela et al.,[5] recommendation algorithms limit our experience of serendipity. They do so because most of these systems are set up to feed content based on our past behaviors, reinforcing them and creating inertia that limits exploration and change. This can lead to what has been defined as *algorithm aversion*—when people prefer humans over AI. One of the reasons for such aversion is *uniqueness neglect* when algorithms tend to ignore a person's unique characteristics, circumstances, and symptoms because they ignore qualitative information and contextualization.

Thus, more variety leads to an openness to receiving external algorithm-based recommendations when deciding on future consumption[6]. Yet, ingratiation has a positive impact on consumers' recommendation acceptance and their evaluation of AI's predictive accuracy when AI is perceived as machinelike rather than humanlike, although most literature states that those consumers are more likely to rely on AI for cognitive/objective tasks versus effective ones[7].

Algorithms and You

Thanks to algorithms, all apps and websites try to get closer to their consumers. The machine learns from the decisions we make online, with the goal of customizing the relationship with us and leading us to choices that are more personal. Whatever turns more personal also turns into something more emotional and judgmental. Take the Zocdoc TV commercial as an example. The person scrolling down the app on their phone makes comments about the doctors she sees listed there: "too old, too young, too middle aged, too good looking to be good, too educated to be trusted...." While none of these personal traits testifies to professional competence, the advertisement seems to suggest that there are all kinds of profiles in their pool of doctors and that some of them will seem to be closer to what each patient would be looking for, assuming that not all patients have the same criteria to choose a doctor. In an attempt to be funny, the advertisement pushes it to the absurdity of questioning the trustworthiness of someone who is highly educated.

The criteria used by the patient featured in the Zocdoc's advertisement would be more appropriate for eHarmony than for the search of a health care provider, but these are the algorithms used by the app to better know their clients at the same time as it provides them with the feeling of being in total control of their decisions.

The willingness to control one's life is the main reason why people turn to magic. Contemporary consumers use technology to control all aspects of their lives. However, getting the right balance between what is done by others and the satisfaction of accomplishing something oneself is not always easy. Self-actualization is one of the five levels of needs described by Maslow,[8] which is the source of self-satisfaction and sometimes needs to be associated with the need of esteem to completely fulfil one's feeling of accomplishment. While the need of belonging has been exacerbated in our societies, thanks to social media, which would have never reached such penetration without smartphones, the comfort of having everything done by someone else has been creating some frustration.

Having spotted such a gap in the market, the almost-ready-to-consume products give consumers the feeling of control and unicity thanks to some customization, while saving them time. This is how companies such as Home Chef, Hello Fresh, and Blue Apron, among others, penetrated the markets. They make you feel like you are the cook without going through the chore of grocery shopping or thinking about what to cook every day. Nutrisystem makes you feel like you are in control of your weight, money, and relationships when you undertake your diet with your better half with results that look like magic. This concept merging comfort and some level of involvement seems to be ideal in helping consumers to feel less frustrated by feeling useless when they live only on ready-to-eat food.

As stated by Allport,[9] our consciousness of ourselves is largely a reflection of the consciousness, which others have of us. This is increased with social media in the quest for instinctive social prestige. It transcends the traditional consumer markets and buying habits require people to satisfy new fundamental needs. With AI we don't just buy products, we experience a self-conscious social and psychical perspective. Thus, the focus shifted from product to consumer experience and self-image. Social media is a global mediatized *Agora*, a place to speak up and express yourself before an audience of thousands or millions of people.

Nothing seems to be impossible with AI, as there is no impossible with magic. The more comfort we give people, the more we increase their dissatisfaction with old resources, and the more they are willing to pay for new ones when their possessions become obsolete after a couple of years, thanks to the accelerated pace imposed by technological progress. In doing so, companies train customers to require immediate and effortless gratification.

Although technological change opens up many new opportunities, it also poses challenges for marketers. New technologies are scary for some marketing managers because they don't know how to incorporate them into their existing practices and avoid what they do not understand. For others, it is easy to fall in love with the latest thing—whether from the firm's R&D lab or someone external selling social media tools—and blindly add it to the firm's marketing strategy. Both approaches can lead to a production-oriented logic, while it is more important than ever for a customer orientation to guide the process. Finding the best applications of technology still requires marketing managers to begin with customer needs.

Everyone Wants to Go to Heaven But No One Wants to Die

As goes the popular saying. In our quest for longevity, we refuse the limits of human mortality; want to defy death, and envy wizards and witches because they are immortal. To do so, we believe in superfoods to make us superhuman like our superheroes in a supernatural world. That is how the Netflix series *Strangers Things* penetrated the global markets: with supernatural creatures. With the support of sponsors such as Lacoste and Coca-Cola, the series was not only extremely successful but has also been promoted through the merchandise created in cobranding between these two brands and the show. Lacoste created a limited edition for their polo shirts replacing their legendary alligator with the creatures from the show, while Coca-Cola launched a limited edition with the name of the show on their bottles' labels.

Supernatural creatures are nothing new and carry strong cultural beliefs. Sirens were stunningly beautiful half-women/half-fish creatures with such an irresistible tone of voice that their singing would attract sailors to end up sinking their ships. One of the most visited monuments in the world is the little mermaid's sculpture in Copenhagen, Denmark, as the story written by Hans Christian Andersen in 1837 describes the red-haired, blue-eyed creature, descendent of Vikings as part of the Danish cultural roots. Disney turned the story into an animation in 1989. Centaurs being part of the Greek mythology are half man/half horse creatures also displayed in the *Harry Potter* saga.

Supernatural and fantastic sell, because just like magic, they take us away from the algorithmic bifocal view of the world. Ironically, while AI exists thanks to a series of 0 or 1, AI ramifications seem to offer unlimited possibilities to users. Likewise, there are countless possibilities to obtaining what we want with magic. This might explain the growing interest in magic and the proliferation of books, schools, and websites on the topic (further discussed in Chapter 3). Because we are attracted to supernatural, science fiction keeps fascinating people and eventually becomes reality, like holograms in *Star Wars* now made possible, thanks to AR and the evolution of spaceships, such as SpaceX taking nonastronauts to a spin in the space. If people did not believe in magic and supernatural phenomena, video games would not sell. The penetration of video games among populations of all ages and cultures is so strong that there are currently advertising campaigns mimicking video games to convey critical messages such as safety on roads and the prevention of suicides due to depression.

But wearing the costume only does not make you Superman. You need to have the power and the mindset. Likewise, having access to AI doesn't make you an AI marketer if you still have doubts about it. A recent study revealed that 64 percent of marketers are using AI to create campaigns and that 51 percent of marketers have used or experimented Gen AI in their work. Yet, 31 percent worry about accuracy and quality, 20 percent have trouble trusting Gen AI, 19 percent are concerned over the skills needed, and 18 percent worry over job safety (www.salesforce.com/news/stories/generative-ai-statistics/).

What Brings Magic and Technology Together?

The main attraction of magic is effortless and immediate gratification. This is exactly what technology provides us. Press a button and you speak to and see someone from the other side of the world in real time. Push another one and your food, medicine, car, and anything else you want is home-delivered. Scan a QR code and the menu in a restaurant appears on your phone or your name and contact details appear to those who scan the QR code on your nametag in an event. You should also use a QR code to provide feedback to the companies you have been buying from, or simply scan it on the back of the packaging to pay for a product. In addition, to make it touchless, you are invited to use your phone and the QR code to get coffee from a coffee machine. It will take longer and more *clicks* than if you order directly from the machine, but you sure look cool. The same thing applies to your washing machine or to get a nice warm coffee at home or even your office with your Ember cup connected to your phone. You can also cook with Tovala to make fantastic foods just by scanning the QR code and letting the oven do all the *magic cooking* as stated in their advertisement. As you manage your Ninja Woodfire barbecue *cooking perfection* with your smartphone, you can send someone a Hallmark greeting card, which, thanks to Venmo's QR code inside, will magically turn into a monetary gift card!

What can two fields, which everything seems to oppose, have in common? Technology is science and most people say that magic is not. Thus, if you believe in science you can't believe in magic. If you believe in technology, you belong to the modern, rational, and logical world; if you believe in magic, you belong to the ancient, irrational, and illogical world.

The success of both magic and technology can be explained by one theory and one personal trait: Theory X—people are lazy! In the 1950s, Douglas Murray McGregor, a professor at Massachusetts Institute of Technology developed theories of human motivation that provide a framework for how managers use behaviors and tools in the workplace to encourage productivity. Both theories are concerned with how best to motivate employees by providing the most relevant provisions, but they differ in what they believe are the most basic and powerful of human needs in the workplace (https://educationlibrary.org/theory-x-and-theory-y-douglas-mcgregor/).

Theory X suggests that human beings are inherently lazy, dislike the concept of work, and are only in the workplace because they need money. Managers who subscribe to this theory will typically see interactions with employees as transactional and feel the need to rely on strong financial incentives, coercion, and authoritarian control to ensure productivity is maintained in the workplace. Theory X managers may be predisposed to seeing human failure as the cause of problems rather than systemic or structural causes. This would mean that whatever happens to us, whether positive or negative, depends exclusively on us.

Au contraire, Theory Y is underlined by a belief that work comes naturally to human beings and that they can both motivate themselves and also exercise self-control. Under Theory Y, employees seek out responsibility and enjoy performing at a high level. Organizations underpinned by Theory Y are more likely to have cultures of trust, transparency, and engagement as well as healthy two-way relationships between managers and subordinates.

One can argue that people are a mix of both theories because they try to reach their personal goals at the same time as they live in societies, which exert some kind of pressure on them to which they react.

If we apply these two theories to the analysis of the commonalities between magic and technology, we can identify two major characteristics: they provide effortless and immediate gratification. People might aim at avoiding making an effort (Theory X), which explains the surge of online shopping with home delivery, although it is often justified as being a gain of time. At the same time, people are under social pressure: they need to own the most recent iPhone, be active on the main social media platforms and upload as many apps as possible to make their lives easier, and be part of specific communities (Theory Y). Magic has the same effect: effortless and immediate gratification. With a simple movement of your magic wand, you get what you want and become part of the selective community of powerful immortals.

Your smartphone is your magic wand; you can't live without it or without Wi-Fi. In a TV commercial, birds from the *Migration* movie observe humans at home while the bird parents tell the children that *humans need Wi-Fi to live*. Then, all of a sudden, there is a power outage but thanks to Xfinity, Wi-Fi keeps working, and humans keep living.

Our desires are quickly fulfilled because we have them mastered thanks to technology. Our wishes are our devices' command, just like a Jeannie would obey with no argument to their Master's requests. Commands are done by facial, voice, eye, or digital recognition because our devices recognize us as their Masters. In some airports, there is no longer need to show boarding pass or identity to board the plane. It is all done by facial recognition even if, right now, the process is slowed down because the equipment has not been perfected yet. In some universities in the world, attendance is taken by facial recognition at the entrance of the classrooms.

With growing nomadism, we are connected from anywhere to everywhere, we can work from anywhere at any time. In airports, on the streets, and on public and private transportation, people are connected all the time. This is how the advertisement for Jeep shows that you can work from the most remote places if you push the *Wi-Fi* button on your truck's dashboard. Yet, the pervasive power of constant connectedness paves the way to new markets for *Me time* and cabanas. People pay a considerable amount of money to be isolated for a weekend in places with no power at all. Some (silent) retreats are meant to disconnect people from their devices and reconnect with nature. It is somehow a way of leaving rationality and logic to yield to spirituality and emotions. This is also where humans interact among themselves without the digital interface. It seems that deviating from standard rationality to be lured by something that, *a priori*, doesn't seem to make sense is illogical, but it creates meaning.

Technology makes everything possible. One would think that nothing could be less compatible than humans and robots, yet, digital humans exist even if the words defining this new being are antagonistic—human and digital or real and virtual. Research shows that people prefer human-oid bots for tasks traditionally associated with humans and those like animals for tasks associated with animals' natural skill sets. They have shown that when a virtual influencer (whether anime-like or humanlike) creates organic Instagram posts, they tend to receive more likes and more positive emojis than do the posts of human influencers, which drives consumers to engage more with virtual influencers, including the novelty of interacting with computer-generated imagery and the different aesthetic it represents. In addition, consumers exposed to virtual influencers' posts show greater willingness to share their favorable experiences with others.[10]

Magic Is Power, AI Is Control

Just as wizards feel unpowered without their magic wands, being without one's smartphone has been proven to be the highest source of anxiety for humans, which is called nomophobia (no mobile phone phobia). This is understandable because you use it to unlock almost everything you need. And with technology, you can have a self-driving and self-parking car or even better—Volkswagen already sells cars with the intuitive sit-to-start, for which you don't need a key anymore. Your car recognizes you as you sit in the driver's seat and starts immediately. It's magical!

Magic is not evolution; it is transformation. Our transformation into vegan beings paves the way for new markets with unlimited options for food and other industries. Our ancestors were not vegan; they would take what nature, including animals, would provide them with. We are built to crave foods high in sugar, salt, and fat because they provided our ancestors with energy, vital nutrients, and stored fat to help them get through times of food shortage. Yet, with the sedentary lives we have today and with the comfort technology has brought us, our needs have dramatically changed and now we can afford eating without sugar, fat, and meat. We have so much choice among all the kinds of diets available: Keto, Atkins, Nutrisystem, Golo, Noon, and so on, that it is almost impossible to see someone without food restrictions. Not to mention the allergies created by processed food.

Just like the druids of Ancient Ireland, we believe in magic potions. Cannabis, cocaine, and assimilated drugs as well as alcohol provide immediate effect, taking people away from reality. Pharmaceutics' advertisements showing the power of their products in making patients' lives so much better in little time follow this trend. The same applies to supplements, without which it seems impossible to have a normal life today. They are advertised for all target consumers from little kids to help with growth to seniors to increase memory and vitality as if without our dose of daily supplements we would be useless. Modern druids are social media influencers. Recommendations about what to eat and what to do for a better life in society proliferate in social media: drink this every morning to lose belly fat, use this product to wake up with a better skin, and so forth. The bottled water industry is following this trend too. Hydration is no longer enough. Now water should contain vitamins, oxygen, collagen, and antioxidants undertaking a direct competition with energy drinks. All these magic potions are supposed to make us healthier to live a better and longer life.

Soon, the devices we depend on so much today will become useless. Transhumanist thinkers state that we are able to augment the brain and mind through brain implants (discussed in the last section of this book). Genetic engineering could alter the mind biologically, increasing intelligence, creativity, or any other desired quality; we should be better than robots. Virtual or AR might become so advanced as to be indistinguishable from reality, connect reality to our nervous system, and allow us to live in a world currently unimaginable.

Superstition Is Bliss

Is superstition a sign of ignorance?

In the era of high technology, we believe in horoscopes and the Chinese zodiac even if we are not Chinese. We upload an app that delivers daily horoscope and tips on how to go through our day. We call California Psychics or upload the Serpent Reading app to know about our future and we go to fortune-tellers for advice about how to make certain decisions. Every soccer game in Brazil benefits from religious prayers and superstitious rituals. In Thailand, there is a lucky and an unlucky color for clothes to wear every day. There are also lucky and unlucky phone numbers and the subsequent proliferation of websites that help in picking the lucky ones. Some carriers have a dedicated person to analyze the potential client's profile and provide phones with a lucky number. It is an argument often used to attract new customers.

The cognitive revolution that began in the late 1960s shone a spotlight on thought processes, but not on beliefs or lay theories. Even in social psychology, where construals and interpretations became popular, little attention was paid to the underlying beliefs or lay theories that fostered these construals or interpretations in the first place. Researchers did not ask the deeper *Why?* which are these fundamental assumptions people make about themselves and their worlds. You can call them lay theories, mindsets, world assumptions, mental models, but they are all about people's fundamental understanding of the nature and workings of the people, things, and phenomena in their worlds [11].

But our worlds are not necessarily reality. Virtual and real worlds are intertwined, one of them sometimes taking precedence over the other. Every 12 minutes is the average frequency of checking the phones, participating in social media, or playing games. Consumers have now the power of creating their own worlds and populate them with people, ideas, and places they carefully choose. The perfect world created by each individual competes or interferes with their real life, which is not perfect, explaining why some people would rather spend more time online than face the challenges of their daily real lives.

Thanks to technology, instant gratification has become a habit and is often taken for granted by consumers. The reward policy is so mainstream that consumers can't understand a brand that doesn't reward them in some way. We get a 20 percent discount when we buy from the app or when there are sales only for online purchases or when we earn money because our video reached the required numbers of views on TikTok. We are also rewarded with likes, shares, and positive comments. Nevertheless, this expectation also generates frustrations when the number of likes and reshares is not big enough or when we are criticized. The obsession with personal recognition and social validation is a new kind of addiction. Our brain needs to fight these unwanted situations and its response can be anger, aggressiveness, cancelation, or worse, isolation.

AI is becoming an unavoidable tool for all individuals and professionals, and it has already been as enticing and addictive as social media.

Most publications about AI explain the rapid penetration of technology in all markets by the fact that it is already there, and if you don't use it, you will be left behind. Along with QR codes, smartphones, smart cars, smart houses, and communication among all devices, it seems to be just impossible not to be a tech-oriented person today. Our devices learn: Google knows more about your life than you do and all the apps and websites record your actions in detail. But AI became an even hotter topic with the recent introduction of ChatGPT, this magical tool that answers all of the questions about any topic, writes reports, and gives advice in a few seconds.

This prompts the following question: Do consumers use technology only because it has become the norm? The mainstream and short answer will probably be yes. However, there might be another explanation for that, and this is the underlying assumption of this book: consumers enjoy the power of technology because it works just like magic, providing effortless and immediate solutions to recurring situations. Technology offers endless possibilities opening the doors to a world where nothing is impossible anymore. This is a plausible hypothesis taking into account the number of existing brands using the word *magic* in their brands and communications.

Indeed, the research we recently conducted with 286 consumers demonstrated that the word *magic* in advertising attracts consumers who would expect effortless and immediate benefits in all product categories. This validation of immediacy as a unique selling proposition explains the fast and growing adhesion of consumers from around the world to technology, which enhances the feeling of unity in consumption, thanks to globalization. This research is further discussed in Chapter 3.

Although beliefs in magic and superstition differ from culture to culture, the use of smartphones as a magic wand to obtain desired products has unified the world of consumption. Better yet, every time you shop online, the products come to you, just if you had pronounced *accio*, the charm that summons objects toward the caster like in *Harry Potter*.

Thanks to vocal recognition, Alexa tells you what to do, and your car self-drives and self-parks. With VR you can travel across time and space, become a superhero, and fight as many enemies as you want, while

ChatGPT answers all of your questions. All this works just like magic; no effort, no waiting time.

The Structure and Content of This Book

This book discusses the omnipresence of technology and AI in marketing, taking magic as the mirror power. We might not realize it, but the world of the supernatural is not only on Netflix or in some video games. It is in our minds and in all the products and brands we have at home. If we didn't believe in magical solutions, half of the existing brands wouldn't be around anymore.

This book is composed of eight chapters, all of them based on science, academic research, and first-hand observation.

When reading the foreword, you get a sense of the important role played by the word *magic* in marketing. It is almost used as often as AI, which is brought together by the same promise: a better life with easier access to all that you need—customize your life, make no effort to get what you want, and enjoy it immediately. In that section, you are also introduced to the three experts on AI, who very kindly spared time to share their knowledge and view of AI with me by explaining the uses, advantages, and issues companies are dealing with that technology today.

This introduction shows you how consistent magic and AI are and why is it relevant to you as a consumer as well as a marketer. We are immersed in a world of algorithms, but most of us don't realize that our own brains work like them. Actually, all that machines do with AI is copy the human brain. Moreover, as science hasn't finished exploring the human brain with all its mysteries, companies haven't finished understanding the extent of AI capabilities and its ramifications. Just like magic, AI is still a mysterious black box.

Chapter 1 takes you to the heights of spirituality by showing you that technology is not that far away from beliefs that move people in some specific directions. We explore the danger for companies of seeing ghosts and wasting their time and energy fighting someone who is not even a competitor or a real threat. The chapter also explores the need for wonder in all humans. If you are unable to imagine or to be amazed, your world doesn't make much sense to you. If you aren't creative, your company's survival is at stake and technology alone won't be able to save it.

Chapter 2 stresses the importance of superstitions in humans' lives and in companies. From the impact of the Groundhog Day on investors' decisions to fortunetellers helping companies to choose the right place and the right people to work with, and to the rationality of machines, there is a whole world to explore and understand. Such a world is the world of marketing because it has an impact on both consumers and companies. Indeed, myths are not only in the roots of our civilization but are also great promotional arguments used by so many companies and brands.

In Chapter 3, we discuss science. It is interesting to see that science and magic have been opposed for so long, while there is scientific research about magic and that Masters' Degrees' programs in witchcraft are proliferating in reputed universities around the world. That is not only about Hogwarts! We also see that everything that was depicted in science fiction movies, sometimes as supernatural and magical powers, is now becoming reality, thanks to technology. We, humans, are on our way to supernatural beings by consuming products that are supposed to make us much better than the original version of ourselves.

Chapter 4 gets you onto the marketing mix. We start discussing magical products. They might not be magical, but the results you get when using them look like magic. At least this is how they are positioned. Thanks to technology, companies create products that better suit you, make your life easier, or anticipate your needs. You have a self-driving and self-parking car, and your smart home opens and closes doors and windows alone. Your vacuum cleaner and your coffee machine work without you. And you can even design or taste the beverages you will drink in the year 3000!

If you expect Chapter 5 to take you back to rational calculations, you might get disappointed. Yes, numbers are magical too, because they are symbolic, and they mean something to most people. Numbers are either appreciated or avoided; it all depends on the kind of magical powers they carry. Thus, if your life is not going well, it is perhaps because you don't have a lucky phone number! Price tags speak to consumers because we don't read them exactly as they are. We focus on one or two numbers only and make decisions based on them. And thanks to apps for easy comparisons, consumers are more price-sensitive than before.

Chapter 6 explores the strengths and weaknesses of online shopping. What will happen with physical stores if consumers only buy online? Consumers are fascinated by the comfort of having everything home delivered, but at some point, they get annoyed or even frustrated and look for other options. Depending on the product, they would rather go to a physical store to try the product for real. Really? Use AR instead! In addition, the time will come (very shortly) when you will not ask for someone's phone number anymore—everyone will have a personal QR code to connect with others. Just like the one you find on the packaging of the products you just bought.

How you communicate with your consumers is the topic of chapter seven. You might not believe it just yet, but you will see a long, but not comprehensive, list of advertisements and taglines promising magic and magical results if you use their products. Marketers are so happy to enjoy the fast and easy way of creating their communication campaigns thanks to AI. Creating content has never been this easy and cost-efficient. You will also be amazed with how carefully thought was the creation of the top digital influencers in the world. They don't exist but are followed by millions of people who do exist. You can also vote for the first Miss AI pageant, something similar to the Miss Universe pageant, but only for AI Misses. Can you believe it?

Chapter 8 takes you to a trip around the world. That could be a virtual trip, which is what VR is for. As much as AI has fascinated everyone everywhere, it does not imply cultural homogeneity. Cultures are still and will remain different. We might use the same tools, but our roots are culture-specific as are our beliefs. Thus, apparent similarity in behaviors does not mean similarity in mindsets and needs. Technology is trying to make AI look as human as possible and to do so, trying to bring some degree of cultural sensitivity to it. But, humans should first acknowledge cultural differences to really input cultural knowledge in their machines.

Chapter 9 examines the ability of using AI as a competitive advantage. Embracing the digital world is also embracing the magical world. Machines speak to machines as they speak to people. They are able to make purchases but they can also replace people, which is one of the main fears triggered by this technological progress. Collecting and analyzing data is the main goal for companies willing to get closer to their consumers, and AI does it much better than a human does.

It is said that the main advantage of AI is to give structure to our lives and remove part of the chaos we live in. Marketers should use AI's rationality to better serve consumer irrationality. If consumer decision making was purely rational, we wouldn't be speaking about magic and superstition and most products promising magical results wouldn't exist. Knowing that all companies are and will be using AI Marketing, marketers' challenge is not to know how to use it and be acquainted with the newest technologies. The challenge is what to use it for so that they can stand out of the crowded market where almost nothing is done without AI. Marketers should use AI to enhance their products' magical powers and to create new products for magical results because this is what consumers believe in.

The book concludes with the hope and certainty that machines will not replace humans. Hopefully, the so-called *human–AI* collaboration will indeed take us to a better life in a better world. I do hope that AI will help us understand each other better and create more and stronger links among people, rather than having them constantly interacting only through their devices. It is exciting to know that we live in a world where everything is possible. That is the magical power of AI.

I do hope that you enjoy the reading!

CHAPTER 1

AI Triggers Attraction and Suspicion

If you don't see shadows, you are in the darkness, because there is no shadow without light

This chapter seeks to explain the reasons why people are so attracted to AI by paralleling it with magic. It is based on two main benefits they have in common: immediate and effortless gratification. The pervasive role of Artificial Intelligence (AI) in our lives is explained through the lenses of magic because their roles lead to the same benefit: making our lives easier. People might not believe in magic and superstition, but they can see ghosts, at least what haunts their lives and puts their businesses at risk. Not everything we see is what we think they are, and spirituality plays a non-negligible role in shaping our vision of people, markets, and life.

In an era where consumers are served by apps that bring them what they want to their doorsteps and where QR codes provide them all the information they need about any product, place, or event, companies can't count on their customers' patience and willingness to make the effort in going to physical stores. AI is that magic that makes life so much easier!

Consumers reward brands that provide immediate gratification by being loyal to them and are rewarded for their loyalty by benefitting from special discounts if they are connected with the company through their apps. Sales promotions and promo codes exclusive to purchases made online or through the apps are extensively appreciated by consumers who feel rewarded by using the tools companies kindly impose on them. Immediate and effortless gratification is exciting and the joy of being on the top of things by being connected all the time acts like dopamine and creates certain levels of addiction. As addiction implies frequency and loyalty, being away from smartphones is a source of immense anxiety for most people, who react like someone in need of drugs.

The addictive dependence on smartphones is confirmed by a research that showed that running out of battery is one of the worst things that can happen: 41 percent of people fear missed calls the most when faced with a dead battery. In addition, 17 percent of males missed a match on a dating app because their phone died before they could swipe. But it is worse for millennials with 42 percent likely to skip the gym when choosing between working out or charging their phone. Smartphone users will even drop everything (32%) and make a U-turn to head back home to charge their phone. Finally, 60 percent have blamed a dead phone for not speaking to a loved one (www.dailymail.co.uk/sciencetech/article-3607598/Do-low-battery-anxiety-90-panic-losing-power-phones.html).

That explains why brands such as Apple and Samsung focus on their smartphones' long-life battery or secondary battery in their respective advertisements. In reality, very few advertisements for smartphones focus on their original role—to be a phone. Other than the battery, they stress the quality of the camera—with an iPhone, you can produce professional movies—the design, the size, and the weight of the device because being just a phone is a secondary function when compared to the endless benefits other functionalities can provide.

Why Is AI in Our Lives?

Technology, in general, and AI, in particular, are in our lives to make them easier and better. That is exactly the role of marketing. Marketing's role is to satisfy consumers' needs and make them happy. Meeting this goal has been facilitated by the use of technology in marketing. Thanks to apps, companies can get closer to their customers and establish what seems to be a customized relationship with them. In addition, and thanks to the data collected online, companies have better insights for segmenting the markets and understating their target customers.

Everything a consumer does online is recorded. Companies know very well where we have been, when, and doing what. Information about our purchases, quantities, amounts of money spent, and frequency is no secret to any company. Based on that, brands can better target their consumers in relating to their needs and sometimes even anticipating them. This generates a positive surprise to those consumers who believe that the companies strive to provide the best solution to all of their needs. Understanding consumers and making them happy is no longer enough; consumers should be delighted to see that you are part of their lives and an extension of their beings. Understanding that social needs take over all of the other needs today, companies rely on social media to collect data and to convey messages to their consumers, what helps in creating communities. Communities bring together people who share the same beliefs and values.

The parallel that can be made with magic is that magic is the science of causing change to occur in conformity with the will.[1] In getting what they want immediately and without effort, just by using an app, consumers have the power of changing their current situation as per their will. To do magic, you need to believe in it, and to be loyal to a brand, you need to believe that it can bring you the satisfaction you are looking for. Put in other words, magic is a trip to your inner world. Consumer loyalty to a brand rests on the belief in the consistency of the benefits that the brand provides to them. If magic still exists, it is because people see results and pass them on to the next generations. Likewise, if you are loyal to a brand, it is because you see some benefits in using it and you pass it on to your family and friends as well as to unknown people when you post reviews online.

When you decide to purchase a specific product from a specific brand, you feel an internal need and a drive that pushes you toward that brand which you trust because you believe in its benefits. Such benefits can be physical, moral, financial, or social. Thus, you can buy a brand because it will make you healthier or look younger, or because it defends a cause you want to support, or because it is less expensive than its competitors, or because it is the brand that enables you to belong to a certain community, where everyone buys the same brand and participates in the same rites, worshipping the same influencers. Brand communities can spread information very quickly and that information is believed because it comes from the community rather than from the company. Thus, some companies are now turning to community as a service—which gives access to a group of people valuable enough to be considered a marketplace [2].

Magic requires rites, some of them being collective. The participation in social media is a collective rite bringing people from around the world together. The need of checking your phone constantly to be immediately aware of posts demonstrates the need of participating in such rites to exist and be part of such communities. Grand anthropological and sociological theories developed mostly in the late nineteenth and early twentieth centuries offer clear structures, and the classic definitions of Edward Burnett Tylor[3], James Frazer, Emile Durkheim[4], and others still reverberate through much scholarly work on this topic. While these theories remain useful, more recent studies have tended to take a much narrower approach in examining the specific forms that magic, magical rites, or witchcraft in particular periods and within certain societies would build long-lasting communities.[5]

The pursuit of magic is, in part, the result of the human desire to control. In the first centuries, there was a need to control the natural environment, the social world, and the outcome of forces people did not fully understand. This desire for control comes to the surface most often in times of change, which trigger uncertainty and instability. This is one of the main reasons why people are resistant to change. Yet, the word *change* has been intensively used in political campaigns, in advertising for new products (game changer), by companies aiming at a new corporate culture, and by organizations asking for financial support. That also means that humans are never happy with what they have and are always trying to change their current situation with the goal or the illusion that with change things can get better provided that they can control such changes.

Since the Old Egypt times, the relationship with the elements has been both a challenge and a policy. When pharaoh Ramses II built his temple in Abu Simbel, he requested that the god Ra (the sun) enter it on two specific dates—his birthday and his coronation day; this way, the sun would rule both the King's life and afterlife. Magic equals control because it is rooted in mastering the four elements: earth, fire, water, and air. With technology, we created a virtual cloud and electric windmills (air), we have spaceships to go to the moon and to Mars, and satellites gravitating around the earth. We also use technology in agriculture (earth). We replaced the fire for light, now cooking and heating with electricity and solar panels. And we have been creating barrages and changing the sense of rivers thanks to technology too (water). It is true that we cannot create or stop rain and we don't know how to handle tsunamis, but we have the technology to cope with the most basic uses of the elements in our daily lives.

Technological progress is admired because we believe that it can make our lives better. It helps us to fight what we fear the most: the lack of control of our lives. By making things more tangible while being virtual, technology seems to protect us from ghosts that haunt us with so many threats.

Ghosts Can Prevent Businesses From Growing

Magical rituals, religion, and superstition are used to protect people from multiple threats that would challenge their lives. For millennia, people have been looking to the stars for guidance and the spirit world for both protection and inspiration. All indigenous people had their own beliefs, gods, and rituals, which were mixed with foreign religions as colonization and immigration intensified. By worshipping gods who would look after those who had died, religions developed in which magic played a central part. The religions of Ancient Egypt, Greece, and Rome as well as the Celtic world and the Scandinavian developed rituals that spread around the world. They rooted what is practiced as religions today.[6]

If magic and religion have proliferated and survived across centuries and overcame all kinds of threats of extinction is because people need to believe to live—believing is living. Both magic and religion rely on beliefs, hope, and faith without which no human can exist. People who commit suicide are those who lost all hope, have no faith in anything or anyone, and stopped believing in a possible positive outcome to their lives. This is when living doesn't make sense anymore, despite wealth and fame for some of them.

More often than not, people use magic to protect themselves from people who are close to them, using spells against people they know; *your worst enemies are the people close to you* as they say. The fear of contamination has always haunted people with the specter of vampires and zombies. Despite the Western incredulity, several countries do believe in zombies and have proven that they exist with testimonies of doctors and journalists. In an intriguing book, *Haïti, la République des Morts Vivants (Haiti the Republic of the Undead)*, French journalists Pradel and Casgha[7] described and documented with pictures (not created by AI) the existence and use of zombies as slaves after having conducted research in that country.

Other than TV shows such as *The Walking Dead* and so many others featuring zombies, the popular way of describing a person who looks lost and undead is calling them a *zombie.* These people are in emotional distress because of a shock, a trauma, or a big disillusion. They look lost because they feel lost, as if the world around them no longer made sense. They lost belief and trust in people and justice. They also lost their hope and lived disconnected from any kind of spirituality or social norm. Those skeptical about religion, superstition, and spirituality, in general, are now members of what has been called *the zombie religion,* which is defined by nihilism and isolationism—that is, a life without beliefs.

Some businesspeople don't believe in magic or in superstition and don't leave their business to fate, yet they see ghosts. They are haunted by the threat of competition. A few years ago, I met a business owner in the international education field. He had a very good concept but no strategy at all: no business plan, no clear positioning, and inaccurate targeting. Because I believed in the concept and could spot the issues preventing the business from growing, I gave him a considerable amount of my time and advice, which I usually charge companies for, in exchange of the promise of incorporating a still-to-be-created advisory board.

The main factor preventing the growth of the business was the owner himself. First of all, he would not invest in hiring capable and stable people. With the only goal of saving money in mind, he would hire students or any transient and inexperienced person who would randomly cross paths with him, as long as they accepted to work for a low wage. Year after year, he would start his program from scratch because of his team's turnover. That was a waste of time, as well as of information, experience, and energy, not mentioning the impact of such lack of consistency on his clients' loyalty to the program and the consequent company's reputation on the market. Rather than building on experience and expertise, he would scatter and waste his company's limited resources by starting repeatedly the same practices over again every year. In addition, and because he himself would not trust the people he hired—he barely knew them—he would not delegate any tasks, while at the same time complaining that he had to do everything himself and spent too much time in operations without yielding time to strategic thinking. He was clearly scared of riding the waves of strategy and got purposively busy with operations as a good excuse to procrastinate strategic decision making.

One day, he decided that a much bigger organization, putting together an educational program, was his competitor. He offered them a partnership, which they declined because the program in question was already well-established and was definitively not similar to his. He's got so frustrated that he got rid of everyone who would participate in that program, including myself. Indeed, I was invited as a guest speaker in that bigger program and accepted because I had no contract with his company and was just helping him out *pro bono*. Most importantly, there was no competition between them because their programs, topics, target markets, and positioning were totally different. In other words, they were not in the same market.

This supposed *competitor* was one of his ghosts. He was haunted by the specter of a competition that only existed in his mind. Because of his lack of clear positioning and targeting, he would see anyone who would hold similar activity as a competitor. In addition, because of his unclear vision of the market and of his own business, he got rid of people who were there to help him out. Typically, blaming others is a way of avoiding taking responsibility for one's own issues. It turns out that he seized the opportunity to avoid conversations about strategy, which was my topic with him. Without me telling him to build a business plan, he could go back to the same old operational comfortable, however unprofitable, safe nest he had created for himself.

A leader who sees competitors everywhere because they have no clear vision of the market and of their own position in it is dangerous to themselves—they are a good example of self-sabotage. While being cognizant of the competition is imperative, being scared of it is not. The best antidote to this fear is having a solid and realistic strategy. Being haunted by ghosts can only increase fear and lack of confidence. If you don't believe in your own company, why would your clients? If you don't have clients, your company's survival is at stake. It is a strategic mistake to focus on competitors. Companies should focus on their clients because this is where the loyalty and subsequent profit comes from. If you are better with your clients, beating your competitors will be a natural consequence of your strategic ability to satisfy them.

Spirituality and the Power of Wonder

Kotler et al.[8] define Marketing 3.0 as the one with the objective of making the world a better place where a new wave of technology sees humans with minds, hearts, and spirits and where the value propositions are based on functionality, emotions, and spirituality.

Most people get confused between spirituality and religion or spirituality and superstition, which come more naturally during our childhood. Young children are born with a unique developmental path that captures the spiritual essence of wonder and each child's signature style of their own capabilities, strengths, interests, personality, temperament, and learning abilities. Spiritual moments experienced by young children are often direct, personal, and have the effect, if only for a moment, of uplifting the child by capturing the essence of spirituality through playful moments.

Children's spirituality involves questioning, exploring, and belonging by building close relationships in comfortable environments in which they grow. Spirituality, together with the ability to make-believe allows young children to be awakened with an awareness of community and purpose for the world around them. Each new discovery made by a young child is a potential source of wonder and delight. Through a child's imagination and make-believe play, teachers and parents are given opportunities to witness children's spirituality.[9,10] Subbotsky and Quinteros, state that belief in magic begins in the consciousness of children (who explicitly accept it) and persists in the subconscious of adults (who explicitly deny it).

Children are naturally curious and question everything. They are observant and nothing is uninteresting to them—they are unfiltered. They are not ashamed of *not knowing* and they want to know. Thanks to this constant questioning, children develop critical thinking, which starts fading out with adulthood when people are more willing to comply with the beliefs of their groups rather than stand for their own beliefs, which leads to denial of several assumptions and facts in real life. To compensate, adults turn to all kinds of virtual entertainment, including video games involving magic, monsters, and supernatural powers. Now, they look cool when sharing their passion for these games, while they would have been mocked if they shared their real beliefs in magic, spirituality, and the power of supernatural.

The attempt of creating a world of science and technology that negates religion because they seem to be incompatible is questionable. The scientific laws and methods that we still follow today were founded by the ancient polytheistic Greek scientists followed by the monotheistic modern ones—Copernicus, Galileo, Newton, and Einstein—they all believed in God. Atheism, in propagating the lack of religious beliefs, becomes a type of *zombie religion*, because as any other religion propagates faith, but in this specific case, faith in God's inexistence.

Nevertheless, there is a lot of faith in AI, because there is a belief that it will provide us a much better life. AI is in a phase that brings together emotions and knowledge with all their contradictions. It triggers energy through motivation, curiosity, and action, but it is also entropic because while it is all based on logic, there is still confusion and lack of complete understating of how it really works and how to have it mastered, as pointed out by Professor Tea-makorn. The excitement about AI engenders a large production of dopamine thanks to its mysterious novelty and the feeling that nothing is ever impossible with AI. Looks like magic!

Spirituality has to do with moments of discovery and amazement, with going beyond what is obvious, and with feeling the essence of our lives. Today, there is a transfer of such amazement from spirituality to technology: it is more tangible. Consumers are constantly amazed with what technology can provide them. Technology makes their lives so much better and easier with daily discoveries of new apps, reviews, influencers, posts, and likes. And such technology takes them back to a make-believe world, which they would have left behind as they grew up. Video games, virtual reality, videos, and pictures created by AI entice consumers by their delusional reality. Everyone was excited when ChatGPT first got accessible to all people. It was just like magic! In a few minutes, they had responses to their questions, impeccable write-ups, pictures, and videos that looked real. Amazing!

With social media, consumers believe that they are a global celebrity each time their posts reach high levels of engagement from others. Although technology has nothing to do with spirituality, it seems to be able to address the same needs and provide similar satisfaction from the same virtual and intangible world as magic. The main difference is that spirituality is an inward-outward expression of self, while technology goes the other way around. It is our mind, or, as some would say, our soul or our inner light, that represents our spirituality and takes us to higher levels of existence and understanding of the world, while technology is an external factor influencing our existence and understanding of the same world. These are different lenses trying to reach the same outcome.

We Should Sense It

The true nature of the senses has never been understood, as they remained savage and animal merely because successive civilizations have not aimed at making them elements of a new spirituality based on instincts and beliefs. We traded instinct against knowledge and rationality. We are unable to be intuitive and to feel rather than see. We don't see future challenges coming up until they hit us and we need to face them urgently—we improvise solutions. We lost our flair too. In the legendary movie *Crocodile Dundee*, Mike, the Australian, uses all of his five senses to assess situations and spot danger. When in his natural habitat, he is able to fight the *bad guys* just by leveraging his knowledge of nature (natural weapons) against their guns. We were able to do the same some time ago. It was natural to humans as well as to any other animal species. Even our pets lost their former capabilities. By being indoor pets and eating processed pet food, they are unable to hunt and are developing the same allergies and illnesses as humans. Today, a dog might choke on a bone and a cat might break a tooth when eating real meat.

Our civilization is so focused on immediacy that everything that belongs to the long term is dismissed. We deconstruct to reconstruct. Just as in teleportation, one needs to be dismantled to be rebuilt somewhere else again, and not always exactly the same way or in the same order. History is rewritten. Rather than waiting until plants grow to feed us, we have them laboratory-processed, which is deconstructing and reconstructing agriculture. With AI we don't need to *waste* time researching through multiple sources: AI delivers what it is assumed to be needed in a few seconds. We are not defined by patience.

Key Takeaways

- Be sure to identify your real competitors.
- Focus on your customers rather than on your competitors.
- Believe in facts and evidence but trust your intuitions.

Implications to Marketers

1. Beliefs are a key word for marketers. You need to make sure that your customers believe in your brand's ability to deliver the benefits you promise them.

2. Understand that because all companies are focusing on immediacy and easiness, these attributes are necessary but not enough to set your brand apart from its competitors. Your brand positioning should clearly state that you offer more than comfort.

3. Instead of offering a magical product, give your customers the sense of control by demonstrating that your brand conveys them magical powers making their lives easier and more enjoyable.

4. Build trust, nurture it by taking your customers' beliefs seriously, and use them as a valuable input to increase product performance and customer satisfaction. Algorithms can help you to do so.

Decoding the TikTok Algorithm (https://buffer.com/)

TikTok's *For You* page, often abbreviated as FYP, has undeniably transformed how we consume content. The For You page is the first page you encounter on TikTok and is filled with recommended content and videos that get more accurate as you spend time on the platform.

Unlike the algorithms of YouTube and Instagram (but similar to LinkedIn), TikTok serves a mix of content from creators you follow and those you've yet to discover from one page. The blend of familiar and new content is tailored meticulously to user preferences, making the platform addictive and fresh.

At its core, the TikTok algorithm prioritizes a few key elements:

- **Engagement**: This includes likes, shares, saves, and comments. The more engagement a video gets, the higher its chances of being showcased.
- **User interactions**: Whom your audience follows and engages with can influence the content they see.
- **Video information**: Details like whether the video was created natively on TikTok, the information in the caption, and any embedded details within the video.
- **Device and account settings**: Factors like location, language preference, and device type also play a role.

Each one of these factors is in pursuit of one goal: **to help users discover new, relevant content**. One of the standout features of TikTok's algorithm is its emphasis on content relevance over creator popularity. Key tools in this discovery process include:

- Hashtags
- Keywords
- Common search phrases

Finally, TikTok won't recommend certain content on your For You page if:

- It's too graphic or endangers the safety of users
- I's tagged as *Not interested*
- You've seen it already

Understanding the TikTok algorithm is the first step, but how does it translate into actionable advice for creators? Here are some ways to harness the algorithm's nuances to enhance your content's reach and engagement.

Follow the Rules to Increase Your Reach

You should be making relevant and engaging content, *but* that only works if your content is seen in the first place. By keeping to TikTok's rules of reach, you can ensure your content is always optimized for reach so you can focus on posting. Here are some evergreen tasks to consider as you make your next TikTok:

- **Use relevant hashtags**. Three to five hashtags are recommended as the sweet spot for boosting discoverability.
- **Incorporate trending audio** from the TikTok Audio Library.
- **Add captions** to your videos and sprinkle in relevant keywords.
- Embrace **native TikTok features**. Whether it's filming directly within the app or using features like Stitches or Duets, staying native can give you an edge. For more robust editing options, use CapCut, which is owned by TikTok's parent company ByteDance.

CHAPTER 2

AI, Superstition, Myths, and Marketing

Don't mock what you don't understand.

In the previous chapter, we explored the role and power of spirituality, which leads us, here, to the analysis of the role of superstitions and myths in marketing. In a world ruled by technology, can AI and mythology coexist? From a cognitive standpoint, they don't seem to be incompatible and marketers know very well how to explore mythological creatures in their communication with customers. This task is made even easier when we understand that our brains work in an algorithmic way.

In a world increasingly dominated by science, superstitious thinking takes a back seat in business affairs even if it plays a central role and remains prevalent in the popular culture of all societies. Superstitions receive considerable attention in several fields including popular psychology[1,2,3], philosophy[4], abnormal psychology[5,6,7,8], and medicine[9,10], which typically frame superstitions as irrational mistakes in cognition.

A notable exception, however, is[11] Shermer, who argues that superstitions are the adaptive outcome of a general belief engine, which evolved to reduce anxiety (proximate cause) and enable humans to make causal associations (ultimate cause). The cause–effect relationship is reassuring because humans want to know why phenomena happen, which is the main goal of science. However, the scientific method can only explain what can be rationalized and concretely defined, and all behaviors and happenings that are not captured by science yield to assumptions and to the quest for answers in mystical settings[12,13]. Interestingly, for several decades, what was not explained by science was attributed to culture, which, among hundreds of definitions, seems to be a complex whole. This is still true today, because culture keeps being the mysterious human trait that is hard to measure and explain despite the constant attempts to quantify it. Perhaps, this is exactly the issue; trying to quantify what is purely qualitative and notoriously subjective.

What Is Superstition?

Just like religion and magic, superstitions are fueled by beliefs, faith, and hope. They link causes and effects in ways that defy logic and fail all impartial tests. They are fascinating because they challenge all intellectual advances and evidence. No one can be rational all the time and totally free from ancient beliefs transmitted as a cultural connector through generations, as improbable as some superstitions may sound to others.

Superstitions are beliefs that run counter to rational thought or are inconsistent with known laws of nature.[14] Superstitions can be classified as either cultural or personal and are invoked either to bring good luck or to fend off bad luck. The degree to which consumers rely on superstitious beliefs in their purchase decisions is likely to depend on the associated level of stress, risk, and uncertainty.[15,16] The prevailing view is that resorting to superstitions provides a sense of control like in magic or, at least, explains why control is not possible.[17]

The effects of superstitions pervade the consumer environment. For example, a 2003 Harris Poll revealed that 31 percent of those surveyed believed in astrology.[18] Similarly, in the 2004 Science and Engineering Indicators report, the National Science Institute Foundation reported that 30 percent of Americans read their horoscope occasionally and 15 percent read their horoscope very often.

Superstitions also influence high-involvement decisions. When the Groundhog predicts an early spring, investors get optimistic. This is the *sell in May and go away* effect—the market tends to be at its worst from May through October. Stocks perform poorly around the full moon and when Mercury is in retrograde. This is proof of an existing correlation between weather and investing behavior.[19] Interestingly, we are far away from the times when witches were burned because they were deemed responsible for the weather variations, which would have an impact on agriculture and thus lead to starvation. Consumers employ superstition as a heuristic device for making decisions and an estimated U.S.$800 to U.S.$900 million is lost in business each Friday the 13th because people intentionally avoid travel and work on that day.[20]

Most people might be reluctant in believing that such behavior could exist in modern and developed societies such as the United States, a society rooted in factual evidence, which would constitute one more argument in favor of AI. Indeed, machines have no superstitions, and these kinds of losses can be avoided everywhere professionals can be replaced by technology. Machines have no unions, no vacations, and don't claim religious holidays. They will not look for guidance on the planets and the stars. Rather, they make logical decisions based exclusively on data. Yet, accuracy depends on the available data and if past data were based on superstitions, machines might simulate the same trends and perpetuate them even if they don't apply to current situations, as explained by Professor Tea-makorn.

Superstitions may be divisible into negative and positive beliefs[21]: *women on board is bad luck* sailors used to believe. Numbers carry magical powers thanks to superstition too: dial 666 for Satan, and avoid 13 in Christian cultures and number four in Asia. While magic and superstition are also used to protect ourselves from any kind of harm, with technology, we use cybersecurity to protect us from technological harm. Brands such as Google, Apple, and WhatsApp (Meta) make their data privacy policy their main promotional argument. With more and more people having their bank accounts, ID, or credit card numbers used by cyber thieves in addition to companies having their systems hacked, cybersecurity became a very fruitful market.

Superstitious beliefs and behaviors permeate our society.[22,23] Many people believe that knocking on wood wards off bad luck and that lucky charms bring good luck. For example, the use of incense to clear and clean a new home or to bring good fortune, and money, as well as enhance spirituality is a common practice across countries. The use of stones specific to one's birthday is also believed to bring positive vibes. Superstitious beliefs are often harmless, but may lead to irrational decisions [24,25], which would never happen with a machine.

Despite the large impact that superstitious beliefs have on the marketplace, we currently know very little about their implications for consumer judgment and decision making. The existence of the influence of superstitious beliefs on consumer behavior has been documented by[26] Kramer and Block, where the authors specify superstitions' conscious and nonconscious underlying properties. In particular, superstitious beliefs have a robust influence on product satisfaction and decision making under risk. However, these effects are only observed when superstitious beliefs are allowed to work nonconsciously.

Belief in superstition also means that sometimes people leave their own decisions to fate: *what should happen will happen*, what leads us to a paradox: using magic and technology to control our lives while leaving part of it to fate. Superstitions are pervasive and resistant across time because they are a source of hope to people. Believing in superstitions is believing in the possibility of the impossible. It is accepting that what one can't control can still happen. Superstition is also this virtual shield against threats; people don't know exactly what can happen but want to be protected in case it happens. In a world of uncertainty, superstitions represent protection and stability.

One could envisage a parallel with AI. Is it able to control, predict, and protect? Does it leave room for fate? Is there a balance between control and randomness? Apparently not for now. Because AI is still a black box, we don't know exactly how data are processed and how we get the outcomes it delivers. Whatever happens in the black box will have an impact on the outcome.

We Exist Because We Believe

Superstitions are strong beliefs, and beliefs are the essence of our existence, because willpower depends on beliefs—what is worth fighting for. It is a human natural need. That is why we observe a behavioral change when there is a shift in belief. There is no hope without belief, and there is no life without hope. Consumers are loyal to certain brands because they believe that those brands will provide them with added value and constant satisfaction. In a world where products come and go with shorter life cycles, brands represent stability. In fact, between

80 and 90 percent of new product launches fail, according to multiple studies, and from more than 30,000 new products launched in the market every year only 10 to 20 percent are accepted by the consumers.[27] That is why consumers are loyal to brands rather than to products.

Superstitions are also incorporated in businesses. In a study conducted in Asia, four types of superstitions were identified as being used by the companies' leadership: feng shui, calculation destinies (date/time of birth, palmistry, meditation), physiognomy (identification of character from facial structure), and consulting the oracle (mediums in Temples). Superstition was used in hiring and location, and blessings were held both for new business hardware (land and equipment) and—more commonly—for the opening of an entirely new venture. For the latter, a cleansing ceremony was especially common if the land on which the premise was to be constructed was once a graveyard or the scene of a disaster. The study found that even in resolutely secular commercial centers an important place is given to esoteric belief systems, where astrology and animism help people to choose a child's name, secure the right job, or find the best location for starting a new enterprise.

In addition, it was noted that superstition is widely used among local managers for the purposes of recruitment, promotion, demotion, and dismissal. In recruiting prospective employees, signs drawn from astrology, numerology, and clairvoyance were used to provide additional information to help secure the *right* individual.[28] This is the absolute opposite of ChatGPT, which can write a perfect job description in a few seconds as long as users input the right keywords to get the right answers.

Cognition and Myths

The opposition between cognition and behavior has been an everlasting discussion in the consumer behavior field. The behavioral models see people as in a black box: there is an input and an output but we don't know what process generated that output initialized by that input. Cognitive models, on the other hand, analyze what is inside of the black box where lie our beliefs, emotions, memory, and so forth. AI is still a black box because we can't figure out the whole process. Despite its fast penetration and use, we don't know what exactly leads to outputs, and there are often surprises. What we do know, though, is that to solve a problem you need to first solve the underlying data problems as stated by Professor Adelakun.

Autosapient systems are something of a black box, not just to users but even to their designers and owners, who are often unable to decipher how the systems arrive at specific decisions or produce certain outputs. Same mystery as in magic! You see before and you see after, but you don't know how the process unfolds.

With that, we now risk a major recentralization of the flow of information and ideas, in large part because of the filtering and synthesizing roles that AI-powered digital significant others will play. They'll summarize our inboxes, organize our digital lives, and serve us elegantly packaged, highly tailored, and predetermined answers to many of the questions we would once have relied on search engines or social media for, rendering the original source material that these tools scrape less necessary and much less visible. A very small number of companies (and perhaps countries) are likely to control the base models for these interfaces. The danger is that each of us will end up being fed information through an increasingly narrow cognitive funnel. In the face of this, leaders and organizations must work to cultivate a breadth of perspectives, strive to combat confirmation and other biases, and avoid overreliance on any one company or interface whose goal is to fully mediate their connection to the world.[29]

In ancient times, a large array of associations among apparent disconnected sources was possible, because people believed that there was a connection between colors, astrology, and planetary bodies, which were ruled over by gods. That is still true in several cultures. In Thailand, for example, color symbolism is influenced by several factors such as politics, religion, and astrology. The latter imposes the color of the day, which means that each day has a lucky/unlucky color, because each weekday has a corresponding planet and deity that influences it.

The symbolic role of animals in marketing is worth noticing as well. From the magical powers of Pegasus, Dragons, the Sphinx, and Griffins, several animals are chosen by companies to represent their values and promises. There is a belief that animals convey different features and traits that can represent a brand, so it is important to choose an animal that symbolizes the characteristics the company wants their customers to associate with their brand.

Arguably, the most famous logo featuring an animal is Ferrari's wild stallion. It depicts everything that Ferrari wants its customers to think about the cars that they produce—fast, sleek, and luxurious. The Jaguar logo is a very memorable one because it is a literal representation of their brand name. The pouncing wildcat was designed to not only mirror the name of the company, but also to illustrate the fundamental values of the manufacturer—ambition, grace, and power.

The Peugeot's lion dates back to the 1800s, when the Peugeot family's steel business needed a logo that reflected the company's activity and strength. The long-standing association between the Austrian royal family and swans allows Swarovski to have a luxurious, classy feel to their branding. Lacoste's crocodile logo dates back to 1923, when tennis prodigy and eventual founder of the company, René Lacoste, had a bet with his team's captain to win a crocodile leather suitcase if he won his upcoming match.

The Penguin Books logo is another famous logo containing an animal. In 1935, 21-year-old artist, Edward Young, visited London Zoo to draw pictures of the penguins and these drawings became the inspiration for the company's logo. Finally, the German company chose the name Puma to highlight its values of strength, agility, and grace. The logo has changed several times throughout the years, but the current logo is the one introduced in 1988. With a sleek, bold wordmark, designed to showcase power, and a leaping Puma to represent agility and sporting prowess. As the elephant is known to have strong memory, Evernote helps you keep track of all your tasks whereas the Hermes horse is a symbol of power and luxury.

It is worth noting here that some Asian parents try to choose the year for their children's birth as per the zodiac's animal representing that year. The child would thus benefit from that animal's attributes for their whole life.

Our Brain Is an Algorithm

Beliefs are complex chains of cognitive algorithms. Our minds were built to find patterns to enable us to recognize people, food, places, and so on. Thus, anything that promises immediate satisfaction and eternal happiness falls in the same pattern. If you hear always the same statement, you end up believing it. Beliefs don't exist in isolation because they are entangled with one another and in doing so they create a context prone to introduce other beliefs consistent with the pre-existing ones. This chain of beliefs determines what is acceptable and what is not acceptable and works as a shield. Ideas and statements contrary to well-settled beliefs are rejected to protect us from cognitive dissonance; we don't like to be shown that we are wrong. On the contrary, all ideas compatible with the pre-established beliefs are welcome and immediately accepted without further examination, added to the pool, and reinforce the chain of beliefs.

When a consumer is loyal to a brand, everything positive said about that brand is coded *yes* and goes to the chain of beliefs and everything negative is coded *no* and is rejected. This is explained by the fact that criticizing the brand consumers accept and defend is taken personally because that brand was their choice and they are resistant to the idea of having made a bad decision. In addition, one of the key roles of a brand is to convey messages of expression. When consumers proudly display the brands they buy, they are expressing themselves socially. In a world where social acceptance and validation are vital, sharing brands with the consumer's community is crucial. Thus, brand communities created around influencers dictate the purchase of specific brands as norms of acceptance and conduct to be a member of that community. The bright side is that it enhances a person's self-esteem, self-identity, and pride in societies having substituted technological diversions for human community.[30]

Algorithms shape our perception of reality. Coding establishes a relationship with the customer through algorithms when for example asking you if you travel for leisure or business. The activities and prices the app will suggest will be different and consistent with the purpose of your trip. Love and hate work like algorithms too. Love is that one-of-a-kind magical feeling that no other event can trigger in us. It works like magic, because it changes our vision of the loved one, which only we can have. Our perception of others (and of the world) is always blurred by love or by its opposite—hate. While we might be able to roughly explain why we hate someone, it is very hard to explain why we love someone because love is such a unique feeling impossible to rationalize and put in words. That is why Kay defines it with diamonds!

Cognition is the gatekeeper of everything we do. It is how we see reality. Our decisions, emotions, and actions are all rooted in our beliefs. Because our brain works as an algorithm creating biases that help us to make choices with the binary codes 0 and 1 to define truth and reality as we like, our vision of the world is based and contained on a simple equation: *if x, then y*. If you believe in magic, then you are crazy. If you trust technology, then I cannot trust you. Alternatively, in marketing, if you buy that brand or support that shop, then you belong to our community, but if you buy a different brand and support a different kind of shop, then you are out. A change in our beliefs is a consequence of a change of programming somewhere in our brain. Cognitions may be triggered by real-world events, but they are ultimately the product of our beliefs and desires. Our vision of the world is processed by an emotional algorithm, which is triggered by the cognitive habits and may or may not be accurate representations of reality.[31] Unlike machines, our algorithms (brain) are the factory of emotions that control human behavior.

We assume that others think the way we do or should think like us without realizing that we all have biased minds. Part of that is inherited from our family who convey their beliefs and historical background to us. This includes cultural traditions and rituals, superstitions, and a way of seeing the world and everything that is in it. As we grow up and interact with others, we add other peoples' standpoints and as we are confronted with reality, we now interpret it our own way based on our own knowledge and beliefs. This is part of our socialization process; we become members of a society. Then, when we go abroad, we face different mindsets, beliefs, and rituals that can sometimes seem surprising. If we live and work in a foreign country, this will indubitably happen and we need to acculturate to be able to survive in an environment that is not our original one.

Indeed, history, tradition, and myths are the accumulation of knowledge as we learn from the past. For instance, mythology is a set of stories about gods. A god is a personification of a motivating power or a value system that functions in human life and in the universe—the powers of your own body and of nature. The myths are metaphorical of spiritual potentiality in the human being, and the same powers that animate our life, animate the life of the world.

Every individual can find an aspect of myth that relates to his or her own life. Myth serves four functions:

1. The mystical function—wonders about the universe and humans —mystery;
2. The cosmological function—scientific answers to limited questions about the cosmos—knowledge about the universe;
3. The sociological function—support and validation of a certain social order—social and ethical norms;
4. The pedagogical function—living a human lifetime under any circumstances—understand the wisdom of nature and brotherhood with it—nature is the divinity.

Mythology can also be strictly sociological, linking consumers to a particular society (culture), or a particular social group (community). The use of mythological creatures by brands aims at conveying an aura of power and mystery. From the Siren in Starbucks' logo to Pegasus on ExxonMobil's, and brand names such as Apollo and Nike, the use of mythology perseveres and keeps the mythical beliefs alive in contemporary consumers' minds.

When Marketing and AI Play With Myths

Branding and marketing communications play a pivotal role in keeping myths close to consumers. The brand Kaleidos sells cookies with Unicorn flavor, which no one will ever be able to question because no one knows what a unicorn tastes like. Nike is named after the

Greek Goddess of Victory, and the logo is the swoosh made by her wings. Danone (Dannon in the United States) created the Greek Yogurt line branded Oikos, with an advertisement featuring Ares, the Greek god of War. Gillette sells feminine razors named after the Roman Goddess of love, Venus. In addition, Amazon sees Yeti using a hair dryer and Medusa wearing sunglasses in their advertisements. In addition, consumers can wear cryptid sweaters featuring Nessie, the Scottish Loch Ness monster with the saying *the important thing is that I believe in myself!* The list is much longer than these few examples that show that myths do have their place in the contemporary collective imaginary. Consumers somehow identify with these myths, even if they are often depicted in humorous situations as if they weren't meant to be taken seriously. Yet, they are part of our civilizations' deepest roots.

Nevertheless, some other brands are real and become myths thanks to their past history and longevity. Chanel N5, the mythical French perfume from Chanel, is more than a century old and has been the top brand for perfume across generations of women around the world. Other than the mystery around the number five and its extravagant creator Coco Chanel, the brand has also benefitted from the endorsement of Marilyn Monroe when she stated that all she wore when going to bed were a few drops of Chanel N5.

Coca-Cola is also more than 100 years old and became a myth not only because of its extensive marketing efforts in communication and an impeccable distribution strategy but also because of the mystery of its top-secret recipe safely hidden in a vault in Atlanta. Coca-Cola has raised successive generations of people enjoying this drink around the world and became synonymous with soda. The brand is also closely associated to Christmas and Santa Claus who wears the same colors as the brand.

McDonald's has a comparable reputation, thanks to its history of pioneering the fast food and hamburger industry. The story of this unique place opened in 1940 in California and having been later turned into an empire by Ray Kroc is today one of the top globalized brands, with all its failures and successes abroad, and has been one of the preferred topics for several case studies in business schools around the world.

These three brands used to be ranked in the Top 10 of the most valuable brands for several decades and became mantras. Today, the most valuable brands are Apple, Microsoft, Amazon, Google, and Samsung. Tesla is growing and reached the 12th place in 2023 (Interbrand). Brands in the technology industry have taken over all of the other industries and their penetration is much faster.[32] Sutherland states that magic does exist, *because we don't value things, we value their meaning*. To him, companies that look for opportunities to make magic, like Apple, figure in lists of the most valuable brands because they make believe that their products are magical, but no one in public life believes in magic.

> This is why marketing doesn't get any credit in business—when it generates magic—it is more socially accepted to attribute the resulting success to logistics or cost-control. The ingrained reluctance to entertain magical solutions results in a limitation in the number of ideas that people are allowed to consider.

That also means that there is more investment in the current leading brands. Thus, Chanel N5, Coca-Cola, and McDonald's face new challenges today. Younger women prefer fruity and lighter perfumes and the new dietary patterns are opposed to sugary and artificial drinks as well as caloric foods, which are all the opposite of what Coca-Cola and McDonald's stand for.

To keep up with the new consumption trends, these companies are incorporating AI in their strategies. McDonald's started a partnership with Google to apply generative AI to its operations, as thousands of stores will get hardware and software upgrades. Along with updates to other systems including ordering kiosks and the company's mobile app, McDonald's will be able to use generative AI on massive amounts of data to optimize operations.

Moreover, Coca-Cola began a digital transformation journey, aiming to use AI to streamline processes, improve efficiency, and deliver personalized customer experiences. The company collaborated with a team of AI experts to develop and implement Cola 3000, a cutting-edge AI-powered system. Among the goals were (www.linkedin.com/pulse/how-coca-cola-used-ai-improve-operations-customer-julia-baranava/):

- **Demand forecasting:** Cola 3000 analyzed sales data, market trends, and external factors to accurately forecast demand. This allowed Coca-Cola to optimize production, manage inventory efficiently, and avoid overstocking or shortages. The result was reduced costs and improved customer satisfaction.
- **Supply chain optimization:** Cola 3000 provided real-time visibility into Coca-Cola's global supply chain, identifying potential delays and suggesting optimal transportation routes. Logistics operations were streamlined, minimizing delays and maximizing cost-effectiveness.
- **Customer personalization:** Cola 3000 allowed Coca-Cola to deliver personalized customer experiences through data analysis. The system gathered insights about individual preferences, purchasing habits, and demographics. This enabled Coca-Cola to target specific market segments, leading to higher customer engagement and loyalty.
- **Social media engagement:** Cola 3000's AI algorithms analyzed public sentiment and customer feedback in real-time on social media.

Coca-Cola's adoption of AI yielded results and benefits:

- **Improved efficiency:** AI automation and optimization increased productivity, reducing manual effort and errors.
- **Enhanced decision making:** AI-driven insights provided by Cola 3000 empowered Coca-Cola to make informed choices faster and more accurately.
- **Cost reduction:** AI-powered demand forecasting and supply chain optimization resulted in cost savings.
- **Personalized customer experiences:** Cola 3000's analysis of customer data improved marketing initiatives, resulting in increased customer satisfaction and loyalty.

- **Competitive advantage:** Coca-Cola gained a competitive edge in the industry, staying ahead of market trends, and meeting customer demands effectively.

In sum, data are the language of business, and stories are the language of consumers. While numbers are no one's native language, everyone is familiar and enjoys stories.[33] If numbers were a natural language people would not be scared of mathematics and calculations. However, we live in a quantitative world where anything that has no figures seems not to matter. No wonder there is resistance to taking superstitions, beliefs, and symbolism into account, because they are not quantifiable. Yet they do influence consumer behavior. AI is somehow able to bridge this gap in translating numbers (codes) into words.

Key Takeaways

- Take your marketing strategy beyond rationality. Consumers do rely on intuition and superstitions.
- Our brains make choices just like AI with algorithms.
- AI is science based on evidence, but humans are also made of beliefs, emotions, intuitions, and superstitions. There is science in magic too.

Implications to Marketers

As much as marketers in developed countries would believe that magic, myths, and superstitions are buried in the past, they should remember that people are intuitive and this is why they are driven by factors other than facts. This can be an issue because a machine might not be able to seize such subtleties of human behavior and leave important intangible variables out of the equation when trying to predict consumer behavior.

When using AI to understand customers, marketers should calculate the error margin generated by the biases introduced by the users and the machine's inability to understand what is not said but is felt by the customers. AI seems to be able to create new products taking current trends into account, which is an amazing asset. Yet, marketers should be well aware of the short product life cycle that such creations would entail. The machine creates products with today's trends or based on future estimations. But trends change quickly and a new product can easily become obsolete if it is not rooted in long-lasting beliefs rather than in transient trends.

CHAPTER 3

AI and Science

Is There Magic in Science?

Science is the daughter of time.

—Galileo

Skepticism about magic and superstitions is nothing new as explained in the previous chapter, but how can they persevere in a world that is more rational than spiritual? While some would argue that AI is science and magic is not, this chapter unveils the science of magic and the numerous academic programs specialized in magic recently created by universities around the world. The science of magic comes also through our smartphones on which we are totally dependent as we use them as magic wands. Other than serving as a premonition, AI makes your dreams come true by surprising you every day with new solutions to your problems.

Science involves constant questioning. Questioning is not skepticism; it is critical thinking and not taking things as they are given. The French philosopher René Descartes used to say that *if I have doubts is because I exist and it is because I have doubts that I think, because the proof that I think is that I have doubts.* However, today you never see people *just thinking*—everyone is busy with their screens no matter what is on there. Thinking became a waste of time; everything we should know comes to us. Need to buy something? Check what people recommend on TikTok.

One would assume that four centuries after the age of science began there shouldn't be any belief in magic, faith, or religion. Yet thanks to technology, there is. Technology enables people to see and speak with others from far away in real time. Fantasy and reality are blurred because many consumers can no longer tell virtual from real lives. And, with the evolution of AI, introducing not only digital influencers but also pictures and videos so well done that they look real, this line between imagination and reality becomes even more blurred.

Consumers live on videos, chats, and pictures posted on social media and they tend to believe all of them. It is known that many people become antisocial and lose the ability to go out and interact with real people because they spend more time online than speaking to people they meet physically. Their lack of ease when being around other humans also adds to the feeling of exclusion and isolation.[1,2] Ironically, people might question the existence of magic, superstition, faith, and religion, but they don't question what they see online. Because they don't question answers from ChatGPT, they don't feel the need of going beyond and fact-checking. The immaterial rules the world.

French King Louis IX aiming at bringing religion and monarchy together once said: *reason doesn't contradict faith, because faith is an act of intelligence leading to rational intelligence and both together can lead to liberty.* After his death, the king was canonized as Saint Louis. The city of Saint Louis in Missouri was named after him. During the Crusades, Louis IX summoned Robert de Sorbon, who believed that only intelligence could save humanity from sins and wars, and invited him to create a place where knowledge would be conveyed to all those who wanted to learn, because the literacy rate was very low in the country. This is when one of the oldest and most famous universities in the world was created in Paris (1257) : La Sorbonne. Today, students from around the world apply to this university and it also became one of the most visited landmarks in Paris. Sorbonne was my home university where I created and ran the trilingual master's degree in international negotiation. I was a professor there for 23 years!

Toward a Science of Magic—The Eternal Paradox

It has always seemed to be a paradox bringing science (technology) and magic together. Yet, we behave in paradoxical ways: we want to save the planet but we keep shopping online and thus, multiplying the air and noise pollution caused by constant shipping and transportation.

For example, and in addition to your daily deliveries from Uber Eats, Amazon, Instacart, and Hello Fresh, Skura tells you that, to protect your home from bacteria, you should change your kitchen sponge frequently, and to help you out with that, they send you a new sponge every two weeks. People use electric doors rather than the revolving ones because the electric doesn't require effort, yet it wastes electricity. Moreover, we know that AI consumes massive amounts of energy and increases carbon emissions as does a spaceship every time it takes off but we are so fascinated by such technological accomplishments that we don't even think of that. We have been trained to focus only on the detrimental use of plastic. We eat impossible meat (who knows what is in there) to save the planet and ourselves from cows but we enjoy the NASCAR and all kinds of car races.

Paradoxical or not, the pervasive penetration of technology triggered the resurgence of interest in the scientific study of magic in the past few years. Despite being only a few years old, this new wave has already resulted in a host of interesting studies, often using methods that are both powerful and original and pave the way to new opportunities available for scientific studies based on the use of magic[3], despite the skepticism of contemporary scientists.

Skepticism, along with what is used to be called common sense, sees beliefs in curses and spells as a kind of hallucination. Hallucination is everything that is confusing and something that humans and AI have in common. AI hallucination is a phenomenon, wherein a large language model—often a generative AI chatbot or computer vision tool —perceives patterns or objects that are nonexistent or imperceptible to human observers, creating outputs that are nonsensical or altogether inaccurate and sometimes with unrealistic estimations and extrapolations. Humans should be there to supervise and correct such outcomes. Professor Adelakun reminds us that qualified professionals are needed to avoid AI hallucination.

Humans can also educate machines to be polite and say please or use capital letters when it is important or urgent, just like speaking to a human. For example, and just out of curiosity, we asked ChatGPT how one could go from Chicago, Illinois, in the United States to Paris in France. The answer was: by car, train, bus, or airplane! We then asked how we would cross the ocean by car, train, or bus. It apologized and suggested to fly to the destination. This simple illustration shows that no one can rely on ChatGPT without checking the answers, which in some cases can be more time-consuming than finding out the answers through more reliable sources.

If people believe everything ChatGPT tells them they will be experiencing the *certainty of hallucination,* which means that we have been wired to believe in nonsensical responses or situations without questioning them or looking for other sources of information. One pertinent example would be the exponential growth in the number of followers of digital influencers. People follow and obey someone who doesn't exist, and they know that those influencers are just computer-generated images. It is illogical, irrational, and yet human. This absurdity doesn't seem to be relevant to them. The same ones will state that magic is illogical and irrational because it doesn't exist—*how could people believe in superstitions in the era of technology?!* Did you say paradox?

Additionally, many customers buy virtual shoes to wear in video games or in photos. Those virtual products fall under the category of nonfungible tokens (NFTs) and include a record of ownership of primarily digital media. NFTs are authenticated as limited in number, thereby increasing their value to collectors. Exclusivity creates value. For instance, the Gucci Virtual 25 trainer shoe was created to be worn by a player's avatar in online games like Roblox or to be worn in photos shared on social media. Users put on the shoes using Gucci's app and take selfies while wearing their latest fashion. Some industry experts predict that in the next decade, virtual clothing may be a large portion of the fashion business. Did you say hallucination?

Look at the Sky to Understand Your World

From the moment they first connected the alternation of night and day with the motion of the heavens, human beings have been fascinated by astronomy. Long before they knew how to write, people knew the phases of the moon, which formed the basis of the first calendars. They noticed the periodic return of the seasons, watched the daily movement of the stars, which they saw as circular and uniform, and observed that every night the stars reappeared in the sky in what seemed to be permanent arrangements. They found it useful to group the stars in constellations and sometimes to label them according to the images they saw in them. There was a search for natural and unchanging laws by which events would occur and be understood, and the temptation to place omnipotent beings in the sky to explain what was mysterious and not understood. It was a search for patterns to enable planning and forward seeing. Imagination and observation, without technology, or fancy instruments, brought us the knowledge we have today which is the basis of our new discoveries.[4]

Followed the Western perception and cognition from the ancient Greeks and forward which has been analytic. The focus is on some central object, with respect to which the individual has some goal, which enables predictions and control. On the other hand, Eastern perception has been holistic. The object or person is seen in a broad context or field, and behavior is understood in terms of relationships and similarities rather than generalized categories and rules. Aristotle's physics focused almost exclusively on the object (intrinsic properties of the object), while the Chinese conception of action took into account the interaction between the object and the surrounding field (context). In addition, this is how the Chinese understood magnetism and acoustic and the real reasons for the tides before Galileo. Objects were composed of particles and atoms for the Greeks, while the Chinese would see waves in matters.

One of the reasons is that the Chinese society was based on agriculture, which would require substantial cooperation at the family and village levels; interdependence and collectivism were the result. The Greek society was based on herding, fishing, and trade that allowed for more independence and individualism. The different understandings of the social world resulted in different understandings of the physical world because if the individual regards himself as being highly linked with other people, other objects and events will also be seen as highly related, whereas if the individual regards himself as an isolated unit, other objects and events will also be seen as unique and unrelated to other objects and events. Thus, the chain of causality won't be the same.

Although science and magic are often seen as incompatible practices, because it is believed that science implies logic and intelligence, while magic stems from ignorance and irrationality, their common roots are found in nature. From the observation of the planets to the relationship with the elements, both science and magic have been evolving in symmetry and penetrating peoples' lives with intensity.

More recently, it has been suggested that it might be time to consider developing an outright science of magic—a distinct area of study concerned with the experience of wonder that results from encountering an apparently impossible event. Science can be viewed as a systematic method of investigation involving three sets of issues: (1) the entities considered relevant, (2) the kinds of questions that can be asked about them, and (3) the kinds of answers that are legitimate.[5] A science of magic could contribute to the study of the mind because it centers primarily around experiential effects.[6] Some experiences are largely unique to magic and have to do with the extent to which our perceptions and beliefs can deviate from objective reality.

No idea is ever examined in all its ramifications. Theories and practices are abandoned and superseded by accounts that are more fashionable. For instance, a few people know Voodoo, but everybody uses it as a paradigm of backwardness. Yet, a study of its manifestation could be used to enrich or revise our knowledge of physiology. The scientific revolution pushed aside, regarded as irrelevant, and often as nonexistent those facts that had supported the older philosophy. Thus, the evidence for witchcraft, demonic possession, and the existence of the devil were disregarded together with the superstitions it once confirmed. Witchcraft and other irrational views have ceased to be influential because reason was overruled at some time in their past.[7]

The experiential effect on consumers is more and more studied and practiced by marketers and materialized by customers' experience management efforts. A study conducted by Pointillist (https://pointillist.com) revealed that 87 percent of marketers believe that exceptional customer experience is very or extremely important to their organization. What consumers really remember is their experience with the product, the brand, and the company. This experience remains in their memory and drives their future purchase decisions. This explains why more than focusing on consumer satisfaction, companies focus on consumer experience. Consumers measure their experience according to their expectations, which are generated by their beliefs. If they believe that the experience will be very good, anything less than that will be a disappointment, whereas if they believe that the experience will be only average, anything higher than that will result in a positive memory.

Therefore, customer service is the most active department for AI deployment today. A study from MIT (MIT Technology Review Insights *Global AI Agenda* survey, 2020) revealed that data sharing has the potential to unlock new value for many industries. In the public sector, the concept of open data is well known. Publicly available data sets on transport, jobs and the economy, security, and health, among many others, allow developers to create new tools and services, thus solving community problems. In the private sector, there are also emerging examples of data sharing, such as logistics partners sharing data to increase supply chain visibility, telecommunications companies sharing data with banks in cases of suspected fraud, and pharmaceutical companies sharing drug research data that they can each use to train AI algorithms. Travel and hospitality, consumer goods and retail, IT and telecommunications, and customer care and personalization of products and services are among the most important AI use cases.

Is Your Smartphone a Curse?

The disturbing dependence of consumers on their smartphones is the best argument for demonstrating that technology and magic are compatible. Consumers attract the products they want just by pushing a button on their phones, and the product comes to them by home delivery. They turn on and off home's lights and they use it as an alarm clock, as a watch, as a step counter and as a wallet. But the best magic trick enabled by the smartphone is seeing and speaking with someone who is far away. It is creating a vision of what others can't see in reality by producing photos and videos and sharing them on social media.

Yet, without your smartphone, you will be locked out of your home and car, unable to order food, clothes, or transportation, and unable to scan QR codes or pay with Apple Pay. You are stuck without your magic wand.

Indeed, online shopping is what nurtures the belief in magical solutions because it is easy, effortless, and provides immediate gratification to consumers. That is why it has been growing exponentially, replacing physical stores, and turning some cities' downtowns into ghost towns. The social experience incarnated by an afternoon of shopping and having a snack with family and friends no longer makes sense. Now physical shopping is more frequently associated with chores than with pleasure. Perhaps shopping online is not that much of a pleasure, but it is easy, immediate, and effortless, just like magic.

Therefore, online retail sales amounted to U.S.$ 4.9 trillion worldwide in 2022 and it is forecasted to grow over 50 percent within the next four years (https://www.statista.com/topics/871/online-shopping/.)

Mobile commerce keeps growing: in 2021, U.S.$ 3.56 trillion in retail e-commerce sales were made from mobile users and e-commerce sites have been optimizing the mobile experience to increase their online sales for years—58.4 percent of internet users buy something online every week. According to Datereportal (https://datareportal.com/reports/digital-2022-global-overview-report), the categories with more spending are consumer electronics (U.S.$ 988.4 billion) and fashion (U.S.$ 904.5 billion). China generates U.S.$ 351.65 billion in revenue from retail e-commerce sales in social transactions made directly on a social media platform; 10 times more than the United States (www.emarketer.com/chart/247600/retail-social-commerce-sales-china-vs-us-2021-billions). Shopping on smartphones is estimated to go up to U.S.$ 420 billion in the United States in 2024.

Smartphones have been so prevalent in consumers' lives that M-commerce (Mobile shopping) has been growing more than shopping through computers and tablets. Anything that consumers want is made immediately accessible with their smartphones, which they can order at any time from anywhere through apps, as they keep their phones constantly with them. Smartphones can also start a car, open and close doors, and command coffee machines without touching any of them. A magic wand can do all of that and more.

Other than smartphones, technology can self-drive and self-park cars. When we see a car moving forward with no driver, it looks like magic. The smart door lock from Xiaomi locks and unlocks your home's door with facial or fingerprint recognition and can also be controlled remotely with your phone. Technology can make consumers younger with new body and face treatments and transport them to anywhere in the past, in the future, or to fictional places, thanks to virtual reality. Before we believed that only magic could do so.

Google does magic too, as the leader in offering AI services to make people's lives easier. After opening an email, Smart Reply suggests possible email responses. The user simply clicks on whichever one is preferred. Over time, Smart Reply learns the user's habits and preferences, and future suggestions become more customized and reflect the user's natural communication style. No need for the user to think or type.

Despite all of these advantages, the total dependence on smartphones is also a curse because it prevents people from learning and remembering—there is no need to make any effort. We document what we hear and see with pictures and videos and this is our memory. But do we really experience what we are recording? Do we really feel the experience as if we have lived it when we filter it through the lens of a camera? Our devices' memory is replacing our brain's memory, which doesn't really help with its plasticity and with learning. Not mentioning that we miss a lot of real-life events surrounding us by focusing only on what we are given to see on a screen.

Holding on to the smartphone also causes ophthalmological issues because of the extended hours of exposure to a small screen, causes posture issues because people bend forward when playing with their phones, favors obesity because of the lack of exercise caused by home delivery, and is an immense source of anxiety when the battery dies or the phone is lost or stolen.

Embrace What You Can't Avoid

The observation of the growing use of smartphones for every simple daily activity sparked the willingness to conduct a study. No hypotheses or assumptions were stated. Instead, the research aimed at understanding the fascination that contemporary consumers have for technology. Thanks to observations, we suggested that a plausible explanation would be that its ability to satisfy their desires immediately and with no effort could be assimilated to the magical powers only witches used to enjoy.

Therefore, a survey was conducted with only three open-ended questions asked to the participants: Do you believe in magic? Do you believe in superstition? Do you shop online? Those three questions were supplemented with a word association technique with the word *magic*. The sample constituted of 460 adult participants was fairly balanced between males (52%) and females (48%) and spanned across five countries (China, Taiwan, Bulgaria, the United Kingdom, and the United States). Findings indicated that 57.5 percent of the respondents believed in magic and 69 percent in superstition. In addition, 92 percent of the respondents declared shopping online, through their mobile phones, for most of the products they needed.

The word *magic* triggered the following associations: amazing, fantastic, Harry Potter, Dungeons & Dragons, happy, exciting, entertaining, abracadabra, witches, supernatural, unbelievable, magician, cards, trick, unexpected, make believe, incantations, miracle, whimsical, deception, and spells.

Official figures from Statista align with our findings: 2 in 10 Americans believe in spells or witchcraft. According to a survey conducted in 2021, 21 percent of respondents from the United States said that they believed in spells or witchcraft. In addition, according to a survey carried out among U.S. adults in April 2022, more than a quarter of them said they believed in astrology and that the position of stars and planets can exert an influence on people's lives. Incidentally, consumers can use the Night Sky app, by holding their smartphones up to the sky for a tour, identifying planets, stars, constellations, and more. They can also make a wish when they see a shooting star! In some cultures, shooting stars are seen as messages sent from the gods.

Accordingly, a global study conducted in 2022, stated that belief in magic is widespread around the world. The results show that about a billion people across 95 countries believe in witchcraft, which is most certainly an undercount, given the sensitivity of discussing witchcraft for some respondents. While at least some people believe in some version of witchcraft almost everywhere—about 40 percent of those who took the survey said they do—the local prevalence of those beliefs seems to vary widely. In Sweden, for example, only 9 percent of participants reported a belief in witchcraft, compared with 90 percent in Tunisia. Although witchcraft beliefs are more common in some countries than in others, they still cut across sociodemographic groups in each country (www.sciencealert.com/massive-global-study-shows-belief-in-witchcraft-is-more-abundant-than-you-might-think).

These results are also consistent with the proliferation of Witchcraft schools and universities around the world including the first master's degree in magic and the occult, starting in September 2024 at the University of Exeter in the United Kingdom. It also reveals the reasons for the success of a plethora of free online tests to assess anyone's ability to be a witch, for example, *15 signs You're a Witch. Do you Have These Witch Powers?* (Spells8—https://spells8.com).

Far from having been buried with the past, witches and witch-craft are flourishing in the era of technology and turning into a promising and juicy industry attracting more and more consumers through products with magical powers. In addition to the educational programs, several publications, including academic articles and books, have been proliferating. The *Harry Potter* saga might have influenced these developments but some other reasons could explain them too. Although AI is in all mouths and writings while fascinating the whole planet, magic appeals to customers because it is warmer, more human, more personal, and sounds closer to them than technology. Magic is exclusive and you need to want it—it requires specific skills, while AI is inclusive—anyone can use it. Using AI is already as straightforward as using one's smartphone. While technology is seen as a tool, magical powers are a rare and exclusive skillset: AI is not capable of warding off bad luck!

When Dreams Come True

Superstitions are often associated with dreams, which are supposed to be meaningful and have predictive powers. Studies about sleep and behavior focus on nighttime physiological processes and their impact on daytime cognition. A recent research suggests that remembering a good dream can help people make headway with the day's tasks. Respondents described the meaning they ascribed to the dream, their emotional response and their progress toward work goals.[8]

In the YouTube video *This is why GOD Wakes You up at 3:00 in The Morning,* the speaker delves into Nikolas Tesla's unique belief system, which held that waking up at 3:00 a.m. was a time of great spiritual and creative potential. Tesla, who was known for his irregular sleep patterns, believed that this rhythm allowed him to access deep insights and solutions, as well as connect with the divine energies of the universe. He saw the early morning hours as a time of tranquility and stillness, which facilitated clear thinking and spiritual growth. Tesla's fascination with the number three, which he considered sacred, further reinforced his belief in the significance of this hour. Whether the above is true or not, science and spirituality are brought together on behalf of one of the most respected scientists incidentally immortalized by Elon Musk's car.

Dreams are seen as unreal because they are structured and organized differently, and we feel as if we do not have control over them, unlike in real life. Yet, there is nothing more real than dreams because they are not bound to social desirability bias: your dreams are between you and yourself. Dreaming is traveling across time and space, and in your dreams, you write your own narrative and create your own life rather than what you have simply been taught to recreate.

Carl Jung defined the collective unconscious as all the inherited information we have as humans. It is a kind of storehouse of all human experience, which is influenced by universal wisdom. Mythology, rituals, and stories of ancient civilizations have grounded the collective unconscious we are part of today. This is how, in the contemporary interconnected world, the shared beliefs are an attempt to explain our own existence, both for what is physically seen and what is in our minds. The Toltecs in Mexico, as well as the Aboriginals in Australia, were known as being dream masters who created a masterpiece of life.

Dreams fight the replacement of common memories by a mass perception or vision of the facts and reality and the concept of truth reflecting an ethical persuasion. There is a dream of a world of common idiom of expression (Esperanto never worked well), of the discomfort with things as they are and the search for virtual amelioration—we always evoke change as having a positive impact on our lives, but there is not always long-term evidence of it. Every change has ramifications that are only measurable over time. Dreams and reality become equated in the world of digital idea generation, and when reality does not conform to the dream, AI reforms reality.

AI is designed to pass through the greatest amount of popular resistance and break down the barrier between thinking and doing. It holds a dream of human happiness molded outside of the human brain and reality, teaching people how to think. Since the 1920s, the *machine civilization* has been seen as a solution to social ills, the foremost imperative being what to dream.[9]

When dreaming, we are free to feel our emotions without filter. Our animal instinct leads us to protect ourselves from any threat, whether it is physical or ideological. The instinctive nature is the undomesticated (nonsocialized) part of us that intuitively and deeply knows how to navigate life's terrain and cycles. However, we can also lose the connection to our instincts because of social or societal pressures, trauma, or self-inflicted choices (following others), which sometimes lead to confusing emotions.[10]

Yet, all emotions are helpful to our development as members of a society. Emotional strength is about being able to move through the expression of emotions without being stuck. Emotions are not final goals; they are meant to take us to a more evolved state of mind; they are fluid markers of the experience of life. When you definitely admit how you feel to yourself, that is when things can actually change. Neuroscience shows that we respond instinctively to anything that looks like a human because our brains are attuned to react emotionally to facial signals. That explains why people are drawn to digital influencers and why bots with human faces work better than regular chatbots.

This human appearance tricks consumers into a one-way emotional relationship. Machines are emotionless logical inventions created to serve you, not to take over you. For some people, all the comfort provided by technology is like a dream coming true. It seems fair to notice that consumers are diving into a void rootless culture where new habits, practices, rituals, a new virtual society, and language emerge with names and acronyms such as SEO, chatbots, ChatGPT, AI, VR (Virtual Reality), AR (Augmented Reality), and so forth. We are acculturating to a highly virtual world.

Key Takeaways

- The more human your company looks, the more your consumers will be drawn to it.
- Consumers are always looking for products that make their dreams come true.
- Treating science like magic can be more persuasive than technology alone.

Implications to Marketers

Make sure that you use ChatGPT in a way that attracts and retains your customers. Help them to use it (https://searchengineland.com/):

Iterate and Refine

ChatGPT's responses may not always be perfect or exactly what you're looking for on the first try. Experiment with different phrasing or approaches to refine your interaction and get closer to your desired unique perspective.

Engage in Dialogue

Instead of asking a single question, engage in a back-and-forth conversation with ChatGPT.

Ask follow-up questions and request elaboration to deepen the exploration of ideas. This iterative approach can help generate more nuanced and diverse perspectives.

Incorporate Real-World Examples

Provide relevant examples or scenarios to ground the conversation in real-life contexts.

This can help ChatGPT draw connections and generate unique perspectives based on its understanding of the world.

Use Your Creativity

AI prompts can act as creative catalysts, sparking new ideas and fresh content concepts.

Experiment with different prompts and instructions to see how AI-generated suggestions can inspire you to think differently.

CHAPTER 4

AI and Products

A World of Plenty and Customization

We live in a make-believe world

Not as many dreams would come true without technology, as discussed in the previous chapter. A visible consequence is the proliferation of products that promise magical results. They carry the word *magic* on their brand names as they promise immediate and effortless results. This also explains brand loyalty from consumers who are rewarded for using the right apps. In this chapter, you will see how companies, such as Coca-Cola, strongly challenged by the new *healthy* trends, are using AI to be ahead of consumers' needs and ensure that their loyalty to the brand will be even stronger in the future.

Who doesn't want a miracle product? You want the one that makes you look fit, sexy, and younger in a few weeks or days, the only one that can get rid of stubborn stains, the one that will make you forever healthy and happy. Everyone wants that, but how many of us believe it? We would laugh today at the magical elixir called *snake oil* in the American Wild West, which would cure any illnesses in no time, but people believed it then. Today, the promises remain the same but to get the same benefits one customer should buy several different products each one targeted to one specific result. This multitude of products is meant to provide consumers with a better life and a better version of themselves.

The hardest task for the contemporary customer is to make a choice among so many alternatives. This partially explains why they follow influencers: someone should tell them what to buy. Plethora of magical promises proliferate on internet: less wrinkles in only two weeks, firmer skin in only two days, get rid of belly fat in five days, build muscles in three days, find real love, and lose weight without dieting or working out. All these promises are supported by revolutionary, exclusive, and unique technology. While Revitalift from L'Oréal promises wrinkle reduction in only one week, thanks to the hyaluronic acid, N7 launches Reverse, a facial care that reverses skin aging in only four weeks, thanks to a new peptide technology. And for your hair, use Fructis Hair Filler to reverse damages of up to one year in only one use. They work like a charm!

Each brand strives to show that they are the only one providing the magical solution to your problems, while saving you time and money. Without making much effort, you will receive, at home, the miracle product that can fix what you have been struggling with for years. You will get the product and its magical results immediately and without any effort. All the brands position themselves as the only option you should consider when making a choice.

For example, and to stand out from the multiple brands selling diets, Noon explains that overeating is caused by psychological reasons and offers a dieting program based on helping you understand why you overeat, which is admittedly someone else's fault for pressuring you. Unlike their competitors, the brand doesn't count calories or present delicious ready-to-eat meals or pills. Instead, they explain that your mind will help you to lose the weight. You are the one in control. It is just like giving you magical powers—you will control your mind and your behavior with visible outcomes.

The search for immortality has been one of the fascinations of humans who have been looking for the Holy Grail and the Philosopher's stone for centuries, which seems to be the perception we have of AI today: THE solution to everything for everyone. That explains why products with magical results proliferate on social media where anyone can be a witch and recommend life potions to extend peoples' lifespan. To do so, consumers buy countless supplements to replace fruits and vegetables, for energy, and for the skin, hair, and nails; they mix green powders with water for protein and have free access to recipes, diets, and tutorials on TikTok and YouTube for free. What a time to be alive!

While no consumer would ever admit being influenced by traditional advertising, they proudly share information about products they bought because of an influencer: *TikTok made me buy it*, as says the tagline—#TikTokMadeMeBuyIt. It is a bold statement, because any brand that would convey a similar statement would be more likely to be boycotted. That is the magic of TikTok. You would never see a consumer saying *advertising made me buy it*. Yet, it is the same marketing tool used by traditional companies to influence consumers in their choices by persuading them of the superior (magical) performance of their products when compared to their competitors. Within those commanded by social media are children and teenagers. A recent study[1] reveals that tweens between ages 8 and 12 spend 5 hours and 33 minutes daily on screens, while the 13 and 18 spend 8 hours and 39 minutes daily. Teenagers are getting less sleep and exercise and spending less in-person time with friends creating a cognitive implosion: anxiety, depression, compulsive behaviors, self-harm, and even suicide. These trends appear across genders, among poor and rich families, in every ethnic and racial background, and in cities, suburbs, and small towns. Heavy users of social media are about 30 percent more likely to be depressed.[2] In other words, it is a universal phenomenon, because life online has become nastier, more polarized, and more likely to incite bullying and shaming.

At the same time, robots have been useful in schools. Nao, for example, is an autonomous, programmable humanoid robot developed by Aldebaran Robotics, a French company headquartered in Paris, which was acquired by SoftBank Group in 2015 and rebranded as SoftBank Robotics. Nao robots have been used for research and education purposes in numerous academic institutions worldwide. In the summer of 2010, Nao made global headlines with a synchronized dance routine at the Shanghai Expo in China. In October 2010, the University of Tokyo purchased 30 Nao robots for their Nakamura Lab, with hopes of developing the robots into active laboratory assistants. In 2012, donated Nao robots were used to teach autistic children in a UK school; some of the children found the childlike, expressive robots more relatable than human beings. In a broader context, Nao robots have been used by numerous British schools to introduce children to the robotics industry.

Can You Believe It?

We have been equipped with an assortment of devices and apps meant to make us feel more productive by developing our expertise in multitasking and splitting our attention among multiple goals. While many people pride themselves on their ability to multitask, research has shown that media multitasking impairs memory by thinning the prefrontal cortex. Now humans should mimic machines. AI doesn't multitask: the machine handles each task at a time and never gets distracted by external sources which coincidentally aligns with MIT's Prof. Miller's words: *There is no such thing as multitasking; you just end up alternating between doing different tasks badly.*[3]

With this, the proliferation of miracle products sold online keeps growing and they all convey the same promise: immediate and effortless gratification while giving you the feeling that you are in control. Here are a few examples:

- **Smile** promises teeth alignment in a few weeks without consulting with a dentist.
- **Audible** reads books to you.
- Hair Lust and **Nutrafol** deliver shampoo and gummies for faster hair growth without consulting a specialist.
- **Warber Parker** delivers five pairs of glasses for you to try on and return those you won't buy.
- **Nutrisystem** home delivers ready-to-eat meals specific for couples' diets, for women over 50 years old, and for people in general helping to save money with less waste.
- **DriveTime** enables you to make your own deals to buy a car on your phone thanks to their app.
- **Instacart** allows grocery shopping while watching a game at the stadium: *You don't need to choose between football and the grocery store,* says their advertisement. Also, the app remembers

the groceries already purchased and makes it easier to renew the cart without bothering to pick products one by one.

- **Uber Eats** delivers any kind of ready-to-eat food.
- **Roomba** vacuum cleans your home without you.
- **Sleep Number** automatically regulates your mattress's temperature throughout the night.
- **Galaxy S24+** smartphone comes with AI integrated and translates your voice to other languages in real time.
- **Chewy** home delivers everything from food to toys for your pets.
- **GoDaddy** helps you create your own website by using AI.
- **Calm** and **BetterSleep** apps fight insomnia, anxiety relative to work or lack of focus by emitting calming sounds.
- **Meetik** helps you to find, online, real love in a few days.
- **BetterHelp** gives you access to online consultations with therapists.
- **MTailor** takes measures digitally and creates tailor-made pants for men
- **ProPhotos.ai** creates your professional headshot with AI.
- **Petivity** smart litter analyzes your cat's litter and allows you to monitor their weight and health on your phone.
- **Mood Magic**—is your uplifting superfood powder.
- **Carnival Magic**—takes you on a magical cruise around the Caribbean.

This noncomprehensive list of products from so many different industries rests on the same appeal to consumers: immediate gratification without effort, which can only be enabled by technology (or magic), and the apps on consumers' smartphones. Of course, other devices such as tablets and smartwatches are meant to make consumers' lives easier too but they are not as extensively used as phones. Thanks to their apps, Uber and Lyft work just like magic too. All consumers have to do is upload their apps, register their favorite addresses (home, work, etc.), and let the app do all the rest, even pay for the ride. The consumer sits in the car and is taken to destination in no time, without the struggle of owning a car. The magic of all these apps to marketers is that they secure customer loyalty and are a priceless source of data.

Only AI can handle this proliferation of products addressing so many different needs for masses of different people. AI accelerates the product innovation and development process, as stated by John Burkey. The use of modeling and simulation techniques can dramatically shorten the lead time to find new ingredients against functional specifications, achieving in weeks what previously required months of testing.

Generative AI is an inspiration to creativity and human brainstorming by introducing ideas other than what was thought by people. It has more references than humans about languages and cultures, and it can support divergent thinking by making associations among remote concepts and producing ideas drawn from them. It can also challenge expertise bias in the early stages of product development. Atypical designs created by generative AI can inspire designers to think beyond their preconceptions of what is possible or durable in a product both in terms of form and function. This approach can lead to solutions that humans might have never imagined using a traditional approach. Generative AI tools can assist in evaluating ideas and also in combining them. It facilitates collaboration between designers and users of a prospective product and thus makes the cocreation of new offerings easier and less expensive.(www.techtarget.com/).

Surprising consumers by anticipating their needs is always a good move. Many products try to forecast what a customer will want next, perhaps even before the customer realizes it. Google does it with Google Now an intelligent agent that operates on Android smartphones. The digital assistant turns information from a user's online search activity, location, email, and calendar into *wisdom* to predict what the user needs next. So when Google Now pulls together information that a business traveler is flying home today and is currently driving a rental car to the airport, it can suggest gas stations near the airport where the tank can be refilled—before the traveler even thinks of this idea. Surprise!

Believing in Brands Is Believing in Magic

Marketing would not be this powerful if people didn't believe in magic. Because of the need of controlling one's own life, consumers' relationships are no longer with products or brands but with a community through the experience provided by the brands they consume.

The interest in magic also grows thanks to movies and TV shows such as *Pirates of the Caribbean*, which includes curses, spells, superstitions, and bringing dead people back to life. The *Harry Potter* and the *Twilight* sagas, movies about *Halloween*, and *The Haunted Mansion* are some examples of movies featuring magic. Other movies entice consumers with superheroes with supernatural powers such as *Star Wars*, *Star Trek*, *Avengers*, *Terminators*, *Pokémon* as well as TV shows like *Mayfair Witches*, *Sanctuary: A Witch's Tale*, *Magic Mike*, *The Watchful Eye*, *Vampire's Diary*, and *Interview with the Vampire*, just to name a few. Some of these become so famous that they turn into copyrighted brands and generate additional income thanks to the merchandise manufactured under their brands as for example *Stranger Things*, *Pirates of the Caribbean,* and *Harry Potter*, which originated higher revenues than the movies.

As explained before, the word *experience* has become one of the pivotal business arguments because it takes into account every interaction consumers have with a product, a place, a person, or a company. The type of experience a customer has with a company determines where they fall in the continuum from highly loyal ambassadors to toxic customers blaming, boycotting, and canceling the company.

Knowing so, some brands such as Meta and Google make it all about you. While Meta immerses you in virtual realities, Google reassures you about their data privacy policy. The immersive experience has also permeated museums, where visitors become a central part of the art displayed on the walls. Playing with optical illusions and peoples' five senses, museums produce a kind of illusionism that can be assimilated to magical tricks. The visitor is transported through time and space, can meet the artists, and partake in their work.

Metaverse is a virtual reality space where users can interact with the environment and other users. In the metaverse, a user has a digital person or avatar, which acts as a graphical representation of themselves in this space. Some companies, especially in the computer gaming and social media space, think this may be the future of entertainment and education. Others believe that it may replace the real world for everyday activities like business meetings.

The big advantage of Metaverse is that it expands access to rich content and wider pools of talent, thus lowering costs and augmenting data-based decision making and personalization. All these added to the use of 3D printing to affordably produce components and products applications to help with simulations. For example, Metaverse-enabled technologies can increase customization by creating digital twins of physical goods that can be very useful to simulate and test a new product digitally.

While the idea has been around for decades, where it goes next is difficult to forecast. Facebook changed its name to Meta to signal its intention to be a leader in using this technology. If more people begin to engage in the metaverse, many companies want to make sure they are there—with products, advertising, and promotion. For example, Nike acquired a company that could help it design and sell virtual sneakers. John Deere, best known for tractors and lawnmowers, created a virtual world called Farmcraft that operates within the popular *Minecraft* video game. And the high-fashion brand Gucci created Gucci Garden for the online gaming platform Roblox.

Admittedly, millennial consumers spending continues to shift from products toward experiences. But as immersive as the customer experience could be, it is insufficient to replace the loyalty to the physical world. It is the same difference between experiencing a live performance in a concert and watching it online. Obviously, the physical world delivers much deeper social, emotional, and sensory experience and a behavioral body language that remain necessary to build trust.

Yet, and as the younger generations of consumers are growing up in a virtual world, they don't find it absurd to pay up to thousands of dollars to attend a concert to which the star is just a hologram. Hatsune Miku is a worldwide pop music megastar. She was created in 2007 by the Japan-based company Crypton Future Media, as a character to promote its vocal synthesizer music software, known as Vocaloid. More than just a face on the box however, Miku is the program, a databank of voice samples that can be manipulated to sing user-composed lyrics over homemade beats, riffs, and hooks. Her concerts consist of a live band playing around a 3D anime image cast onto a transparent screen by an array of high-powered projectors. But that doesn't mean she's not real to the tens of thousands of fans who commune at her concerts. And people don't believe in magic because it is not real!

In this context, generative AI plays a vital role in delivering personalized experiences by analyzing large volumes of data and generating insights that drive targeted marketing campaigns. By leveraging generative AI, marketers can create directly personalized content, product recommendations, and advertisements that cater to individual preferences and behaviors. This degree of personalization enables customer satisfaction and fosters long-term brand loyalty. AI has even been used as a sales argument. If you write a post on LinkedIn, it will suggest you to rewrite it with AI as long as you subscribe to their Premium offer.

Who Is the Customer?

While the difference between customer and consumer is not always made clear in marketing, AI states that customers and consumers can be two different entities: the one who buys and the one who uses the product. With AI, a customer is a nonhuman economic actor who obtains goods or services in exchange for payment—a digital agent that acts on a human's behalf. It can be a virtual assistant or a physical object connected to the internet such as home appliances or factories' robots.

Rather than looking for customers, companies will be able to manufacture their own customers and thus create mega markets very fast. It is believed that 15 to 20 percent of companies' revenues will come from machine customers by 2030, when there will be around 18 billion connected devices, most of them with the potential of behaving as customers that can shop for services and supplies for their owners and themselves. They can reorder capsules for coffee machines, replacement filters for cars, brush heads for electric brushes, as well as tools for professionals.[4]

The advantage specialists see in machine customers is that, unlike humans, their decisions will be only rational. They will rely on calculations, rules, and logic, which will certainly take away most of the efficiency of current advertising and branding. Humans have a utilitarian connection with products and a hedonic relationship with brands. Machines will only focus on product functionalities and cost. There is no guarantee that these machines will be a loyal representation of their owners because their creation and maintenance won't be conducted by the end users.

The machines will obey a programming, and consumers will comply with it. While the feeling of control and easiness will persevere, end consumers won't have any control over their devices. With magic, they control the situation and obtain what they want. Here, they will make much less effort but will lose control. The providers of machine customers aiming at scale effects will operate the same way as mobile operating systems, digital commerce platforms, and social media platforms: the consumer will choose among the limited possibilities someone else offers to them, while having the feeling that they control the situation and have unlimited choices. Marketers should realize that this would be the end of impulse purchases, which currently count for 73 percent of the purchases for several product categories—clothing (35%), food/groceries (30%), household items (29%), shoes (28%), and technology (27%) (https://money.slickdeals.net/surveys/slickdeals-impulse-spending-survey-2022).

As machine customers won't be seduced by impromptu purchase decisions such as promotional efforts at the point of sale, they will also control the kind and quantity of food you should consume. There will be less waste and more control over your cravings. Thus, there will be a lack of control on the consumer's end because someone/something else will make decisions for them, as they will barely participate in their own shopping activities.

Furthermore, the impact of packaging on consumers will also be ignored by machines. Shapes and colors are codes that attract consumers because they convey messages that make sense to them. The beauty, originality, and pragmatism generated by the packaging are partly responsible for the choices made by customers. Some consumers even collect some containers, which they keep at home even when they are already empty. If people are attracted to immersive experiences it is also because of the colors, movements, and symbols they contain. Machines are insensitive to all of that. Therefore, marketers should re-evaluate the weight of symbolic codes on packaging when addressing machine customers.

And because they are exclusively rational and follow logical calculations, machine customers will look for cost-efficiency based on functionality, availability, and price and will be thus, insensitive to appeals such as *women/black/LGBTQ+ owned businesses*. Deprived of human consumers' sensitivity, machine customers will not care about supporting local or small businesses either, which might hurt the quest for diversity, equity, inclusion, and sustainability.

In marketing, we know that shopping is a social experience, and neuroscience confirms this statement. Shopping triggers adrenaline and activates some areas of the brain that influence human mood. People who enjoy just browsing without a shopping list and without looking for something specific are not likely to leave their shopping decisions to a machine. Yet, the more connected devices they own at home, the more they are going toward having a digital shopping assistant.

Do You Miss the Good Old Days?

Diving into paradoxes, again, nostalgia, an emotion exclusive to humans, is making its comeback in the AI world. Nostalgia marketing taps into the profound emotional reservoirs of consumers, leveraging the innate human tendency to reminisce about *the good old days*. This strategy resonates because it exploits the psychological phenomenon where past memories, especially those evoking happiness and comfort, influence current perceptions and decisions. A study from *Frontiers in Psychology* highlights that consumers' purchasing choices are significantly swayed by emotional satisfaction and psychological recognition(www.frontiersin.org).

This emotional connection is particularly potent in a world that often feels uncertain and rapidly changing. By rekindling positive memories, brands can create a sense of familiarity and safety, making consumers more inclined to engage with and remain loyal to them. Nostalgia marketing, therefore, is not just about selling a product or service; it's about selling an experience, a trip down memory lane that feels both personal and universal, fostering a deeper brand affinity.

Social media has revolutionized nostalgia marketing by serving as a digital time capsule, preserving and reviving our collective past. It provides a platform where memories are not only shared but also celebrated, allowing brands to weave their narratives into the fabric of cultural nostalgia. This digital immortality ensures that nothing truly dies on the internet, making social media an invaluable tool for marketers aiming to evoke nostalgia.

Platforms like TikTok have become breeding grounds for niche communities, where both old and new fans can explore retro infatuations together. Through nostalgic ads, retro-themed product launches, and interactive challenges inspired by past trends, social media enables brands to spark conversations, foster loyalty, and amplify their reach. The dynamic nature of these platforms allows for a seamless blend of past and present, creating compelling narratives that resonate across generations.

However, implementing nostalgia marketing requires a delicate balance between reverence for the past and relevance to the present. First, tuning into the nostalgia melting pot on social media is crucial. Platforms are awash with conversations about past trends, enabling brands to tap into these discussions with authenticity. For instance, leveraging social listening can reveal what consumers miss, allowing brands to reintroduce products or themes that resonate. Second, focusing on audience and relevance ensures that nostalgia marketing does not alienate but rather broadens appeal. Understanding that nostalgia varies across demographics is key to crafting messages that resonate universally.

Lastly, reintroducing products back by popular demand, informed by social listening, can surprise and delight customers. McDonald's successful reintroduction of the McRib demonstrates how nostalgia can drive demand. These strategies underscore the importance of emotional connection, relevance, and consumer engagement in nostalgia marketing (www.clickz.com/the-rise-of-nostalgia-marketing/269496/).

The Future as Designed by Coca-Cola (www.coca-colacompany.com/)

In December 2023, Coca-Cola invited fans to imagine what the future tastes and feels like with a limited-edition drink and a new AI-powered experience. Coca-Cola® Y3000 Zero Sugar was cocreated with human and artificial intelligence by understanding how fans envision the future through emotions, aspirations, colors, flavors, and more. Fans' perspectives from around the world, combined with insights gathered from artificial intelligence, helped inspire Coca-Cola to create the unique taste of Y3000. *We hope that Coca-Cola will still be as relevant and refreshing in the year 3000 as it is today, so we challenged ourselves to explore the concept of what a Coke from the future might taste like—and what kind of experiences would a Coke from the future unlock?* states Oana Vlad, senior director of global strategy at The Coca-Cola Company. *The Real Magic brand platform celebrates unexpected connections that make the ordinary extraordinary, so we intentionally brought human intelligence and AI together for an uplifting expression of what Coca-Cola believes tomorrow will bring.*

The zero-sugar offering was available for a limited time in select markets including the United States, Canada, China, Europe, and Africa. Coca-Cola® Y3000 Zero Sugar sported an equally futuristic—and optimistic—visual identity. Cocreated with AI, the design showcased liquid in a morphing, evolving state, communicated through form and color changes that emphasize a positive future. A light-toned color palette featuring violet, magenta, and cyan against a silver base gave a futuristic feel. The iconic Spencerian Script featured a connected matrix with fluid dot clusters that merge to represent the human connections of our future planet.

Consumers could scan an on-pack QR code to access the Coca-Cola Creations Hub, where they could filter photos through the custom Y3000 AI Cam to envision what their reality could look like in the future. And the futuristic fun continued through the Y3000 capsule collection, cocreated with the genre-defying fashion brand AMBUSH. Inspired by a vision of the year 3000, the limited-edition collection included a necklace resembling the top of a Coca-Cola can, a graphic tee featuring AMBUSH® and Coca-Cola logos, and a silver sequin shirt that spotlights a futuristic version of the Coca-Cola can on the back.

> The role of every drop is to leverage the latest, most advanced technologies and cultural trends to create novel experiences. After leaning into AR last year, we're embracing the power of AI and continuing to build our company's capabilities in this exciting space. Coca-Cola Creations has created new pathways to deepen our engagement with existing fans and those who may not have considered our brand before

Vlad stated.

It is worth noting that this new creation is part of the *Real Magic* communication campaign, launched a few years ago, which featured video gamers. By using technology, the company aims at enticing both acquired and potential consumers to the magical world of the immersive experience with the future as they imagine it.

This new imaginative product aligns with the limited editions the company has crafted in the past, such as Coca-Cola Starlight and Coca-Cola Dream World. Because no one knows what starlight and dreams taste like, no one could counter the company's statement. All that consumers could assess was whether they liked the beverage's taste or not. These attempts disconnect consumers from reality taking them to a virtual world where, unlike in the real world, the brand does not go against the new trends—natural, vegan, and low-calorie beverages.

Takeaways

- Let your customers define *experience* their way.
- Invite your consumers to be part of the creation process whether it is AI-assisted or not.
- Understand that the introduction of AI and machine customers will dramatically change your relationship with your consumers.

Implications for Marketers

As we reach a transitional period in the history of marketing, marketers should understand the ramifications of the easy use of AI by their customers and consumers. With all the enticing advantages that AI proposes and consumers' fascination with the power they think they have at their fingertips, their behavior is likely to change very frequently in an unpredictable way. For example, the Y3000 was a valid attempt to create excitement about the use of AI in the food industry, but it was also delusional to think that any technology could, today, predict the flavors and colors consumers will prefer in the year 3000. However, Coca-Cola enjoys the use of technology and created the first-ever drinkable advertising for Coke Zero several years ago (www.youtube.com/watch?v=IQovoot_ZUM).

Tracking consumers down with apps is a good idea, but the most important one is still to try to keep them loyal to your brand by leveraging consumer engagement with apps, social media, and AI. Consumers can cocreate packaging, advertisements, and influencers with you. This will generate and increase a sense of belonging thanks to which they will be able to spread more happiness.

And never lose sight of your own engagement: connect purpose to your product—the magical solution your consumers have been looking for.

CHAPTER 5

AI and Pricing

A World of Accessible Value

Life is like a boomerang: whatever you do comes back to you.

Everybody knows magic tricks with cards, but numbers carry magical powers too. The products described in the previous chapter charge customers who believe in their magical powers, some amount of money. All customers need to feel like they got a good deal when they buy a product. Here we discuss pricing strategies and price sensitivity, because thanks to smartphones and apps, consumers can easily compare prices in real time.

Ask someone if a hundred dollars is a fair price and they will answer that it depends what for. Price is relative to products, brands, and income. We might pay more for some brands, while we wouldn't pay the same amount for a similar product from a different brand. Moreover, there are several products that we can afford but we don't buy them because the price is not right or because we just don't want them.

In the human world, price is perceptual because it is subjective and relative. There are several product attributes that consumers take into account to determine the appropriateness of a certain price. Some of these attributes relate to personal preferences, and some others to emotional cues—brand reputation, nostalgia, and influencers. These pricing considerations will change with machine customers, because price will be assessed by logic and cost-efficiency calculations without yielding to subjective attributes.

The human loyal customer is the one that leaves the checkout with the feeling of having done a good deal (machines too). If they paid more than expected, they will regret it and probably blame the company (unlike machines that will critique themselves and learn to do better next time). If they are charged much less, they question the product's quality and the company's honesty: Is this product authentic? That is why *low price hunters* will never be loyal customers, because they are loyal to low prices rather than to brands for certain product categories. Some companies address only these consumers, as for example Walmart — *Always low prices* - or Aldi which stores are very simple and most products are unbranded. On the contrary, Whole Foods and Trader's Joe target different consumers for which price is not the main criterion for purchase and are thus more expensive because of their fresh and organic products positioning.

Magic Numbers and Price Endings

The belief that consumers always look for the lower prices is not true. If that were true, Apple wouldn't be around anymore, because consumers could purchase similar devices for lower prices from other brands. Consumers are willing to pay more for Apple's devices because they believe in the superior quality of their products and because the brand is a myth, thanks to the legendary Steve Jobs. While well-known for its innovative technology, Apple is first and foremost a marketing company. They deal beautifully with their consumers in creating suspense about their new products, which are, after all, just a new version of the old ones, and have amazing communication campaigns. In addition, the Apple stores are strategically located in all main cities in the world where everyone is welcome even those who don't buy their products. The synchronization among their devices and their incompatibility with all other operating systems greatly help with customer loyalty to the brand as well.

Price correlates with value. If the customer sees value in the product, they are willing to pay the required price for it. Rarity is one of the factors that make people pay more for a product, which explains the very high prices charged by luxury brands; you don't see them everywhere, and they are not accessible to the majority of consumers. The more customized and exclusive the product, the higher the price.

Consumers often actively process price information, interpreting it from the context of prior purchasing experience, formal and informal communications, and point-of-purchase or online resources. Price endings have a magic impact on consumers. Customers perceive an item priced at $299 to be in the $200 range rather than in the $300 range; they tend to process prices *left to right* rather than by rounding them up. Prices that end with 0 and 5 are also popular and are thought to be easier for consumers to process and retrieve from memory, that is why most discounts are displayed as 30 or 35 percent rather than 32 or 34 percent.

For better determination of pricing strategies, the marketing information system should have a wide range of internal data readily accessible to marketing managers. For accounting, tax, billing, and production planning, data on sales and cost information for different products are required and are already in a company's computer system. The data are also segmented into specific geographic areas and by customers. The company can also collect data on visits to its website and apps, from order placement to delivery, in addition to competitors' new product announcements or pricing changes and articles about customers, at the same time as monitoring information on industry growth trends and relevant legal and regulatory issues.

As stated by[1]Duani et al., advancements in data processing, coupled with increased access to volumes of customer data, have dramatically improved companies' ability to estimate customers' willingness to pay and tailor prices to individual consumers.

Price Sensitivity

When consumers are not loyal to a brand for a certain product category, they compare prices across brands. This task has been facilitated by price comparison apps such as Trivago, which compares prices from different websites for the same hotel room. The ability to easily compare prices in real time has made consumers more price sensitive.

Price sensitivity means that when the price for the same product goes up, consumers buy less, whereas they buy more when the price goes down. If, thanks to apps, the consumer can easily compare prices for the same product, they will be obviously drawn to lower prices. This is what characterizes the demand's elasticity. The higher the price sensitivity, the more elastic the demand. This means that consumer behavior changes when the price changes, while in inelastic demands, such price changes have little impact on consumer's willingness to buy.

Price incorporates two main variables—the monetary (also called economic value) and the nonmonetary (also called perceived value). The monetary price is the one featured in a currency; it is the amount paid by the buyer to obtain the product—the price tag. The nonmonetary price is the effort made by the buyer to obtain the product. Thus, people usually try to compensate for the time and effort of driving for miles and the cost of fuel with lower prices paid for the products that they might buy in bulks. Other customers might agree to pay more for their comfort and buy the same product at a convenience store next door. This also explains why customers buying online are willing to pay for shipping and delivery fees just for the comfort of staying at home even if sometimes the shipping fees are higher than the prices charged for the products.

The nonmonetary price also refers to the effort made by the consumer to get the product ready to consume: the less effort needed to be made, the higher the willingness to pay more for the product. Thus, if you go grocery shopping and you cook from scratch, by the end of the month, you would have saved money when compared to home-delivered ready-to-eat food despite the discounts and coupons for loyalty you might earn. Because we live in societies where everything is timed, grocery shopping and cooking are seen as a waste of time, which reinforces the value of nonmonetary prices and increases the likelihood of accepting higher monetary prices—paying more for what is ready to consume. This circles us back to the previous discussion about immediate and effortless gratification. Consumers are willing to pay more for making less effort and getting products ready to consume and home-delivered.

Some companies having understood that for some people having everything ready to consume turned out to be frustrating at some level, created the almost-ready-to-consume products. Most part of the effort has already been made by the company, and all that the consumer has to do is add their personal touch. This is how companies such as Hello Fresh, Home Chef, Blue Apron, and Green Chef, just to name a few, found their target market in the meal and food kit delivery industry. Their promise is: *Sign up for a meal delivery kit and cook restaurant quality meals at home.* Taken together, the restaurant quality, the comfort of home delivery, and the satisfaction of cooking without grocery shopping justify the acceptance of the high prices charged by these companies.

Haunted by the Feeling of Loss

Value is a subjective feeling dependent on income, contextual stability, product category, and brand, among the most relevant ones. That is why value is a dynamic concept, which constantly evolves. When customers think they are paying the best prices possible, it increases customer satisfaction, which increases loyalty and makes the customer become a returning one. Consumers have several references in their minds when judging a product based on its price:

- The fair price—This is what consumers feel the product is worth based on the value they assign to it.
- The typical price—When all the similar products charge more or less the same amount.
- The last price paid—Consumers expect to pay the same price as the last time they purchased the same product.
- The upper-bound price—This is the highest price consumers would agree to pay for that specific product.
- The lower-bound price—This is the lowest price consumers would agree to pay for that specific product.
- The competitor prices—Consumers look for significant price differences among competitors.
- The usual discounted price—Consumers buy products with promotional prices.

All these variables, taken together, should lead companies to define the price consumers would be willing to pay, while making a profit. With this goal, AI has become a precious tool for pricing optimization—using algorithms and marketing analytics to analyze large amounts of data and determine how the customers will react to certain prices so the company can set a relevant price for their products. To do so, AI uses historical data, unstructured data such as images and videos, and competitor's prices through their websites to suggest the most favorable ones for the company.

The use of AI improves accuracy because of its ability to analyze large amounts of data bringing together more variables than a human would use in their predictive analysis as explained by Professor Adelakun. Other than speeding up the process, the machine can continuously analyze pricing influences from different sources at once instead of doing it at every period, which enables faster decision making in today's fast-changing world. AI also helps to personalize pricing strategies, dynamically adjust prices, anticipate demand, analyze competitors, and allocate resources efficiently. These factors collectively contribute to higher profit margins by capturing the maximum value from customers while optimizing costs and resources.

Data become information when they provide answers to questions of *who, what, where, how much,* and *when.* So, for example, sales data might be presented in a table that shows the sales of different products over time and in different geographic locations, answering questions such as: Who is buying our product? Where do they live? How much do they buy? What products are they buying? Information becomes knowledge when it helps marketing managers answer *how* and *why* questions. Marketing managers combine experience with information to generate knowledge. So, a marketing manager may observe growth from a particular target market (information from sales data) but combine this with experience and market research to find out why the target customers purchased more. Other questions that require knowledge include: How did our largest competitor gain access to an international market? Why did that Instagram post generate so many reactions? Why did a competitor sell its product through grocery stores?

Knowledge and wisdom involve an ability to accurately predict the future, which is exactly what fortunetellers do. Marketing models can provide predictive analytics by forecasting customer behavior. A model can predict or estimate what will happen if a new product is introduced, an advertisement is run, or a price is lowered. AI uses past consumer behavior to predict future behavior. AI and machine learning can generate information and implement strategies as data can be used for predictive analytics—potentially indicating when a particular customer is interested in making a purchase. Yet, we should not forget that all these are estimates and that human behavior remains somehow unpredictable. In addition, if the machine is not imputed with all possible variables accounting for consumer behavior, it might not see factors that explain behavioral shifts as discussed before.

By leveraging AI-powered pricing optimization and in coordination with their marketing communication strategy, businesses can focus their promotional efforts on the right customers, offer personalized and targeted promotions, optimize timing and discounting, and allocate promotional spending more efficiently. This leads to reduced spending on ineffective campaigns and a higher return on investment for promotional activities. In doing so, companies can handle large data sets, adjust prices in real time, automate pricing processes, personalize pricing strategies, conduct rapid experimentation, and integrate pricing optimization with existing systems. This scalability allows businesses to expand their pricing optimization efforts efficiently, cater to a growing customer base, and adapt to changing market dynamics while maintaining consistent and effective pricing strategies.

When it comes to the pricing strategy, the attraction of machine customers to companies is their cost-efficiency to realize more revenue from existing customers, gain market share, and expand their reach to new markets. A virtual assistant can connect a car to other devices and take the order from the restaurant to reduce waiting time. It can also indicate restaurants nearby where the type of meal envisaged can be enjoyed for a lower price and with little waiting time. Other advantages are reducing volatility, being consistent and reliable, spending within the budget, complying with company policies, operating 24/7, and securing business continuity independent of changes in the staff.[2]

Rethinking a pricing paradigm requires creative thinking. At most organizations, discussions around pricing focus on simple price-setting: whether to charge $27.99 or $29.99 for a restaurant entrée, for example. Those decisions depend largely on costs, customer demand, and value relative to other options. Some companies adopt a more sophisticated approach, such as good-better-best pricing. That involves bundling product elements or services into distinct pricing tiers (typically three) and encouraging customers to decide which set of offerings makes sense for them.[3]

As ideal as this seems to be, the risks are numerous too. Other than operating failures causing serious accidents and big losses, everything that is digital is prone to the action of hackers, who lately have been successfully relying on the big amounts of ransom paid by companies to have access to their own operational systems again. Machines are not this infallible. Remember how many times you were in trouble because your computer crashed or your smartphone just stopped working. Relying solely on machines and entrusting all strategic data and decisions to them might not be a wise decision.

Key Takeaways

- The biggest advantage of segmenting the market based on big data is that companies are able to adjust their pricing strategies to the different target markets they address
- Personalization helps immensely with customer loyalty, which, in turn leads to higher profits. Micro-segmentation is facilitated with AI.
- It is easier for companies to address several different consumers at the same time, because of the overview of the whole market provided by constant data collection.

Implications to Marketers

If charging the right price keeps your customers happy, knowing what the right price should be is still a challenge. A customer might pay a price today and refuse to pay the same amount for the same product tomorrow, because they found a better deal online.

Monitoring the market is an obvious need for all marketers, but with AI it can be constantly done and any fluctuations can be spotted in real time by the machine as long as it is given access to macro and micro economics, customers' habits, interactions on social media, the action of influencers, and so forth. All these factors can play with your customers' price sensitivity.

An AI-proficient team is necessary, because marketers should always supervise the machine, not only to adjust the algorithms as per changes in the company's policies and objectives but also to ensure that the brand positioning is not likely to be hurt by the machine's decisions.

CHAPTER 6

AI and Distribution

A World Where Everything You Wish Comes to You

One wish was enough to change Dorian Gray's destiny

Paying more for one's comfort is part of customers' equation. Customers are used to home delivery, and that is the role of distribution in marketing. Shopping in physical stores became a chore to customers, and online shopping has been growing, more so through smartphones than from any other devices, which led to the expansion of M-commerce. More recently, QR codes are running the show, as consumers just need to scan them to purchase a product.

Known as the third P of the 4Ps (Product, Price, Place, Promotion) of the marketing mix, placement is the way a company ensures that its target market has access to its products in the location they would be most likely to look for them.

Distribution is the strategy whereby companies give their targeted consumers access to their products. While for several decades companies have been using only in-person channels, an integrated marketing channel system, in which the strategies and tactics of selling through one or more channels bring online and offline shopping together, is more likely to be successful. In doing so, companies mechanically enlarge their potential markets. The main advantages of an integrated marketing channel system are the increased market coverage, lower channel cost, and the ability to do more customized selling.

When Products Come to You

A distribution channel is the network of businesses or intermediaries through which a good or service passes until it reaches the final buyer or the end consumer. Distribution channels can include whosalers, retailers and the internet. Distribution channels are part of the downstream process, answering the question *How do we get our product to the consumer?* This is in contrast to the upstream process, also known as the supply chain, which answers the question *Who are our suppliers?*

A distribution channel is a path by which all goods and services travel to arrive at the intended consumer. They can be short or long and depend on the number of intermediaries required to deliver a product or service to the end consumer. Increasing the number of ways a consumer can find a good can increase sales but it can also create a complex system that sometimes makes distribution management difficult. Longer distribution channels can also mean less profit for each intermediary along the way.

Selecting and monitoring distribution channels is a key component of managing supply chains. Technology can replace humans' labor across a broad range of supply chain activities enlarging the opportunities to operate worldwide. It becomes possible to locate affordable factories closer to the plants, can save time on the assembling lines, and can offer new ways to reduce costs thanks to *cobots*, which are robots that directly interact with humans in manufacturing facilities.

There are several components of a distribution channel:

- **Producer**: Producers combine labor and capital to create goods and services for consumers. They manufacture the products to be sold on the market.
- **Wholesaler**: A person or company that buys from the producer and sells large quantities of goods, often at low prices, to retailers.
- **Retailer**: A person or business that sells goods to the public in small quantities for immediate consumption.
- **End Consumer**: A person who buys a product or service.

Among the different types of distribution channels, we find:

- A direct channel, which allows the consumer to make purchases from the manufacturer. This direct, or short channel, may mean lower prices for consumers because they are buying directly from the manufacturer.
- An indirect channel allows the consumer to buy the goods from a wholesaler or retailer. Indirect channels are typical for goods that are sold in traditional brick-and-mortar (physical) stores.
- Hybrid distribution channels use both direct and indirect channels. A product or service manufacturer may use both a retailer to distribute a product or service and may also make sales directly with the consumer online.

Basically, direct distribution channels are those that allow the manufacturer or service provider to deal directly with its end customer. A company that manufactures and sells directly to its customers using an e-commerce platform would be utilizing a direct distribution channel. By contrast, if that same company were to rely on a network of wholesalers and retailers to sell its products, then it would be using an indirect distribution channel. For example, drivetime.com seems to be a direct distribution channel enabling cars' acquisition without intermediaries. The same strategy is applied by Opendoor.com where homeowners can sell their houses directly to house seekers by skipping the intermediaries.

Distribution Channels in the Digital Era

Digital technology has transformed the way businesses, especially small businesses, use direct channels of distribution. With increasing consumer demand for online shopping and easy-to-use eCommerce tools, direct selling means more success for businesses of all sizes. In addition, most online transactions are subscription-based, which ensures customer commitment and recurrent purchases from the same company at least for some time.

Rather than having to rely on relationships with retailers to sell their products, software and artificial intelligence sales technology allows companies to manage sales and automatically achieve high customer relationship management. It also helps target specific areas or demographics and social media networks, which are increasingly considered in marketing strategies. If a company uses indirect channels of distribution, digital technology also allows it to manage relationships with wholesale and retail partners more efficiently.

For example, AI has become an important ingredient for the liquor industry as it involves sales and marketing tactics, alcohol production, packaging design, and how brands are built and engage with drinkers. Four years ago, Pernod Ricard, the French-born global leader in wines and spirits and owner of well-known brands such as Jameson, Absolut, and Malibu, began a comprehensive review of big digital investments that could potentially boost growth, the company spending roughly U.S.$1.7 billion on marketing annually. One of the projects now deployed across 13 countries uses AI to make store visits more efficient for Pernod Ricard's sales representatives.

The sales team can have up to 1,000 stores in their purview, but they can only visit a few dozen each week. The mix of stores that could be visited each week could result in millions of unique combinations. But today, data and AI help ensure store visits. Pernod Ricard looks at what each store sells, the nearby population, the size and assortment of the store, and other factors to create clusters of stores that should behave the same way based on that data. Sales representatives are then advised to visit the underperforming stores within those clusters where there would be potential to upsell. AI is also used to highlight whether a promotional effort is needed to support a Pernod Ricard's brand in some points of sales (https://pernod-ricard-usa.com).

Not all distribution channels are appropriate for all products, so companies need to choose the right ones for them. The channel should align with the firm's overall mission and strategic vision including its sales goals and its brand positioning. The method of distribution should add value to the consumer as well. Do consumers want to speak to a salesperson? Will they want to handle the product before they make a purchase? Or do they want to purchase it online with no hassles? Answering these questions can help companies determine which channels are more suitable to them. The company should also consider how quickly it wants its products to reach the buyer depending on its perishability. If a company chooses multiple distribution channels, such as selling products online and through a physical retailer, the channels should not compete with one another. Companies should make sure that one channel doesn't cannibalize the other ones.

Online Shopping

It is a pleasant feeling to be recognized as soon as we land on a company's website or app. There, we find our favorites, our cart, and the items we purchased in the past. It is also very handy to have customized recommendations, because it feels like the company works for us, exclusively!

These are a few of the main advantages of online shopping when compared to in-person shopping, because unless you are a regular shopper in a physical store, the staff won't recognize you and know all of your preferences. In addition, there is the comfort of shopping 24/7, from anywhere, and being home delivered. There are disadvantages too: the package not delivered, the product arrives damaged, the color, size, or texture are different from what was displayed on the website, and sometimes, the shipping fee is higher than the price of the product itself. These bad customer experiences have been detrimental to several brands, which do not always listen, understand, or try to amend the issue. Consumers spend hours on the phone and sending emails until they get a response, which is sometimes not satisfactory. This is the opposite of comfort. Had they purchased the product in a physical store, they would have left the shop with it and if any problem, they would be speaking to humans. However, that would have also increased, *a priori*, the product's nonmonetary price as discussed in the previous chapter. Sometimes, the postpurchase rationalization turns into regret, but the psychological advantages of the trending of online shopping take over again, thanks to the confirmation bias dictated by conformism to the main widespread norm.

It is clear that today's bots are not performant because they are unable to respond to customers' issues. Ideally, the main advantage of the use of AI in distribution is having a better-targeted distribution and increased customer experience, because the machine learns from visitors' behavior in real time—and so incorporates machine learning—anticipating the visitors' intents, and adapts the results to rank the most relevant products higher. Consumers expect a personalized experience to remain loyal to the brand. But we are not there yet.

Turning window shoppers into buyers has always been the main goal for any e-commerce site. That is why we receive reminders of our carts, are offered enticing promotional rewards, and are often pulled back to the website or the app. AI can help fine-tune these interactions because machine learning algorithms can deliver smarter search results. They can understand what is typed in the search bar, thanks to natural language processing. After that, they will use what they have learned from previous searches to show what the searcher wants to find. Algorithms can analyze visitors' behavior on an e-commerce site and recognize products that a visitor buys or browses. That way, when an individual returns to the site, they get product recommendations based on what they have shown interest in before.

Machine learning refers to a type of computer algorithm where a software application becomes more accurate in predicting outcomes without actual programming. Through machine learning, a program makes predictions, receives feedback on whether it is correct or not, and then updates the program. With access to big amounts of data, machine learning can help a software program learn a specific skill rather quickly.

To do so, companies use chatbots to help inform customers when products are out of stock and suggest alternatives. They can also be used to inform customers about delivery, order status, or even suggest products based on what the customer is looking for. Another benefit of using chatbots in e-commerce is the functionality to remind customers about their abandoned shopping carts knowing that some of them don't abandon their carts on purpose and are happy to complete the purchase. The use of chatbots can significantly reduce customer service costs.

Virtual Reality Is Magical

With the help of interactive visual design such as virtual reality (VR), augmented reality (AR), and three-dimensional imagery, the customer can get a better sensory experience and a better understanding of what to expect from products while shopping online. According to Marxent Labs, 77 percent of shoppers want to see the product's features like colors or style, 72 percent of shoppers purchased items they had not planned to purchase because of AR, 68 percent of shoppers spent more time with products when AR was available, 65 percent want product information through AR, 61 percent of shoppers prefer retailers that offer AR over those that don't, and 55 percent say AR makes shopping fun (https://marxentlabs.com).

For example, AR seems to be very useful when shopping for furniture (you can place them in your space), clothes and footwear (scanning your body and feet to find the appropriate sizes), cosmetics (determining the best makeup from facial recognition), jewelry (simulating with different attires), toys (playing with them), and cars (test drives).

Navigation is crucial because it can help increase the average time spent on the site. An easily navigable e-commerce site allows visitors to spend more time to explore and discover the site and get the information that they will need. Visitors should quickly understand what you are offering, without having to scroll and click too much. If a potential customer visits your e-commerce site and finds that it is too difficult to navigate, they may not take the time to go through the site properly. They may bounce and search for another e-commerce site instead. Remember that consumers look for effortless gratification.

Therefore, visual search has been used as a novel technology, powered by AI, which allows the user to perform an online search by employing real-world images as a substitute for text. Visual search optimization boosts conversion and engagement and is easily operated with a smartphone. The customer experience can be much better if you offer an image-based search where users can use pictures to search for other similar products. That way, customers can quickly find what they're looking for. This is exactly what Etsy explores in their advertisements showing customers taking pictures of the products they want in real life and finding them on Etsy's website or app thanks to image search.

AI and automation are powerful tools that can help you optimize your distribution strategy and efficiency, by improving your distribution channels, processes, performance, innovation, and challenges. However, to leverage these tools effectively, you need to have a clear vision, strategy, and plan for your distribution goals, objectives, and actions. You also need to have the right skills, resources, and partners to implement and manage your AI and automation initiatives. By doing so, you can achieve distribution success and growth.

The Magic of QR Code

From websites to apps and to QR codes, online shopping has undertaken a speedway. As it is depicted in Tovala's advertisement; *discover the* ***magic*** *of Tovala—it makes cooking as simple as scanning a QR code.*

QR codes are the interface between the physical and digital worlds and are often used to more targeted marketing campaigns. It is a big advantage for smaller businesses and it helps to follow the supply chain as highlighted by Professor Adelakun. The code enables consumers to have immediate access to a big array of information such as ingredients, recipes, recycling, and directions for use, just to name a few. The QR code is meant to replace the scan bars at the point of sales by 2027.

QR codes work very well on packaging and labels so the consumer can quickly scan them for convenient shopping and browsing. The possibilities exceed the products that are available in the store alone. In addition, sharing AR experiences with consumers inspires them to create new looks, decorate differently, compare alternatives, and give other people they know referrals to brands they like, especially by posting on social media.

There are many creative places to put retail QR codes in smaller shops and larger retailers for the convenience of the staff and the shoppers—tags, different departments, at the cash register, and even in public places that show adverts to direct consumers to m-commerce shops. Since QR codes are scanned from mobile phones, shoppers need the ease of making quick purchases from mobile-optimized virtual stores. Being able to compare prices, sizes, colors, and reviews, these shoppers will buy from the best source, which, by the way, increases their price sensitivity as discussed in the previous chapter.

Whether updating a digital sales promotion or adding to an e-commerce shop, dynamic QR codes are a versatile option for making edits as frequently as necessary. The physical QR code does not have to be reprinted and can be designed as a QR code specific to your brand and logo for easy brand recognition. Whereas printed materials alone get tossed in the bin, consumers can share QR codes between mobile phones, expanding brand awareness. Anyone from any type of industry can use QR codes to enhance their digital marketing strategy, attract followers to social media, and connect codes to their e-commerce stores.

AI and automation can, however, pose some challenges for the distribution strategy and efficiency, such as ethical, legal, and technical issues. For example, it is imperative to make sure that the use of AI and automation is transparent, fair, and compliant with the relevant regulations and standards. In addition to ensuring that the use of AI and automation is secure and reliable, respecting consumers' data privacy.

When AI Was Not Artificial Intelligence

As exciting as it was to get in and out of an Amazon shop without human contact and without paying thanks to AI, we know now that the story was somehow distorted (www.businessinsider.com/amazons-just-walk-out-actually-1-000-people-in-india-2024-4).

Amazon's Just Walk Out technology had a secret ingredient: roughly 1,000 workers in India who reviewed what you picked up, set down, and walked out of its stores with. The company touted the technology, which allowed customers to bypass traditional checkouts, as an achievement powered entirely by computer vision. But Just Walk Out was still very reliant on humans. About 700 of every 1,000 Just Walk Out sales had to be reviewed by Amazon's team in India in 2022. Internally, Amazon wanted just 50 out of every 1,000 sales to get a manual check, according to the report.

The revelation came as Amazon is planning to replace Just Walk Out at Amazon Fresh stores with its Dash Carts. The smart shopping carts also allow customers to avoid waiting in a checkout line, though they have to place their purchases in the cart, which keeps track of their selections and debits their accounts. While customers used Just Walk Out at Amazon Fresh stores, they also wanted the ability to easily find nearby products and deals, view their receipt as they shop, and know how much money they saved while shopping throughout the store —all options that the company's Dash Cart provides. Yet, marketers should consider the opposite effect on customers' mind, who could stop shopping as they see the amount spent going up. It could also have a negative impact on impulse buying.

Just Walk Out first appeared in Amazon Go convenience stores. The technology allowed customers to enter a store by identifying themselves with their Amazon account on their phones. From there, they could pick up items, put them back on the shelves, and walk out with their final picks, all without having to interact with a cashier. In the last few years, Amazon has rolled Just Walk Out to larger-format stores. Twenty-seven of the 44 Amazon Fresh stores currently have the technology. Amazon also added Just Walk Out to some Whole Foods stores.

The lack of transparency of AI being still a black box for marketers associated with the lack of understanding of what it really is on the customers' side can lead some companies to be deceiving. While testing a new technology, companies should avoid misleading their consumers. The incident with Just Walk Out can hardly harm a company like Amazon because it enjoys high loyalty from its customers and usually serves them well in other distribution channels. Nevertheless, a similar situation can be highly detrimental to other companies.

Key Takeaways

- Make sure that all of your distribution channels are integrated and consistent with your positioning.

- Don't leave critical parts of your distribution strategy to unreliable sources.
- Remember that your consumers purchase YOUR products and should receive them as promised by you even if you entrust other parties with delivery. Your brand is at stake.

Implications to Marketers

AI and automation can help you identify, select, and manage the best distribution channels for your products or services. For example, you can use AI to analyze customer behavior, preferences, and feedback, and then tailor your distribution channels accordingly. You can also use automation to streamline your channel operations, such as inventory management, order fulfillment, and delivery tracking. By using AI and automation for distribution channels, you can increase your reach, relevance, and retention.

AI and automation can also help you innovate and transform your distribution strategy and efficiency, by enabling you to explore new opportunities, challenges, and solutions. For example, you can use AI to discover and test new distribution models, markets, and segments, such as subscription, direct-to-consumer, or niche targets.

You can also use automation to experiment and scale new distribution methods, technologies, and partnerships, such as chatbots, blockchain, or platforms. By using AI and automation for distribution innovation, you can create and capture new value and growth.

CHAPTER 7

AI and Communication

A World of Self-Expression

We live in an age when men treat art as if it were meant to be a form of autobiography.

—The Picture of Dorian Gray

If consumers are willing to look for a specific product, order it online, and pay for it is because they were told to do so. As described in this chapter, the communication mix has several methods to reach out to consumers, including influencers, among which, some are humans and some are digital. The promise of magical results motivates consumers to buy those brands. Using generative AI, companies create communication campaigns that target consumers with more accuracy and can even create micro targeting, for example, by using SMS marketing.

Massive social changes in markets start with a small and even serendipitous social nudge. Someone perceived as credible in some community states an opinion or engages in an action, which is seen as a green light to all the others to do the same. The movement grows strong, and it can even turn around a business, because it can be about a product, a person, or an advertisement, and what seemed to be a trickle becomes a flood especially when social media gets involved[1].

This is also when words, mostly adjectives, are constantly used, whether accurately or not, to describe a situation, a person, a brand, or a company, which will be recaptured and propagated by other influencers through all social media platforms. Just as mentalists can read other peoples' minds and convince them of the rightness of their ideas, these words become incantations meant to change our views of the world, or even change the world. Common words used in all types of media are currently: green, diversity, equality, inclusion, freedom, liberty, sustainability, technology, magic, and of course, AI.

The relevance of these words changes as current events unfold and contemporary values evolve, imposing the greatest challenge for marketers in today's society, which is to stay relevant in a world that is constantly and quickly changing. The amount of new information that is created every day is astounding and it is practically impossible to keep up.

In this fast-paced environment, marketers can use AI to speed up processes such as rote tasks or idea generation, by reducing workload and increasing efficiency. Marketers can use AI to produce unique concepts for advertising and promotions as well as analyze consumer data to gather insights and improve performance.

The use of AI in marketing communication is also relevant for creating immersive advertisements more likely to capture consumer's attention. As discussed before, immersive experiences are taking over all flat relationships consumers have with companies, such as museums, movies, games, and so forth. Knowing that consumers skip advertisements or simply don't pay attention to them, having them immersed and interacting with products and situations depicted in the ad constitutes a great added value. Put in other terms, consumers will pay attention to advertisements in which they have a role to play, because the advertisement will be all about them and, just like magic, they can virtually create the world they want for themselves.

Magic Sells

Consumers became so used to technology that its progress is almost taken for granted while magic came back as an exotic way of obtaining immediate and effortless results. Therefore, number of companies employ the word *magic* in their marketing communication campaigns. Having magic as their common trait, several brands have been using different approaches in their advertisements. Here are some examples:

- **Ikea** relates to the magic of **Mary Poppins** when the child and his family, moving in a new house, take one by one all of their furniture from an apparently empty Ikea blue plastic bag.
- Sthil sees their gardening tools clean up a messy yard in a few minutes with no human operating them with **Fantasia Sorcere's Apprentice** song in the background.
- **WeatherTech** shows mother and daughter in a car changing the weather by pushing a button on their smartphones.
- Which hotel? Depicts the **witch** who takes you to **Choice Hotels.**
- **Hyundai**'s tagline in their cobranding with Disney, promises that *there is **magic** in the journey.*
- **Mr. Clean Magic** Eraser factually demonstrates how to, immediately, erase stubborn dirt.
- **Disney,** the Kingdom of Magic promotes Disney Cruises as the place *where **magic** meets the sea.*
- **Coca-Cola** launched the *One Coke Away From Each Other* campaign representing the first creative experience under the **Real Magic** platform, when creating the new *hug* logo in 2021
- **L'Oréal**'s **Magic Roots** shows that their temporary *root* touch up spray covers gray hair in three seconds, with Eva Longoria as their spokesperson.
- **Cirkul** promises to *Bring **magic** to the way you drink water.*
- **Fudge Stripes** from Keebler states that *Magic is here*
- **Farmer's dog promises that** *the food preparation looks like **magic***
- **Lucky Charms** *is **magically** delicious!*

On a very different approach, *Magic* Johnson is the spokesperson for GlaxoSmithKline's TV Spot about RSV, his nickname having been inspired by his accomplishments as a basketball player, which looked like **magic**.

AI uses customer-centric targeting based on data, particularly behaviors, which enables advertisers to track the performance of campaigns in real time to make the necessary adjustments and bring more magical effects to their products.

To increase credibility and look like being closer to consumers or mimicking consumers' lives, some TV advertisements look like TikTok videos. Knowing that user content generation (UCG) enjoys more credibility than any other communication content, looking like someone who has no financial interest in the products being promoted can lead to more trust and willingness to buy the product.

That TikTok has been growing exponentially around the world is nothing new. What is new is that now they advertise on TV—traditional media—with a campaign named *TikTok Sparks Good*. In these communications, you see people sharing what seems to be of public utility—a surgeon, a nun—rather than influencers promoting products. This corporate communication discloses the human side of TikTok showing that it is a medium that serves all kinds of people for all kinds of causes, which is a very cost-effective public relations campaign. Another trend is seeing founders of small companies showcasing their offerings on TV in videos just like videos similar those from TikTok, demonstrating closeness with consumers and suggesting a direct distribution channel as discussed in the previous chapter. They start their story by stressing the fact that, as consumers, they spotted an unsatisfied need and thus decided to offer a solution for that issue. This brings them closer to the consumers because it feels like UCG.

Humans Are Influenced by Humans

There are different factors that explain consumer behavior[2]: anchoring, availability, and representativeness. *Anchoring* establishes a parameter around which adjustments enable consumers to make decisions and exist as a member of a community. *Availability* of information shapes consumer behavior, knowing that this information is shaped by algorithms leading most people in the world to crave the same products and brands and to behave the same way, complying with what seems to be a universal norm. *Representativeness* means that consumers follow someone who seems to be representative of who they are or aim at being. Influencers play this role in creating the stereotype of the cool person who would buy that specific brand and behave in that specific way.

Humans live in societies and in today's digital communitarian world, identity-based cognition is recognizing that each individual is a member of groups and to keep belonging to those, they should comply with the sometimes-implicit norms that rule such groups. Everyone follows the same influencers, purchases the same brands, and speaks the same jargon. Thus, doing what others do is understood as learning. As we remember, socialization is learning to be part of a specific society by complying with its norms as is learning to be part of a specific community.

The power of communities rules peoples' lives and several industries wouldn't exist if it weren't for social media. At the same time, social media wouldn't be this powerful without the astounding penetration of smartphones, which will be shortly replaced by Rayban Meta smart glasses, which take pictures and post them on social media without the use of a phone. Unlike the one-way traditional communication conveyed by traditional media, a new power arose when the capacity to produce and share content was decentralized and put in the hands of billions of people, creating a huge premium on ideas and information (and disinformation) that spread sideways instead of from the top down. The big winners in this world are the technology platforms that capture our data and attention within this mass of information and interactions.

The more people remain clustered with those who are alike, rather than looking for diversity (ironically), the more easily they are influenced by those who run the show and more clearly they represent a homogenous target market to companies. They buy the same brands, speak with the same vocabulary, and share the same ideas, stories, and of course, beliefs and rituals. It is a net compliance. The actions and attitudes of others compel us to conform, even if we know better. When we are young, we hear about the power and the dangers of peer pressure, and although it takes different forms, social pressure does not go away with adulthood; we should comply with the norms of our communities. This explains shopping decisions made with the goal of social identification, or the suggestion that a certain decision is characteristic of *people like you* or *just for you*. Not only does your identity shape your behavior, but your behavior shapes your identity as well. People in communities are people under influence. We all are.

Indeed, around three million people in the United States call social media content creation their full-time job—about the same number as are in the manufacturing sector. Results like that helped influencers earn some $21 billion in 2023.[3] It seems to be so easy to become a celebrity overnight and earn money in a few days just by posting oneself on TikTok. Another example of social media's impressive power is the resurgence of Uno, the traditional family cards game, by reaching millions of followers in a few days thanks to social media and a young unknown *Chief Uno Player Officer*, who would meet with people to play in person and post all of that on TikTok. The before unknown *CUPO* became famous and earned significant amount of money in a few weeks just to be seen playing cards. No wonder new generations aim at being social media influencers!

Indeed, a study conducted by Lego to know what kind of job children wanted to have when growing up revealed interesting results. The company surveyed 3,000 children between the ages of 8 and 12 from the United States, the United Kingdom, and China, as well as 326 parents who had children aged between 5 and 12. Almost a third of the kids in the survey said they wanted to be a YouTuber when they grew up, while 11 percent said they wanted to be an astronaut.

However, the responses varied depending on where the children were from. More than half of those in China said they wanted to be an astronaut, making it the most popular career aspiration. In the United States and the United Kingdom, that number fell to just over 10 percent, with vlogger (video blogger) or YouTuber ranked as the top aspiration in both countries. Three in four children believed humans would eventually live in outer space or on another planet, according to the research, with 96 percent of Chinese children believing this to be true, compared to 63 percent in the United Kingdom and 68 percent in the United States (www.cnbc.com/2019/07/19/more-children-dream-of-being-youtubers-than-astronauts-lego-says.html).

Despite the fact that all these children belong to the same generation and that social media has the same penetration in all three countries, their views of the future significantly differ. For the short-termed cultures such as the United States and the United Kingdom, children aim at short-term results, knowing that social media is the speedway to fame and wealth. In the long-termed Chinese culture, and in spite of the massive use and creation of platforms such as TikTok, children see the future somewhere far away from where they are today and start paving their way to what is expected to happen in the long term.

The Magicverse—Digital Humans and Digital Influencers

There are 10 million active influencers worldwide, from which, more than 50 percent perform on Instagram (Social Star, 2023; https://officialsocialstar.com/blogs/influencer/how-many-influencers-are-there-in-the-world). The role of influencers being to influence shopping decisions and beliefs in customers, they could be assimilated to witches, because they are so blindly followed by humans that it looks like they are under a spell. The most impressive of these witch-like people are the 150 active human-like influencers called digital or virtual influencers, which are totally illusionary because they look just like people but are purely digital, that is, nonexistent in the real world. More than 20 million people follow these nonhuman influencers (www.stryvemarketing.com/blog/virtual-influencers/#:~:text = As%20of%202023%2C%20there%20are,on%20the%20internet%20in%202018).

The above explains why influencer marketing's landscape continues to grow at such an impressive pace. In short, a virtual influencer is a digital character that was created using computer graphics software. This character is then given a personality and will at all times act on social media platforms as if they were a human being. A study in the United States found that 58 percent of respondents were following a virtual influencer. As much as believing and following (obeying) a person who doesn't exist could be defined as madness, the big advantage for marketers is that virtual influencers can do anything that human influencers can do, but with total control and higher engagement. And you don't need to pay them! In fact, virtual influencers can offer nearly three times the engagement rates of real influencers. Here is the top 12 digital influencers for 2024 according to HypeAuditor and VirtualHumans.org (https://influencermarketinghub.com/virtual-influencers/):

1. In 2022, Lu do Magalu was the most followed virtual influencer. Currently, she is also the virtual human with the most visibility in the world. She boasts more than 14.6 million followers on Facebook, 6 million followers on Instagram, more than 2.6 million YouTube subscribers, and over 1.3 million followers on Twitter and TikTok, respectively. However, her fame and reach is mostly limited to Brazil from where she originates.

2. Miquela Sousa, or better known as Lil Miquela, is a virtual robot model who has worked with some of the top fashion brands like Prada, Dior, and Calvin Klein. She also released one single, *Not Mine*, in 2017 and debuted her first music video, *Hard Feelings*, at Lollapalooza's online festival earlier this year. This freckled Brazilian-American beauty was created by Brud, a startup based in Los Angeles. She has three million Instagram followers, dubbed as *Miquelites*, 3.6 million TikTok followers and more than 31,000 Twitter followers.

3. Barbie has her biggest following on Facebook, but she also has huge followings on other platforms, particularly on YouTube where she assumes the role of a vlogger. She boasts 2.2 million followers on Instagram, 11.1 million subscribers on YouTube, close to 320,000 followers on Twitter, and more than 440,000 monthly listeners on Spotify.

4. Guggimon, originally from Montreal, Canada, made his appearance in June 2019. He was created by Superplastic, the world's leading creator of animated synthetic celebrities, apparel, and designer toys. His obsessions include anything horror related. In his own words, he has described himself as a *fashion horror artist & mixtape producer with obsessions*: handbags, axes, designer toys, Billie Eilish, & *The Shining*.

5. Originally from Brazil, Any Malu is a fully animated virtual influencer that is recognized across the globe. She first made

her appearance in 2015, and in five years, she managed to grow from an idea to a YouTube star to a transmedia experience. The Brazilian virtual influencer has more than one million fans across Twitter, TikTok, Facebook, and Instagram. Her videos on YouTube have received more than 280 million views. As a matter of fact, she is one of only a few virtual influencers with their very own TV show. What sets her apart even further is that her TV show is powered by Cartoon Network.

6. Anna Cattish is a Russian animator and illustrator. She is part of the HonkFu visual label that creates specialty animation and character-based imagery. She has gained close to 472,000 followers on Instagram. Her work is cute, yet edgy with a touch of attitude.

7. Originally from Jakarta in Indonesia, Thalasya travels all across her home country exploring its balconies and shops. Though, while staycations are currently a thing, this has not stopped her from traveling all the way to the United States to a recording studio in Florida. As we all know, traveling can be an expensive hobby. So, to fund her hobby, she has advertised for hotels, restaurants and even health pills. What's more, she also has her own clothing store. She was developed by Magnavem Studio and made her first appearance in October 2018. Since then, she has gained over 469,000 followers on Instagram.

8. Janky was created by Superplastic. Originally from Los Angeles, this part-time cartoon stuntman first made his appearance in June 2019. His brand mentions include big names and luxury brands like Tinder, Prada, and Red Bull. In the little over a year that he has been around, he has already gained more than one million followers on Instagram.

9. Noonoouri was created by Joerg Zuber, the founder of Opium Effect, a creative agency in Munich, Germany. The 19-year-old digital character has taken the fashion industry by storm and has worked with the majority of top luxury fashion brands that include Lacoste, Versace, and Bulgari. While her goal is to entertain, she also aims to inform her audiences about various

social causes. She is much more than just a digital character. She is also a vegan who publicly supports sustainable fashion. She does not really use Twitter and mostly uses Instagram to reach her 402,000+ followers. Alternatively, you can also follow her on TikTok where some of her videos have received 50,000+ likes.

10. Originally from Paris, France, Bee is the very first influencer bee. He/she first buzzed onto the social media scene in April 2019. The Fondation de France created this virtual influencer to help brands across the globe collect money to help save bees. While his/her Twitter account is quiet, his/her Instagram account is a hive of activity with over 254,000 followers already.

11. Originally from Tokyo, Imma has the prestigious title of being Japan's first virtual model and made her first appearance in July 2018. Since then, this virtual girl with the distinctive pink bob is featured in many headlines. As a matter of fact, the Japan Economics Entertainment has picked her as a *New 100 Talent to Watch*. Her interests include Japanese culture, art, and film. She boasts brand mentions such as Burberry, TikTok, Adidas Tokyo, and IKEA Japan. In the two-plus years that she has been in the business, she has gained more than 407,000 followers on Instagram and two million likes on TikTok already.

12. Bermuda is one of the older virtual influencers. Originally from Los Angeles, she first made her appearance in December 2016. She aims to motivate young entrepreneurs to go after their business goals. She especially wants to motivate more women to follow careers in the field of robotics. She also hopes to further her music career. She has already released a cover of Under the Bridge by the Red Hot Chilli Peppers on Spotify.

Another amazing power AI has is turning old habits into new creations. Fanvue, a subscription-based content creator platform recently teamed up with the World AI Creator Awards (WAICA) to launch the world's first Miss AI competition. A team of judges, comprising two humans and two virtual models, will sort through AI-generated pictures of women and choose one to crown as Miss AI. The winner gets cash prize along with the chance to monetize their creation on Fanvue.

The AI creator of the crowned Miss AI will receive $5,000 cash plus access to Imagine Education's Mentorship Program worth $3,000 and PR support worth over $5,000. The runner-up in the inaugural Miss AI awards will receive free access to an Imagine Education course worth $500 plus $2,000 promotional package and PR support worth over $2,500. Finally, the third-placed contestant will receive a free consultancy call with Imagine Education worth $500 plus a $500 promotional package and PR support worth over $1,000.

Judges will assess the looks, the size of the character's followings, and their *personalities*. The application includes questions like: *if your AI model could talk, what would be their one dream to make the world a better place?* The technical skills behind the character's creation will also be taken into account by the judges. A press release from WAICA notes that the competition *signifies a monumental leap forward—launching almost 200 years after the world's first ever real life beauty pageant took place in the 1880s.*

The two AI models who are judging the competition are Aitana Lopez and Emily Pellegrini. Pellegrini was designed by an anonymous creator who has said they asked ChatGPT what the average man's dream girl is, and then designed the model exactly along those lines. Which means long hair, big breasts, flawless skin, and a sculpted body. Pelligrini—who, again, is a purely digital creation—reportedly makes thousands of dollars on Fanvue and has famous footballers sliding into her Instagram because they think she is a real person. The other judge, Lopez, who is billed as *Spain's first AI model* and can apparently *earn up to €10,000 (U.S.$ 10,736) a month* doing modeling work for brands. (https://www.dailymail.co.uk/news/article-12877501/ai-model-footballers-billionaires.html)

Ironically, this seems to be incompatible with feminist movements that had protested against the Miss Universe pageant because it stereotyped (real) women, depicting them as objects of men's desire in patriarchal societies! In a world where everything virtual is more willingly accepted than what is real, the emergence of digital influencers does not come as a surprise. What is, however, intriguing is that technology and AI promote rationality as being their best strength while creating a totally irrational world to humans where no behavior can be explained by rationality. How is this different from magic?

Idea Generation, Content Creation and Curation

In today's digital age, marketing strategies are constantly evolving to keep up with the ever-changing consumer landscape. One of the most significant advancements in recent years is the integration of generative AI into marketing practices. Generative AI has already reshaped the marketing industry in various ways, revolutionizing content creation, personalization, customer engagement, and more. As we look ahead, it's crucial to explore the potential future applications of generative AI in marketing.

In the past, marketers relied heavily on human creativity to develop compelling content. However, generative AI has emerged as a game-changer, automating content creation processes and expanding the boundaries of creativity. Using advanced algorithms, generative AI can generate text, images, videos, and even music that mimic human-like qualities. This technology enables marketers to produce vast amounts of high-quality content quickly and efficiently, saving time and resources. Yet, the authorship issue has to be taken into account: Who is the author of a computer-generated image taken from several existing images? (https://research.aimultiple.com/generative-ai-in-marketing/)

AI technologies generate entirely new content, from lines of code to images to human-like speech. New startups continue to enter the market at a swift pace, supported by advances in generative infrastructure like Large Language Model (LLM) and vector databases, with $14.1 billion in equity funding (including $10 billion to OpenAI) in 2023. Even excluding the OpenAI deal, that's a 38 percent increase from full year 2022. Startups are using the technology to create new proteins and drugs, design new products, power the next generation of search engines, develop building architectures, create experiences in virtual worlds and games, and much more (www.linkedin.com/pulse/buzz-around-generative-ai-all-you-need-know-allphatech/).

Generative AI can revolutionize advertising by enabling hyper-targeted campaigns. By analyzing vast amounts of customer data, generative

AI algorithms can identify specific patterns, preferences, and behaviors. Armed with these insights, marketers can create highly focused and personalized advertisements that resonate with individual customers. Hyper-targeted advertising not only improves the effectiveness of marketing campaigns but also reduces advertising fatigue for consumers by delivering relevant content, in line with what was explained by John Burkey.

On average, Americans spend more time online and on mobile devices than they do watching television—and much more than reading newspapers and magazines. That varies by age, with younger generations (millennials and Generation Z) being more active in digital media as compared to baby boomers and senior citizens. Yet, most digital platforms and pure players are now reaching out to older generations by promoting their services on traditional media: YouTube, WhatsApp, Meta and TikTok, are now broadcasting commercials on traditional TV.

As the internet allows consumers to socialize, review information, enjoy entertainment, and shop, this change in behavior creates challenges and opportunities for marketing managers targeting specific customers or segments through digital media on computers and mobile devices. Precise targeting can be automated with artificial intelligence too, which learned that emailing a promotional offer to a customer is most effective at certain times. This learning occurs after trying to mail offers earlier and later than this timing and discovering the most effective lead time. Similar learning may occur around the type of offer or wording of an offer. In this case, the software does not know why the timeframe works, but it does know what works best.

Programmatic delivery refers to the use of software and artificial intelligence to automate placing online advertising on websites or in social media to target users. The process increases the efficiency and effectiveness of media planning. The low cost also means that advertisers spend less to target customers more precisely. Most online advertisers seek a direct response—they entice a customer to click on a link, gather information, and engage. Advertising on the internet continues to evolve quickly, with marketing managers receiving rapid feedback in the form of clicks and other engagement measures. This information allows an advertiser to put more efforts behind effective advertising and withdraw from those that are not working well.

Furthermore, advances in technology continually open doors for new types of advertising. To get the attention of web surfers, online advertisers have created different types of ads that work to achieve different objectives. Each offers some advantages and disadvantages. Banners are a type of online advertising that places an ad on a web page, often across the top or to the side of the page's primary content. Pop-ups are similar to banner ads but usually cover an entire browser window— *popping up* in front of a user's web page. For these ads, the click-through rate—the number of people who click on the ad divided by the number of people the ad is presented to—can be low (less than 1 in 1,000). Although click-through rates are low, banner ads often have the goal of generating awareness and building brand reputation, so click-through may not be the best measure of effectiveness. Evidence suggests that these ads can be combined with offline advertising to increase purchase intent. Click-through rates are also higher when video content is used in an ad (https://research.aimultiple.com/generative-ai-in-marketing/).

While the loss of cookies hurts social media sites, these sites still have a lot of data about each user. These data can still be used to target advertising. For example, response to Facebook ads declined after the social network lost access to third-party data showing its user's behavior off the social media platform. While click-through rates had been growing and were as high as 2.5 percent, these numbers have since declined. At the very least, because customers conduct searches and access social media from mobile devices, advertisers must have mobile-friendly versions of their ads.

As the digital landscape becomes increasingly saturated with content, the challenge for marketers is to cut through the noise and deliver relevant content to their target audience. Generative AI can play a crucial role in content curation and recommendations. By analyzing user behavior, preferences, and contextual information, generative AI algorithms can curate personalized content recommendations tailored to each individual user. This level of content personalization ensures that customers receive relevant and engaging content, fostering deeper connections between brands and consumers.

The power of generative AI extends beyond content creation and personalization. It can also contribute to predictive analytics and forecasting, enabling marketers to anticipate trends, consumer behavior, and market demands. By analyzing historical data and identifying patterns, generative AI algorithms can generate accurate predictions and valuable insights. This information empowers marketers to make data-driven decisions, optimize promotional strategies, and stay ahead of the competition (https://research.aimultiple.com/generative-ai-in-marketing/).

SMS Marketing—The Revenant

With AI-powered strategies and compliance with data regulations, SMS marketing is experiencing a revival, offering a potent way to engage customers. The emphasis on personalized, relevant content and respect for consumer privacy has breathed new life into this tried-and-true marketing approach, elevating customer satisfaction and brand loyalty in the digital era.

SMS marketing is indeed making a comeback thanks to AI advancements and stricter data regulations. Brands are leveraging text messages to build customer loyalty, capitalizing on high open rates. However, they must tread carefully to avoid spamming customers, as opting out is as easy as replying *STOP*. By delivering personalized and targeted content, businesses can keep subscribers engaged and valued, leading to increased conversions and customer satisfaction. Adhering to proper opt-in practices, offering relevant deals, and respecting SMS marketing guidelines ensures campaigns remain effective while safeguarding consumer privacy rights and preferences (www.dmnews.com/).

Often neglected and almost forgotten by marketers, with new technologies and privacy regulation shifts, text messaging has emerged as a more effective approach to building a robust customer base compared to email or social media. Conversational commerce, including SMS marketing, is projected to experience a remarkable 30 percent growth in the upcoming years. The surge in text messaging as a marketing tool is attributed to its immediacy, personalization, and impressive engagement rates. Companies are capitalizing on SMS's power to foster lasting relationships with customers, offering exclusive deals, targeted messaging, and real-time support, ultimately elevating customer satisfaction and fostering loyalty. Here again, immediacy appears as being one of the main pillars of customer satisfaction.

A recent report from Simple Texting (https://simpletexting.com) reveals that 71 percent of consumers willingly subscribe to receive texts from businesses, and 53 percent desire the ability to text companies back. As a result, a staggering 86 percent of businesses have been utilizing text messages to connect with customers. The report highlights the growing demand for swift and convenient interactions through text messaging, pushing businesses to adapt and meet customer expectations: effortless and immediate gratification. This has led to a greater focus on providing value and building trust, which ensures that customer relationships remain authentic and mutually beneficial (www.dmnews.com/sms-marketing-making-a-come-back-discover-how-ai-and-data-rules-are-changing-the-game/).

Just like magic and witches, the comeback of SMS marketing and the use of traditional TV commercials by pure players such as Amazon, Google, Meta, YouTube, WhatsApp, and, more recently, TikTok, show that nothing is definitely buried in the past, and Nostalgia Marketing confirms this trend. In a supernatural world, these would be called revenants!

Key Takeaways

- It is easy for consumers to get confused with so many sources of information flowing toward them every minute of every day. While using AI to shape your communication is very helpful, make sure that yours is distinguishable from your competitors as everyone else will be using the same tools.
- Using AI to hyper target or micro target your consumers is the best way of getting closer to them.

- As much as advertising is still a powerful technique, try to keep it well incorporated with your new tools in your communication mix.

Implications to Marketers

Since content plays such a vital role in educating audiences about your products, its benefits are also substantial (https://blog.hub-spot.com/marketing/benefits-high-quality-content-consistency-brand).

1. **Increased brand awareness:** Content marketing raises brand awareness by positioning your business in your industry.
2. **Build trust:** Demonstrate your expertise by consistently producing high-quality, informative content. This helps you to establish yourself as a reliable source of information and build trust with consumers.
3. **Sales acceleration:** Successful content marketing accelerates sales by providing consumers with the information they need to decide. Once potential customers get all the necessary information, they can finally have the confidence to make a purchase.
4. **Improved customer satisfaction:** Content marketing provides customers the support they need to use your products effectively. This makes it easy for them to get the help they need when they need it, enhancing their experience and giving them a reason to return.
5. **Use a Variety of content formats**: While some may prefer to read, others may be better at processing information in an audio-visual format. So make sure you experiment with different content formats to appeal to a wider audience.
6. **Track your results**: After your content goes live, it's important to track performance to see what's working and what's not. Use Google Analytics and other content analytics tools to see which pieces of content get engagement and shares. This will help you identify the topics that resonate with your audience and the **content formats** they prefer. So that you can keep refining your strategy to maximize your results.

CHAPTER 8

AI Around the World

Magic is just like culture; a survival kit based on beliefs and rituals.

While the product, brand name, price point, distribution and communication can be locally adapted, we still believe in global markets. Yet, cultural differences persist and one would wonder if AI will help companies to better understand such cultural differences or rather try to make marketing strategies more homogeneous. Cultural sensitivity is a human trait, but can a machine learn it? The confrontation between deep cultural roots and the tendency of globalization with technology should call out to marketers. This is the main topic discussed in this chapter.

In nearly every documented society, people believe that some misfortunes are caused by malicious group mates using magic or supernatural powers. In using the Mystical Harm Survey,[1] Singh shows that several conceptions of malicious mystical practitioners, including sorcerers (who use learned spells), possessors of the evil eye (who transmit injury through their stares and words), and witches (who possess superpowers, pose existential threats, and engage in morally abhorrent acts), recur around the world. The author argues that these beliefs develop from three cultural selective processes: a selection for intuitive magic, a selection for plausible explanations of impactful misfortune, and a selection for demonizing myths that justify mistreatment.

Differences in Meaning and Practices

Over the last two decades, almost all the research on this field has involved attempting to identify reliable psychological and behavioral correlates of beliefs in magic and supernatural powers.[2] Paranormal, superstitious, and magical beliefs have been found in a diverse range of cultures for thousands of years[3], polls show that these beliefs continue to thrive in modern times[4], and researchers have long speculated about the origins and functions of such beliefs.[5,6,7]

Admittedly, the pair good luck/bad luck has been ruling our lives forever. Words have different meanings and some of them can summon curses. Numbers carry positive and negative vibes too and symbols can serve to do good as well as bad to ourselves and to others. Those exist in all cultures but differ from culture to culture. If in the United States, there is no 13th floor in buildings; in China, there is no 4th floor. Thumbs up is positive in most Western cultures but it is offensive in some Arab countries. Moreover *tomorrow* has no universal meaning and can mean 24 hours from now or any other day than today, depending on the culture.

Superstitious beliefs are typically acquired and used in contexts involving the native language because they are culture-dependent, which shapes a language-dependent memory.[8] As a result, the native language evokes them more forcefully than a foreign language, which explains why in some situations foreign languages prompt less negative feelings toward bad-luck scenarios and less positive feelings toward good-luck scenarios. This also explains why skeptical people from other cultures use some of the foreign words (and beliefs) for mockery.

Differences in cognitive and perceptual domains explain some of the behavioral differences across cultures. For example, Easterners are situation-centered; they are sensitive to their environment and more consonant with fate; they take things as they come, while Westerners are individual-centered; they expect the environment to be sensitive to them and actively try to control it. These cultural differences lead to differences in causal attributions: *what should happen happens* as opposed to *I failed to make it happen.*

The short-termed and controlling behavior explains why frustrations grow in most Western cultures, while in the East, people seem to be more easygoing because they are more patient. They are taught to wait and see. These differences are also explained by the relationship to the past. Eastern cultures are more contextual because, to them, history, traditions, and myths are the accumulation of knowledge (we learn from the past) while detachment from the past leads to starting anew when analyzing each isolated situations, without relating it to past events (there is not much to learn from history), which characterizes most of the Western cultures where myths are considered to be just silly superstitions.

The relationship to time also explains those differences. In most Eastern cultures, time is circular, and the past, present, and future coexist in a way that explains most of the phenomena observed in the world. In addition, the circular vision of reality makes people more patient too: what goes around comes around. Or, *if it didn't happen today it is because it was not meant to happen today.* On the contrary, Western cultures have a linear perception of time. The past is gone, the present is ephemeral, and the future is tomorrow: what was not done today is lost and thus perceived as a failure and experienced as a frustration. Tomorrow we should start all over again. Westerners stick to strict deadlines and planned behavior. We can thus see that with AI, we are drawn to the Western standards because the machine will always behave in a strictly planned way, without straying away from what it is meant to do: AI does more in less time.

How much of the context a machine is capable to take into account is still a mystery, but it can become an issue. If the machine is change blind, it might leave out critical information having an impact on decision making. Change blindness is a phenomenon that takes place when individuals are unable to identify differences in the context. When focusing on the object, people cannot assess the contextual situation because they do not see it and thus cannot identify changes in it. Thus, despite the numerous explanations one can provide them about a specific object or event, they will keep insisting and repeating the same story about the object because this is all they can see. Context is ignored because everything is assessed in absolute terms rather than relative to the context.[9]

Magical beliefs are contextual. Some of them, such as belief in luck and precognition, are presumably universal; however, the extent to which such beliefs are embraced likely varies across cultures. Over and above the effects of demographic factors, culture has been a significant predictor of luck and precognition and behavioral shift. Indeed, when culture was added to demographic models in research, the variance accounted for luck and precognition beliefs approximately doubled and its impact on behavior was evidenced.

When it comes to marketing, superstitious beliefs can be the basis of product performance expectations and their impact on initial purchase likelihood and subsequent satisfaction. Superstition-driven expectations cause consumers to make purchase decisions that run counter to economic rationality. In Asia, for example, consumers are relatively more likely to purchase a product with positive superstitious associations based on its lucky color and are more willing to pay more money for a product with a smaller but lucky number of units contained in the package (eight tennis balls compared to four). In contrast, consumers who do not hold such superstitious beliefs adhere to the more rational choice paradigm—value for money.

Such differences in purchase likelihood are driven by superstition-based performance expectations. Consumer expectations play an important role in marketing because of their impact on initial purchase decisions, satisfaction judgments, and subsequent repurchase behavior [10,11,12]. Research has shown that expectations can be based on a variety of factors, including advertising or published quality ratings[13], trial[14], and company promises and word-of-mouth.[15]

As shown by multiple examples presented in the previous chapters, marketers rely on superstitions in their communications, potentially creating or changing consumer expectations. We remember that superstitions are beliefs that run counter to rational thought or are inconsistent with known laws of nature[16] and can be classified as either cultural or personal, and are invoked either to bring good luck or to fend off bad luck. This power attributed by the consumer to the products they are likely to purchase can represent a determinant factor in their decision-making process. We all know that we hang on some travel souvenir, or a gift or even clothes that we define as our lucky ones, which we make sure to carry with us when we go through important moments in our lives. In several cultures, it is believed that the color of the underwear you wear on New Year's Eve will determine your degree of satisfaction and happiness throughout the upcoming year.

Indeed, consumption rituals include using a particular product before an important event that is associated either with a high likelihood of failure or a high level of uncertainty.[17] The degree to which consumers rely on superstitious beliefs in their consumption decisions is likely to depend on the associated level of stress, risk, or uncertainty.[18,19] Examples of personal superstitions or rituals relevant to marketers include consumers' buying and wearing lucky accessories, like charm bracelets, lockets, pens, or cufflinks. The brand Pandora understood it very well in selling multiple options of charms to add to consumers' bracelets, each charm carrying highly emotional value.

The big risk for marketers is to have their products associated to acts and events for which they have no knowledge and even less power. If the charm does not work, consumers are likely to blame the product associated with the event.[20] Kramer and Block found that superstitious associations influence consumer behavior to a great extent, and furthermore often do so through an automatic process. Specifically, they found that following product failure, consumers were less/more satisfied with a product for which they hold positive/negative superstitious associations.[21]

Superstitions also influence high-involvement decisions. While there is an Amulet Market in Bangkok, Thailand, the number of weddings scheduled on 07/07/07 increased dramatically in the United States in order to capitalize on the lucky number 7.[22] China waited for August 8, 2008, at 8 am to start the Olympic Games in Beijing. Likely, Chinese investors more frequently select stocks with a surplus of 8 in the ticker number.[23] The Chinese brand LONGFENGXIANG has developed a jewelry collection that incorporates traditional Chinese auspicious symbols, such as the dragon symbolizing good luck, prosperity, and protection attracting consumers who value cultural heritage and believe in the power of these symbols. LONGFENGXIANG trains employees to have an in-depth understanding of the meaning of different auspicious symbols and designs special packaging for jewelry, using red (good luck) and gold (prosperity) boxes.

The technology-oriented Japan, with its last-generation robots, is also a highly superstitious culture with several rituals and objects specific to the country's beliefs, including special editions of Kit Kat for students facing challenging exams. Indeed, Japanese parents often give Kit Kats to their children before a big test or exam as a good luck charm, telling them they will surely win and do well on their exams. Sales spike in January when the Japanese college entrance exams are held. Most of the time, students don't eat these Kit Kats, but rather keep them as an amulet. Nestlé created a postcard-like packaging, accepted by the official post office, for writing words of encouragement or blessings. The company cleverly rides the waves of superstitions in the country of technology by associating their brand with local words: Kitto Katsu, which means *sure winner*. Kit Kat is a lucky charm in Japan. Who said that technology and superstitions couldn't coexist?

In Taiwan, people put snacks of the brand *Kuai Kuai* next to or on top of machines, because they believe that its name (obedient, well-behaved) will make a device function without errors. Thus, green bags—the yellow and red ones represent abnormality—are commonly found in offices, placed next to the devices of server rooms, computers, ATMs, ticket booths, control systems, and toll booths, but users should ensure that the snacks are not expired.

Belief in astrology is also prevalent in other areas of the world including Europe and Asia. For example,[24] Kramer and Block reported that Taiwanese consumers were willing to spend nearly 15 percent more money for a product when the price point included the lucky number 8. Similarly, they found that Taiwanese consumers were willing to pay more for a neutrally priced product, forgoing a discount, when an identical product was offered at a lower price point that included the unlucky number 4. We mentioned in previous chapters the apps enabling Asian consumers to pick a lucky number for their phones even if they have to pay a higher price for them. Similarly, there are financial firms that recommend stocks based on their astrological sign.

Superstitions influence the selling of homes in the United States. In order to increase their chances of selling their home during the recent housing market crash, some homeowners purchased a statue of

St. Joseph—the patron saint of home and family. As instructed, they buried it upside down and facing away from the home in order to symbolize leaving.[25] However, the impact of superstitious beliefs on the marketplace extends far beyond hopes of bringing luck to a marriage or the sale of a home. As seen in previous chapters, superstitions guide management decisions in some Asian countries as does the Groundhog Day at Wall Street.

When consumers look for signs of good/bad luck or take actions to influence chance outcomes, they are using superstition as a heuristic device that acts as a shortcut in the decision-making process. It is just like inputting the machine with all the superstitious codes (numbers, colors, names, signs, etc.) and waiting for the decision to be made by the compilation of these inputs. Not all consumers are triskaidekaphobics (afraid of the number 13), use astrological signs to purchase stocks, or bury statues to increase the likelihood of selling their home. Admittedly, there are individual differences in the propensity to express superstitious behavior and the effect of superstitious beliefs and risk-taking behavior is not likely to be the same for all consumers around the world.

Despite the technological progress, marketers should not forget that culture matters. In some cultures, the fortune teller would be engaged by companies to make specific calculations regarding the suitability of the individuals concerned by the business. This evaluation would then be considered alongside other more standard criteria such as strategic fit, credit rating, and so forth. If the person has an inauspicious birthdate then they may opt for an entirely different partner company or, between them, to arrange for a different person to sign some contract.

Prior to meetings, the advice of the fortune teller would focus on the optimal venue/place and favorable days and times to meet and advise on the best time to begin the meeting itself. The fortune teller would also stipulate what kind of food or drink to imbibe before attending the meeting and what color clothes to wear, what kind of gemstone to carry on one's finger, and what type of flower scent to apply about one's body and hair.[26]

In contrast, in Western cultures, the person–organization (PO) fit model is more likely to be used. PO fit is the compatibility between people and organizations that occurs when: (a) at least one entity provides what the other needs, or (b) they share similar fundamental characteristics, or (c) both[27]. Companies have different ways of PO fit in measuring the congruence of a candidate's own beliefs and values with the mission, values, and ethics of the organization, which are reflected in the company's culture. The PO fit is often followed up with the person–job fit, where a candidate has to be able to fulfill the job description requirements in terms of qualifications, specific hard skills, soft skills, cognitive ability, and experience to carry out the role. It seems to be a more rational approach than reaching out to a fortune teller.

Deep Cultural Roots Versus AI Universalism

Industrial and technological evolution can be seen as a process of transforming the habits and life patterns where AI provides the freedom of creating, playing, communicating, and much more by entering the consumer market as a new paradigm of a personal yet global experience. Its ability to shape consumers' needs and wants leads to homogeneous patterns of a lifestyle in which almost nothing could be done without the help of AI. This makes consumers more predictable and profitable by increasing the quantity of people behaving the same way through the same limited array of options thanks to universal notions of freedom of a customized life. For example, Nike allows consumers to customize their shoes by offering a limited amount of variations in colors and symbols that can be combined in what the consumer will see as unique and specific to them.

All over the world, there is a widespread belief that norm adherence is rewarded and punished by supernatural entities.[28,29,30,31] White et al.[32] state that supernatural beliefs provide a culturally supported mechanism that can encourage the adoption of particular norms (by framing certain actions as especially valued by supernatural agents) and inhibit norm violation (by positing supernatural punishment for counter-normative behavior). Subsequently, supernaturally enforced prosocial norms can foster increased cooperation and support the long-term success of large groups of unrelated individuals.[33,34] In many world religions, supernatural norm enforcement takes the form of a moralizing God, and experimental reminders of this have been found to encourage pro-sociality among believers.[35,36] There is also growing cross-cultural evidence that commitment to such Gods is associated with adherence to social norms prescribing cooperation, honesty, and generosity toward strangers.[37,38]

Norms have always existed and have been reinforced as communitarian behaviors have been proliferating in all societies. Whether those norms are ancient or contemporary, based on facts or superstitions, they serve the same goals: reward and punishment. As much as the quest for universalism has been enhanced by the belief in global markets, cultural differences have never been so salient. Countries having been categorized as underdeveloped or as developing economies are running the show today. They impose their own terms in business negotiations as well as their own currency for trading. Most of these countries constitute big markets with big populations that, although fascinated by technology, are proud of their native cultures and promote them through social media. Put in other words, those cultures that used to be shy and almost ashamed of their country and would happily accept foreign products are now proudly extending their brands to foreign markets, and selling them for much higher prices than in their domestic markets. But these are also cultures that believe in magic and superstition, which partly explains the recent growth in superstitious beliefs spreading around the world.

For example, Brazil exports its flip-flops Havaianas around the world, with the Brazilian flag inscribed on the product itself. This traditionally inexpensive basic product in Brazil afforded by all social classes became trendy, and thus much more expensive after some international celebrities were portrayed wearing them on social media. Today, the brand is sold in most countries in the world at much higher prices. The same situation applies to other cultures: if we have chai tea everywhere is because India has been exporting the recipe and the habit of consuming it, but we pay six to seven dollars for it at Starbucks. If we eat tacos in the United States is because Mexico has introduced them to the rest of the world and if we drink Bubble tea is because Taiwan showed the way, it is worth noting that superstitious beliefs predominate in all these cultures.

Undoubtedly, consumers from these countries have access to the same technology and use their smartphones to accomplish their daily activities as anyone else in the world. They are very active on social media and follow influencers, both human and digital. This access to technology and the universalism in the use of smartphones suggest an opening to standardization of marketing efforts. Knowing that populations of all countries are on social media and that AI is following the same trend as did internet a few years ago, might give companies hopeful of standardization the illusion that cultural differences won't matter anymore. Yet, evidence shows that they matter even more today.

The challenge for marketers is to bring together consumers with different beliefs and practices requiring specific products but unified by technology. It is not because they all are on TikTok, Instagram, and other platforms that they abdicated to their cultures of origin. Beliefs and practices are deeply rooted in every culture and they should be understood because they generate different needs. Technology only satisfies part of those needs: the rootless and universal need of effortless immediate gratification, because they relate to human nature rather than to culture.

The magic of technology is that it is borderless, not only because of its reach but also because it gets rid of several barriers, including language barriers. Google can translate for free, but with AI, the accuracy is much higher. It is not just about linguistic accuracy; it's about recognizing and appreciating the richness of different cultures by providing authentic representations and avoiding misinterpretations. It is vital in transcending language barriers to allow stories to reso- nate more deeply with audiences from various cultural backgrounds. Therefore, AI is transforming the dubbing field of movies, TV shows, and advertising by elevating the efficiency and reach of content localization. Dubbing, a key postproduction process, involves replacing the original voices in visual content with new ones, aligning with the audience's language and cultural nuances.

AI leverages deep learning and neural networks to create synthetic voices that are indistinguishable from human ones, analyzing speech patterns to generate accurate voiceovers. This not only speeds up the dubbing process but also significantly cuts costs compared to traditional methods, which require hiring voice actors and painstakingly synchronizing audio to video. AI's multilingual capabilities in dubbing are transformative, offering the ability to localize content swiftly into a multitude of languages. This is not just about word-for-word translation; it's about adapting content culturally and contextually for each audience. By leveraging AI, creators can ensure their content is accessible and resonant with viewers worldwide, significantly broadening their reach (https://slator.com/).

Unlike traditional dubbing, which is limited by the availability and scheduling of voice actors, AI can process and dub extensive large volumes of content simultaneously. This capability is essential for platforms with expansive libraries, where timely updates in multiple languages are crucial. AI's robust processing power enables content providers to keep their offerings fresh and culturally relevant across different regions without the bottleneck of human resource constraints. This ensures that as the content volume grows, the dubbing process remains efficient and consistent.

By automating translation and voice generation, AI can turn around a dubbing project in a fraction of the time required for traditional methods, which involve manual script translation, voice actor casting, and recording sessions. This expediency is vital in an industry where content needs to be released quickly to satisfy the immediate demands of global audiences and capitalize on trending topics. AI's quick turnaround times facilitate a more agile production cycle, enabling content creators to stay competitive and relevant in a fast-paced digital marketplace.

As perfect as it would seem to be, the use of AI in multicultural settings is not without risks. One of the most significant challenges facing AI dubbing is the ability to replicate the natural flow and emotional nuance of human speech. Despite technological advances, AI-generated voices often lack the subtle variations in tone, pacing, and expressiveness that characterize authentic human interaction. Audiences can usually sense when a voice lacks the warmth and familiarity of natural speech, which can diminish the immersive experience of the dubbed content. As discussed in previous chapters, the use of AI in audio description by some TV channels has been strongly criticized by the audience for being monotone, inexpressive, and thus totally disrupting the show's tone and pace.

In addition, AI dubbing also presents legal complexities, particularly in copyright and licensing. When dubbing content for commercial purposes, such as advertising, navigating the rights associated with using AI-generated renditions of human voices is essential. These challenges involve intricate negotiations and a thorough understanding of intellectual property laws. Not mentioning the ability of ensuring cultural references, especially when dealing with idiomatic expressions specific to each country rather than to each language. Actually, not all countries speaking the same native languages use the same vocabulary and have the same accent. Witches could speak several languages without translation!

Thus, human oversight is pivotal in AI dubbing to safeguard cultural accuracy. This involves linguists, cultural experts, and native speakers who review and correct AI-generated content, ensuring it aligns with the cultural context of the target audience. Their role extends beyond mere proofreading; they imbue the AI's output with the cultural empathy and understanding it currently lacks. This collaborative human-AI approach helps fine-tune the nuances that AI alone may overlook, providing a layer of cultural authenticity and sensitivity that only human experience can offer (https://murf.ai/resources/ai-dubbing-cultural-sensitivity/).

Can AI Be Culturally Sensitive?

Plethora of examples of companies having failed abroad populate the marketing news, blogs, and academic case studies. Most of these failures are due to cultural insensitivity and the belief that consumers worldwide are willing to accept globalized marketing offers. In addition to the financial losses counting for millions or billions of dollars, the brand reputation can suffer irreparable damage. Few examples of such losses are Starbucks in Australia (U.S.$ 105 million), Walmart in Germany (U.S.$ 43 billion), Uber in China (U.S.$ 42.4 billion), Coors in Spain (U.S.$ 50 million), and Target in Canada (U.S.$ 2.5 billion). Yet, those companies possess all the needed resources to study the foreign markets prior to settling there. They just assume that people around the world want them as they are, with no local adaptations.

The fast penetration of technology, smartphones, and AI in all countries in the world might reinforce companies' assumption of universalism leading to by-default standardized marketing strategies. Although its penetration differs across markets because of power of purchase discrepancies and local technological infrastructures, AI is definitely everywhere, which should come as good news. However, marketers should ask themselves how AI can help them in facing their main dilemma: Should we locally adapt or can we standardize our marketing strategy across countries? If AI can help with better and faster understanding of cultural differences and show how to adapt to them, it will be a win! But if, because of AI's widespead, marketers assume that everyone in all markets aim at the same things and behave in similar ways, companies might keep failing their ventures abroad. The risk is that AI reinforces the illusion of global markets accepting standardization by default.

AI has the potential to make a profound impact in shaping cultural sensitivity as stated by John Burkey during our interview. With its ability to process vast amounts of data and analyze patterns, AI can help bridge cultural gaps, foster understanding, and promote inclusivity. Advanced machine learning algorithms can now accurately translate text from one language to another, helping people understand and appreciate different cultures. AI algorithms are increasingly being used to personalize content recommendations based on individual preferences.

This is an opportunity to promote cultural diversity. By incorporating cultural sensitivity into recommendation systems, AI can expose users to a wider range of content from different cultures. One of the challenges AI faces is the potential for bias in its decision-making processes. This bias can perpetuate stereotypes and inadvertently exclude certain cultures or communities. However, AI can also be used to detect and mitigate such biases. By analyzing vast amounts of data, AI algorithms can identify patterns of bias and help developers create more inclusive and culturally sensitive systems. AI can also play a crucial role in preserving and promoting cultural heritage. Through techniques like image recognition and natural language processing, AI can help digitize and preserve artifacts, documents, and languages that are at risk of being lost. A recent advertisement from Dell depicts a person finding an old family recipe written on a highly damaged piece of paper, which, with the help of his daughter using AI, brings the recipe back to life.

With the rise of VR and AR, AI is enabling immersive cultural experiences that transcend physical boundaries. Through AI-powered simulations and virtual tours, consumers can explore different cultures, visit historical landmarks, and engage with cultural practices from the comfort of their homes. This technology allows individuals to gain a deeper understanding and appreciation of diverse cultures, foster-ing empathy and cultural sensitivity. While giving access to traveling without leaving home constitutes an immense advantage of AI, it can also contribute to the assumption that because consumers around the world have access to the same information, adaptation of marketing strategies is no longer needed (https://fastercapital.com/content/Impact-of-ai-on-content-diversity-and-cultural-sensitivity.html).

In marketing, understanding and embracing cultural diversity is not just a courtesy; it's a business imperative. The power of AI should be to enhance customers' experiences, and to do so, it becomes crucial to ensure that technology is attuned to the cultural sensitivities of your diverse clientele. Every consumer carries their own cultural baggage influencing their expectations and experiences. An AI that recognizes and adapts to these cultural nuances can deliver a more personalized and satisfying experience. When challenged by competitors that standardize their offers a culturally nuanced marketing strategy can be a winning differentiator.

Despite its advanced algorithms, AI lacks the inherent under-standing of cultural contexts that humans possess. This gap can lead to misunderstandings or offensive interactions, inadvertently causing discomfort to consumers. In this context, training AI for cultural sensitivity appears to be critical. To do so, the AI system should be fed with diverse data sets, including various cultural contexts, ensuring a broader understanding of cultural norms. It is important to develop algorithms that can adapt to cultural information and learn from interactions, which enhance the AI's ability to handle diverse scenarios. Involving human sensitivity in the training process ensures that AI decisions are aligned with cultural empathy (www.linkedin.com/pulse/training-ai-culturally-sensitive-guest-interactions-manos-karagiannis-av6jf?).

Training data means that AI should be trained to use the right data, which is currently a challenge knowing that several legal loopholes exist because all of the possibilities have not been thought of yet. As a new yet unavoidable topic and practice, several marketing organizations are proposing trainings and webinars about how to use AI in marketing strategies. Indeed, AI presents various challenges related to bias, privacy, and accountability, all of which require careful consideration to ensure responsible development and deployment. It is, however, a powerful tool, which can be used in a diverse range of daily digital environments.

Cultural diversity plays a significant role in shaping ethical values and norms. What may be considered ethical in one culture could be perceived differently in another one. Recognizing these cultural differences is essential when implementing AI solutions on a global scale. In the realm of AI ethics, it's crucial to grasp the concept of cultural relativism, which acknowledges that ethical standards are not universal but rather context-dependent. As explained before, different cultures hold distinct beliefs, traditions, and worldviews, which influence their ethical judgments. The coexistence of various ethical perspectives and moral values, known as moral pluralism, is particularly pronounced in our interconnected world. AI developers and organizations must know how to navigate this complex landscape (https://labelnone.com/labelnone-marketing-blog/navigating-ethical-landscape-of-ai-a-cultural-perspective/).

With AI, it is possible to learn about a company, a country, or a culture in a few minutes to get prepared to work with multicultural teams. But the information search goes inwards, unlike someone who travels, observes, and discusses with people, experiencing the real life in that culture. It might go faster learning about cultures thanks to AI, but unlike humans, a machine cannot capture the vibe of a place and observe peoples' behavior in their native habitat in real time.

Based on the aforementioned, marketing strategies' adaptation continues to be critical to its success across cultures. AI is not a magic wand that makes all consumers identical with the same needs and wants or expectations for the same products. If AI can be culturally sensitive, marketers should be even more. If AI acknowledges cultural differences, marketers should do the same and understand that beliefs in colors, numbers, and superstition are cultural traits and should be taken into account because folkloric beliefs are impossible to be harmonized Karsaklian (2023)[39].

Key Takeaways

- Don't take cultures for granted.
- Universalism due to extensive use of technology can be deceptive.
- Use AI to start getting familiar with your customers' cultural beliefs then go to see them for real.

Implications to Marketers

The temptation to standardize your marketing strategy can be big if you believe that AI harmonizes cultures. It might do so in some measure, but your role will be, as always, to look for the perfect balance of standardization and adaptation of your international marketing strategy.

AI is a tool you can use to better understand cultures and, consequently, to better translate your advertisements as well as for a more accurate segmentation, targeting, and positioning, but not to replace cultural experience in the real world.

If you don't want to travel to get to know the cultures you will address with your marketing strategy (which is a shame) use VR to at least virtually travel to those places and try to grasp some of their cultural habits.

CHAPTER 9

AI as a Competitive Advantage

There is nothing either good or bad, but thinking makes it so
—Shakespeare

Previous chapters made it clear that with all its magical powers, Artificial Intelligence (AI) is here to stay, at least for a while. But how will marketers use it now and in the future? Companies will deal with machine and human customers at the same time, knowing that they do not aim at the same benefits: there is an emotional side to human decision-making, whereas machines are all about data. Right now, everyone is both fascinated and threatened by AI: too mysterious, too intrusive, too fast, and too magical. AI represents rationality, which is perfect in a quantitative world. But what will marketers do with those huge amounts of data? How will they use it to make our world more inclusive while keeping their competitive advantage?

One of the most fascinating magical powers has always been moving objects without touching them. We saw this phenomenon in the 1960s TV shows with *I Dream of Jeannie* and *Bewitched*. It kept going on with *Star Wars*, where the power of nonhumans' minds was enough to make appear, disappear, and move people and objects around without touching them and even without a magic wand. The mastering of such powers required much training and concentration.

This prowess idealized in science fiction, became possible in a mortal's brain in February 2024 when for the first time, a human was able to move an object without touching it and without having supernatural powers. Indeed, the first human patient implanted with a brain chip from Neuralink was able to control a computer mouse just by the strength of their thoughts. The robot surgically placed a brain–computer interface implant in a region of the brain that controls the intention to move. The company's founder, Elon Musk, said that this scientific progress would facilitate speed up surgical insertions of its chip devices to treat conditions like obesity, autism, depression, and schizophrenia.

We cannot expect all consumers to be willing to accept this kind of surgery in their brains just yet, but most of them would dream of enjoying the same powers. Technology, same as magic, takes people on a trip to fascination and fear. Fascination because what seems to be impossible becomes possible and fear because we are unable to measure the current consequences and future developments of such technological advances involving our bodies and our brains.

This situation prompts the following questions: why would people in good health want to make less and less effort to get what they need and want? Do people use technology because they want it or because there is no other choice today? Why is this turn of events happening so quickly? There is not a single day without news about a breakthrough in the technology field. That might count for something.

In this book, I tried to suggest some plausible answers to the above questions. We might not know exactly the causes and consequences of such evolutions, but we can see that we are entering a new rootless cultural era where a new language is created: AI, augmented reality (AR), virtual reality (VR), Bot, chatbot, ChatGPT, Large Language Model (LLM), Open Ai, and so forth. An era where people can shape their bodies and their brains as they wish through implants, changes of sex, and future children programmed physical appearance, as if we were creating a new species from the void. It seems to indicate that humans feel diminished in a world dominated by machines that can do everything better and faster than them. It looks like to live (survive) in a highly technological world humans need to be augmented.

In line with the above Apple Visions Pro, the company's first 3D camera provides consumers with the ability of *capturing **magical** spatial photos and spatial videos*, and then relive those moments like never before with immersive Spatial Audio. Immersive panoramas wrap around users making them feel like they are standing right there where they took pictures and made videos with their iPhone 15 Pro.

Apple Vision Pro makes it easy to collaborate and connect wherever you are. FaceTime video tiles are life-size, and as new people join, the call simply expands in your room. Within FaceTime, you can also use apps to collaborate with colleagues on the same documents simultaneously. Environments let you transform the space around you, so apps can extend beyond the dimensions of your room. Choose from a selection of beautiful landscapes, or turn your room into a personal movie theater with the cinema environment. The Digital Crown gives you full control over how immersed you are. You have an infinite canvas that transforms how you use your apps. You can arrange them anywhere and scale them to the perfect size, *making the workspace of your **dreams** a reality*, all while staying present in the world around you.

Apple Vision Pro can transform any room into your own personal theater. Expand your movies, shows, and games up to the perfect size while feeling like you are part of the action with Spatial Audio. And with more pixels than a 4K TV for each eye, you can enjoy stunning content wherever you are (www.apple.com/apple-vision-pro/).

Just like this example from Apple appealing to magic and making dreams come true, companies often seek to add customer value to a core product offering. These days, many find that technology—often a website or software application—provides additional value and improves the customer's experience and satisfaction. The addition of technology can also help differentiate a product and offer a competitive advantage in markets where competing products are seen as undifferentiated. Accordingly, many firms look at integrating technology with a core product as a major product decision area. Yet, when all companies have access to the same technology, the way they use it and what they use it for will make the difference. As technology emerges, advances, and revolutionizes every industry, profession, and culture, we have barely scratched the surface of how devices, networks, and AI will change human behavior, displace jobs, and impact organizations, communities, and lives.

Conventional logic and the use of the same resources can lead companies to the same place as their competitors. Marketers would want to take distance from the worship of reason, which reflects the love of the obvious. Marketers should fear the obvious instead. This situation can create a renewed energy for the use of counterintuitive creativity. Marketers use AI to deal with large amounts of data but end up making decisions based on the few options offered by the output. Did the data take context and consumer irrationality and emotional unpredictability among other variables into account? As stated by Sutherland,[1] the problem with logic is that it kills off magic because large effects are not always the outcome of large inputs.

For example, companies are enchanted with their ability to easily gather data from the visitors to their websites. What they do not understand is that part of those visitors are scared away by the first pop-up window requiring filling out a form with their personal data. People who are just trying to browse, figure out the website and collect information to then decide if they stay on or not are shut away by those forms. It is a very rude way of saying *Hello*. Instead, websites should be welcoming; *we are happy to have you here!* Those companies who understood that added a *Continue as a guest* button that shows the visitors that the company wants you to spend time with them and is not there just to collect your data.

Admittedly, the nature of marketing is changing, as is the nature of technology. The average half-life of skills in the technology field is now less than 5 years, and in some of them, it is as low as two and a half years due to the fast pace of technological evolution. Reskilling and upskilling are and will be critical in marketing to build competitive advantage by developing talents that are not readily available in the market and filling skills' gaps that are instrumental to achieving strategic objectives.

As much as highly specialized professionals are needed, citizen developers can be seen as a threat to IT professionals. They are employees, with no coding background, increasingly using generative AI and other easy-to-use software tools. Nevertheless, Professor Adelakun explains that those citizen developers have limited knowledge to replace highly skilled professionals. The same happens with marketing as, thanks to AI, anyone can create a website, an app, an advertisement, a packaging, a digital influencer, fake photos with celebrities, and bogus videos involving any brand and post them on social media. It is imperative that professional marketers know how to work around that. In the era of traditional media, it was impossible for consumers to challenge marketers this way.

How About Market Research?

The issue of legitimacy with AI in marketing also challenges the market research reliability because it has been more and more difficult to know if the respondents to online surveys are humans or robots. Marketers tend to believe that when they purchase databases, these are likely to have been generated by AI. When conducting the surveys themselves, marketers use some filter questions or some software to spot responses coming from robots. While we know that no market research is free of biases, AI introduces one that can have serious repercussions in the design of marketing strategies: inaccurate data leads to inappropriate strategic decisions.

Yet, the use of bots should also be considered as a way of data collection. Bots learn faster and put more ideas together because they have more references than humans with the ability to process information faster, as highlighted by John Burkey. It is also easier to ask respondents embarrassing questions because a robot will not judge them.

Some marketing managers make decisions based heavily on their own judgment with very little hard data. A good marketing information system stores data collected from inside and outside the company and from various market research studies. The big data explosion, advances in computing power, and the internet have created an invaluable access to data for today's businesses. Estimates suggest that organizations process more than 1,000 times as much data today as they did in 2000. At the same time that the amount of data has grown, the cost of storing data has plummeted, making it easier for companies to save almost all data for possible later use (dmnews.com).

Today, data are more than just sales numbers. For example, Coca-Cola takes data from webcams that monitor consumers' facial expressions while watching its ads. Other companies have machines that analyze photos on Instagram. From those photos, a software identifies social media users' emotions, the activity they are engaged in, logos on their clothing, and products they might be carrying. New wearable technology (such as the Fitbit or Apple Watch) collects health data. It is estimated that 30 billion pieces of content (such as articles, photos, songs, and emotions) are shared on Facebook each month and more than 400 million tweets are sent each day on X (dmnews.com). Social media represents the biggest treasure for companies for being the place where they can find the most valuable and spontaneous data about their customers. Thanks to that, and if marketers do a good job, they can surprise their consumers with unexpected new offers that they will willingly accept because that company just read their minds!

However, there remain ethical issues about the data customers give to websites when the advertising is based on an advertiser knowing where a customer is physically located at any given time. One could wonder if it is appropriate for advertisers to track people—what they do online and even where they go—especially because most have not knowingly given the advertiser permission to track their where-abouts. Research has suggested that these are serious concerns for many consumers. In addition, some influencers have been caught buying more followers. Others have used bots that engage with their posts—to make it look like they have a more engaged following.

The role of market research is to get to know the company's consumers and should remain as is. There are several consumers' traits and preferences that marketers can observe when analyzing consumer behavior. Through their consumption habits, consumers choose the personality they want to have and establish through a lifetime of choices precisely what kind of a human being they are or want to become. Consumer decisions disclose a certain kind of personality, along with specific fears, habits, customs, levels of confidence, and intellectual abilities. Because they are well-informed people, consumers expect much more than satisfaction from companies. They want to be surprised and delighted. They want experience rather than products. They are used to having everything coming to them and grabbing their attention has never been this challenging. Your product should be the one that brings some magic to their very busy lives or they will ignore it.

Conducting surveys and asking questions provide biased data because questions trigger rational responses strongly influenced by the Social Desirability Bias (SDB). A good defintion of SDB is proposed by David Ogilvy; *the trouble with market research is that people don't think what they feel, they don't say what they think, and they don't do what they say.* Thus, logic and psychologic overlap frequently. Some problems remain unsolved because they are logic proof. For example, it seems to be self-evident that *the way to improve travel is to make it faster and for food is to make it cheaper,* but it does not work that way, as pointed out by Sutherland (p. 55).[2] The search for productivity with what is commonly called the generalized rationalization of existence leads to the accounting measure, which, in turn, always leads to greater excess.[3] We must always do more, break records. We live in a culture of measuring things over understanding people. Magic is about psychology.[4]

There is nothing more obvious than being rational, but you are required to explain your irrational behaviors. One problem with metrics is that they destroy diversity, because they force everybody to pursue the same narrow goal, often in the same narrow way, or to make choices using the exact same criteria. Neglected variables influencing consumer behavior can be hidden in preformatted questions that lead to obvious answers. If everyone asks the same questions, they are likely to get the same answers. That is also why benchmarking is important because some solutions might have already been found by people operating in other industries.[5]

We are much bothered by the uncertainty of waiting than by the duration of the wait because we are used to immediate gratification. That is why AI is welcome—it responds in a few seconds. Whether we use logic or psycho-logic depends on whether we want to solve the problem or simply be seen to be trying to solve the problem. Promising that a product has been updated to a better version is not convincing enough. However, showing its magical powers thanks to such change makes it very enticing to consumers.[6]

Humans should use their unique creativity, go beyond the first answer displayed on the screen, and challenge AI responses to dig deeper. Critical thinking is a human privilege. Keep questioning. See and enjoy something that others do not see. *Being logical when everyone else is being logical won't set you apart. Logic may be a good way to explain a decision, but it is not perhaps the best way of reaching one. Conventional logic is a straightforward mental process that is equally available to all and will therefore get you to the same place as everyone else.*[7]

Being rational sounds scientific and is easier to explain and justify, but it neglects intuitive or counter-intuitive options. An approved process of reasoning leads to ignore possible solutions not because they have proven to be inefficient, but because they are the *off norm*. Intuitive and counter-intuitive ideas are frequently treated with suspicion as is magic. Yet, some of these ideas can be more powerful than what is seen as normal or logical. Interpretation is a deduction, from a subjective opinion based on an external event, which is part of biased reasoning and oriented by a personal delusional conviction.[8]

Embracing Gen AI

AI opens the door to new business opportunities as new markets are created by technology. While it enhances the likelihood of success when backed by technology, this same technology brings competitors closer to each other because they have access to the same tools. Thanks to technology, more companies can diversify and expand globally what interferes with several local markets. Unexpected newcomers from other industries emerge because diversification is made easier with technology. This is how Google, originally a search engine, penetrated the home security market with Nest and the smartphones' market with Google Pixel. This is also how Uber, capitalizing on their app for transportation, introduced Uber Eats, challenging food delivery companies such as Grubhub, and is now trying to challenge Amazon and Instacart in delivering products other than ready-to-eat food as well.

Right now, AI is a synonym for flexibility, creativity, and scalability. And it is drawing an S curve with a very fast-growing pace. Eventually, it will reach the plateau and marketers should know what to do then because AI alone will not constitute a competitive advantage anymore.

Generative AI has already had a profound impact on the marketing industry, transforming content creation, personalization, and customer engagement. As we look to the future, the potential applications of generative AI in marketing are vast. From hyper-targeted advertising to predictive analytics and enhanced customer experiences, generative AI will continue to reshape the way marketers connect with their audiences. Embracing generative AI technologies and leveraging their capabilities will be essential for staying competitive in the ever-evolving marketing landscape. By harnessing the power of generative AI, marketers can unlock new opportunities, drive innovation, and deliver exceptional experiences to their customers.

Nonetheless, generative AI systems will need formal guardrails written into the programs so that they do not violate defined values or cross red lines by, for example, acceding to improper requests or generating unacceptable content. Companies including Nvidia and OpenAI are developing frameworks to provide such guardrails. GPT-4, for instance, promises to be 82 percent less likely than GPT-3.5 to respond to requests for disallowed content such as hate speech or code for malware.[9]

Red lines are also defined by regulations, which evolve. In response, companies will need to update their AI compliance, which will increasingly diverge across markets. Consider a European company that wants to roll out a generative AI tool to improve customer interactions. Until recently, the bank needed to comply only with the EU's General Data Protection Regulation, but soon it will need to comply with the EU's AI Act as well. If it wants to deploy AI in China or the United States, it will have to observe the regulations there. As local rules change, and as the company becomes subject to regulations across jurisdictions, it will need to adapt its AI and manage potentially incompatible requirements.

Therefore, values, red lines, guardrails, and regulations should all be integrated and embedded in the AI's programming so that changes to regulations can be keyed in and automatically communicated to every part of the AI program affected by them.

There are many use cases for generative AI, spanning a vast number of areas of domestic and work life across countries. The use of this technology is as wide-ranging as the problems we encounter in our lives. It can be used for work and leisure, for creative as well as technical endeavors, and to help us think, learn, do, solve, create, and enjoy. The most common use case is idea generation. We naturally think of content (text, images, and synthetic data) as the output to expect from generative AI—it is virtually built into the definition. But it seems that out in the real world, people have developed a wider concept of what the technology is generating, and it includes ideas. This is not just semantics: human-plus-machine collaboration feels less threatening to the reluctant majority for the main applications in the list shown in the following Figure 9.1:[10]

Customers Might Be Machines but Consumers Are Not Digital Humans

Because we respond instinctively to anything that appears to be human, research from neuroscience shows that our minds are attuned to and react emotionally to facial signals. That is why most people prefer to communicate face-to-face rather than over the telephone. In the case of digital humans, we know that what we see on the screen is an artificial construct, but we still connect instinctively to it, and we do not have to be computer experts to interpret the facial signals and make the exchange work properly. While being human is a biological fact, perceiving humanness is a psychological process. For example, it is important to understand how consumers perceive the humanness of chat agents and the consequences of these perceptions for consumer decision.[11]

Digital humans are thus more likely to provide a meaningful experience than other automated channels, and customers are more likely to extend interactions with them beyond their initial search or transaction. Digital humans are not appropriate for every application. When customers seek a quick transaction, they are likely to prefer

How People Are Using GenAI

Have people found ways for generative AI to help lighten their workloads, increase their productivity, or think through problems in new ways? To understand how individuals are using the technology, researchers mined web forums like Quora and Reddit, filtering through tens of thousands of posts to identify 100 different use-case categories, which they then organized into six themes.

TECHNICAL ASSISTANCE & TROUBLESHOOTING	CONTENT CREATION & EDITING	PERSONAL & PROFESSIONAL SUPPORT	LEARNING & EDUCATION	CREATIVITY & RECREATION	RESEARCH, ANALYSIS & DECISION-MAKING
23%	22	17	15	13	10

Themes

Categories

1 Generating ideas	36 Critique & counterargument	71 With MS Office apps
2 Therapy/companionship	37 Knowledge checks	72 Understanding movie plots
3 Specific search	38 Coding for amateurs	73 Coding for a basic video game
4 Editing text	39 Meeting summaries	74 Tracking medical symptoms
5 Exploring topics of interest	40 Cleaning up notes	75 Healthier living
6 Fun & nonsense	41 Explaining legalese	76 Preparing for meetings
7 Troubleshooting	42 Spotting logical fallacies	77 Explaining idioms
8 Enhanced learning	43 Creating a holiday itinerary	78 UX/user story writing
9 Personalized learning	44 Editing a legal document	79 Suggesting code libraries
10 General advice	45 Business advice	80 Writing poems
11 Drafting emails	46 Replying to emails	81 Work buddy
12 Simple explainers	47 Generating code (pros)	82 Editing video transcript
13 Writing/editing CV/résumé	48 Getting past writer's block	83 Motivating yourself
14 Excel formulas	49 Generating a lesson plan	84 Packing for travel
15 Adjusting tone of email	50 Rubber ducking (debugging code)	85 Sampling data
16 Evaluating copy	51 Negotiating a deal	86 Technical use of software
17 Enhanced decision-making	52 Fact-checking	87 For people with ADHD
18 Language translation	53 Career advice	88 Special needs education
19 Improving code (pros)	54 Practicing difficult conversations	89 Special needs education
20 Drafting a document	55 Seeing blind spots	90 Spotting anomalies
21 Reconciling personal disputes	56 Data entry	91 Building a business plan
22 Summarizing content	57 Legal research	92 Refining prompts
23 Making a complaint	58 Writing job postings	93 For entrepreneurs/startups
24 Recommending movies, books, etc.	59 Strengthening an argument	94 Building a website/app
25 Cooking with what you have	60 Jumping to the useful info	95 Writing blog posts
26 Generating appraisals	61 Generating video	96 Writing a funding proposal
27 Creativity	62 Safe space to ask	97 Writing a press release
28 Medical advice	63 Interpreting song lyrics	98 Editing digital images
29 Generating a legal document	64 Dungeons & Dragons	99 Planning workouts
30 Fixing bugs in code	65 Generating relevant images	100 Project management
31 Drafting a formal letter	66 Data manipulation	
32 Writing & editing a cover letter	67 Homework	
33 Personalized kid's story	68 Writing social media copy	
34 Explaining technical documents	69 Translating code (pros)	
35 Preparing for interviews	70 Realistic web copy	

Source: Filtered   ©HBR

Figure 9.1 How people are using GenAI

traditional user interfaces, chatbots, and voice-only assistants such as Siri or Alexa. However, digital humans can be a much better choice when it comes to communicating complex instructions or describing features of a product.

A humanlike face will better address the emotional aspects of an interaction, such as providing reassurance or empathy. If customers need specific information, then normally they are keen to see the details in written form so that they can quickly digest them. But if they are unsure, scanning pages of text is painful and time-consuming, and they often prefer to be able to ask for help. Unlike straightforward online transactions such as buying groceries or booking a movie ticket, interactions such as shopping for clothes or working with a career coach have open-ended trajectories involving give-and-take. When speed is not the primary requirement, consumers often like to linger and explore.[12]

Next comes identifying what compliance with values looks like and tracking progress toward that. For example, social media and online marketplaces have traditionally focused on developing recommendation algorithms that maximize user engagement. But as concerns about trust and safety have increased for both users and regulators, social media platforms such as Facebook and Snapchat track not only time spent on their platforms but also what customers are seeing and doing there, in order to limit user abuse and the spread of extremist or terrorist material. And online gaming companies track players' conduct because aggressive behavior can have a negative impact on the attractiveness of their games and communities.

Embedding values in AI requires enormous amounts of data—much of which will be generated or labeled by humans. In most cases, it comes in two streams: data used to train the AI and data from continuous feedback on its behavior. To ensure value alignment, new processes for feedback must be set up. A common practice for doing this is called Reinforcement Learning from Human Feedback, a process whereby undesirable outputs—such as abusive language—can be minimized by human input. Humans review an AI system's output, such as its classification of someone's CV, its decision to perform a navigation action, or the content it generates, and rate it according to how misaligned with certain values it may be. The rating is used in new training data to improve the AI's behavior (techtarget.com). Needless to say that the values predetermined by humans are biased as well, because they depend on their own values and beliefs of what is acceptable and what is not. In many ways, AI is like humans in this regard: no matter our formal education, we continually adjust our behavior to align with the values of our communities in the light of feedback. As people use AI, or are affected by it, they may observe behaviors that seem to violate its values. Allowing them to provide feedback can be a significant source of data to improve AI.

Fear Not—AI Is Here for Your Good

Digital humans mimic human behavior and communication and are currently used as sales assistants and social media influencers and might change the business landscape when deployed at scale. They present clear advantages when it comes to cost, customizability, and scalability. A personality is given to this artificial construct because humans respond instinctively to anything that appears to be human. Neuroscience explains that our minds are attuned to react emotionally to facial signs. Thus, digital humans are more likely to provide a meaningful experience than other automated channels through extended interactions with consumers. Digital humans work from text and sentiment analysis and from camera input containing human emotional feedback such as body language and facial expressions. Four types of digital humans can be listed as follows:

1. **Virtual agent**—serves multiple users and does not develop personal relationships with them. Its role is to complete scientific one-time tasks. They can respond in any language and can tailor their appearance to the background or ethnicity of each customer. Used in customer service.
2. **Virtual assistant**—supports the user in completing specific tasks and over time develops a relationship: personal shoppers and home organizers. Can answer questions and arrange schedules.

For example, Bank of America offers a digital assistant to help you find the best investment options for you.

3. **Virtual influencer**—are carefully designed to appeal to a certain type of consumers, any relationship a person might feel like developing with them stems from that person's projection only, rather than from an individual customization.

4. **Virtual companion**—develops a deeply personal relationship with the user. Their role is to simply be with the user and accept their emotional dependence on them, like robot pets.

The *humanization* of robots has sparked unexpected results. Recently, a civil servant robot at Gumi City Council in South Korea was found unresponsive after what appears to be a deliberate plunge down a two-meter staircase. (https://interestingengineering.com/innovation/robot-commits-suicide-south-korea).

Local media and social media users have called it the first *robot suicide* in the country. The robot, affectionately known as the *Robot Supervisor*, had been a model employee since its appointment in August 2023. The official stated that the robot *worked diligently*, handling daily document deliveries, city promotion, and information dissemination to local residents. Witnesses reported *seeing the robot circling in one spot as if something was there shortly before the incident,* sparking speculation about the cause of the fall.

Some experts have suggested that the robot may have experienced an emotional breakdown due to the stress of its workload, while others believe a technical malfunction could be to blame. The exact circumstances leading to the robot's demise are under investigation. *Pieces have been collected and will be analyzed by the company,* the official said.

The incident has sparked a wave of mourning and curiosity across the nation. Local media headlines questioned the apparent *robot suicide*, asking, *Why did the diligent civil officer do it?* and *Was work too hard for the robot?* Social media has also been abuzz with reactions ranging from poignant tributes to the fallen robot to serious discussions about the ethical implications of AI sentience and the potential for robot suffering.

Talking about its quality, the robot was unique in its ability to call an elevator and move between floors autonomously. It reportedly worked from 9 a.m. to 6 p.m. and even had its own civil service officer card. Notably, South Korea is a global leader in robotics adoption, and it boasts the highest robot density in the world. With one industrial robot for every zero employees, the nation has embraced automation in various sectors, from manufacturing to public service.

While the mystery around the robot's suicide remains unsolved, the above most certainly explains why companies are drawn to machine customers. Throughout history, technologies have been our tools. Whether used to create or destroy, they have always been under human control, behaving in nonhuman predictable and rule-based ways. Today, a new generation of AI systems are no longer merely our tools—they are becoming an active part of our lives, behaving autonomously, making consequential decisions, and shaping social and economic outcomes. These systems have distinct characteristics and capacities that deepen their impact. No longer in the background of our lives, they now interact directly with us, and their outputs can be strikingly human-like and seemingly all-knowing. They are capable of exceeding human skills in everything from language understanding to coding. And these advances, driven by material breakthroughs in areas such as LLMs and machine learning, are happening so quickly that they are confounding even their own creators.

AI was first an LLM designed to understand and respond to humans in their own words that it listened on the chats. It was fine-tuned to recognize phrases that led to good customer service outcomes in various situations. But because of the risk of *confabulations,* or plausi-ble sounding but incorrect responses, the system also used a machine-learning technique called *in-context learning,* which drew answers from relevant user manuals and documents.

The LLM monitored the online chats for specific phrases, and when one of them occurred, it based its responses on the information in the in-context learning system. As an additional safeguard, it did not respond to queries directly. Instead, human agents were free to apply their common sense in deciding whether to use or ignore the LLM's suggestions. Both the average number of issues resolved per hour and the number of chats an agent could handle simultaneously increased by almost 15 percent; the average chat time decreased by nearly 10 percent; and an analysis of the chat logs showed that immediately after the new system was implemented, customer satisfaction improved and expressions of frustration declined. Companies that build LLMs are well aware that these systems confabulate and are working on ways to minimize the problem. However, marketers using an LLM to generate copy for a website or a social media campaign can look at what the system comes up with and quickly assess whether it is on target.[13]

Interestingly, this concept of confabulation points to one more reason for everyone to be vigilant about AI responses. Etymologically, confabulate means to discuss with oneself and fabricate memories and is studied in psychiatry when individuals confabulate with themselves. A machine that discusses with itself could be as concerning as people who speak to themselves. One thing is to think out loud and it often helps with idea generation; confabulating is something else. The risk, for both machines and humans, is the resultant decision-making, which can lead to dramatic unrealistic consequences.

Despite all of its advantages, it seems fair to ask ourselves how willing consumers are to live with pervasive technology. As thrilled as they are at the comfort of getting rid of repetitive chores such as vacuuming, dishwashing, laundering, driving, and parking their cars, after a certain threshold, they feel threatened by those machines, which imply that they are unable to accomplish such tasks. In reality, consumers tend to reject automation when there is a symbolic attachment to some activity or when products help them express their beliefs and personalities. Thus, identity-motivated consumers are less likely to purchase automated products than those who are more interested in functionality and time saving.

This is a crucial point for marketers to understand. As handy and cost-effective as AI can be, it remains just a tool. The main goal for a company is still basically to satisfy consumers' needs and enjoy their loyalty and profitability. Technology alone cannot ensure that, because it cannot be a source of satisfaction to consumers: it can only be a vehicle to convey satisfaction through a product. A company that does not understand its consumers will not be saved by technology. Consumers are not digital humans; they are vulnerable and unpredictable physical and psychological beings. Understanding consumers requires longitudinal research based not only on surveys and big data but mainly on motivational methods to dig deeper into their realm of consumption.

As stated by Oscar Wilde:[14] *There are only two tragedies in life: not getting what one wants, and getting it.* AI is here: we wanted it, we have it. So now what? How will you use this new power? What kind of magic will you practice? Do you know its limits? What place will you yield to AI in your company and your life?

When You Embrace the Digital World, You Embrace the Magical World

Many of the most sophisticated applications of AI ranging from smart assistants such as Alexa and Siri to self-driving cars are based on neural networks—computer programs that mimic, in an abstract way, how learning happens in the human brain. Each time a neural network is trained to learn a fact, connections between simulated neurons in the network are modified. As the neural network is trained to learn more and more facts, the simulated cell assemblies in the model are constantly rearranged, no longer voting for any particular fact that was learned, but instead of representing an entire category of knowledge.[15] For instance:

An eagle is a bird. It has feathers, wings, and a beak, and it flies.
A crow is a bird. It has feathers, wings, and a beak, and it flies.
A hawk is a bird. It has feathers, wings, and a beak, and it flies.

Eventually, the computer model becomes good at learning about new birds because it leverages what it already knows. If the network learns that a seagull is a bird, cell assemblies in the model can fill in the blanks and figure out that a seagull can fly. But if the input is:

A penguin is a bird. It has feathers, wings, and a beak, and it swims. Now the machine has an issue—the penguin fits all the characteristics of the bird except for one. A penguin is an exception to the rule that all birds fly, so when the computer learns the exception, it forges what was previously learned about all the characteristics of birds.

This problem is called catastrophic interference, and for machine learning, it is very bad. The solution is to make sure that the machine learns very slowly, so that it does not immediately let go of the rule to learn the exception. Humans are more used to the exceptions and idiosyncrasies of the real world and can better cope with variations and novelty. Thanks to our episodic and semantic memory, we are able to store and index every event differently, we can learn rules and exceptions at the same time and both make sense to us.

We also learn thanks to the association of imagination and memory. All stories in the world share the same backbone: an ordinary person unwillingly navigates a dangerous and unfamiliar world, does something extraordinary, and eventually saves the day, better yet, the world. The same link between imagination and memory is practiced in the field of generative AI, where companies create sophisticated programs, trained with a massive number of examples that can generate new outputs.

Because of that, definitions and accuracy in naming are imperative, because it is through the word that we manifest everything. The word is not just a sound or a symbol—it is meaning. It is the power we have to communicate with other humans. Words are triggers—call to action, orders, hurtful, and comforting. *The word is the tool of magic.*[16]

The word is pure magic and its misuse is black magic, because the word is also a spell. Thus, every human is a magician. When we give positive feedback, the word uplifts others' hearts; when we criticize is feels like a spell. Gossip is black magic and works like poison because it is the opposite of fact, evidence, the truth. It can be compared to a computer virus—a destructive code with harmful intent.[17]

AI Will Take Your Job

Unlike in science fiction, people in general do not believe in a robot's revolution taking over humans, but they are genuinely scared of losing their jobs to a robot. It is said that AI is cost-cutting because it can do routine tasks better and faster than humans can, which leads to feelings such as *I am not good enough; AI does it so much better than me.*

When employees are excluded from the automation process—the end-to-end automation of as many business processes as possible—they become averse to working with AI, never develop trust in its capabilities, and resist even the positive changes that come from using it. If employees do not understand it, they resist it and fear the loss of autonomy. In addition, AI can create silos within the employee population.

In a recent study simulating a video game, after the first six rounds, one member of some teams was replaced by an intelligent agent and led to the conclusion that when AI teammates come on board, team's performance drops. Despite the AI's superior individual performance and the fact that bonuses were paid to the entire team if it performed well, 84 percent of respondents preferred to play with their human teammates: AI causes team sociability to fall and that lessens members' motivation, effort, and trust.

All-human teams playing alongside an AI-and-human team also saw drops in performance in the first round after the teammate change. However, the introduction of an AI player uniquely extended this disruption to the adjacent all-human teams. Those teams, despite not undergoing a direct change, encountered vicarious challenges in adapting to the new AI-influenced dynamics within the interconnected environment. Therefore, it is advised that companies looking to introduce AI to teams might start with employees who are skilled enough to make the best use of automation. In other words, high-skilled humans and intelligent agents working together can be highly performing.[18]

Nonetheless, done correctly, human-AI collaborations represent the most promising way of working. They may not always be the fastest, cheapest, or easiest way to introduce and use AI, but the alternative that excludes workers should not be considered.

In the midst of what AI is or is not, employee-generated content (EGC) is flourishing. It is content created and shared by employees themselves. It is authentic, unfiltered, and reflects the real faces behind a brand, which is an added value when it comes to credibility. EGC takes many forms, including:

- Employees sharing their experiences and success stories;
- Sharing industry insights or expert knowledge through webinars or blog posts;
- Candid photos of office life, events, or team outings;
- Employees leading tutorials or showcasing their work;
- Announcing professional milestones on personal social media;
- Writing reviews on platforms like Glassdoor or Indeed.

Among the benefits of EGC, there are (https://moz.com):

- **Share authentic brand moments**—the power of storytelling in marketing is undeniable. People are drawn to brands that forge authentic emotional connections. Instead of writing generic posts, focus on celebrating real employee achievements. Such posts boost team morale and showcase your company's culture to your target audience and potential new hires. Furthermore, this approach creates a triple benefit: enhancing employee engagement, building brand authenticity, and attracting future talents.
- **EGC gets more engagement on social media** - EGC is shared 24 more times than branded content, and employee profiles receive eight times more engagement. EGC creates a buzz on social media and transforms that chatter into SEO benefits for brands. Positive interactions with your content on social platforms boost your search rankings. Although this impact is indirect and not a ranking factor, the benefits are clear. Employees typically have a network 10 times larger than your company's follower base. Moreover, leads generated through employee advocacy are seven times more likely to convert. Imagine the potential of amplifying your conversions with the additional reach provided by EGC. This is the substantial impact EGC can have on your brand.

- **Your audience trusts EGC more than brand content**—people trust people. When an employee endorses something, it feels more genuine. It is a form of social proof, like user generated content. Developing an employee advocacy program is critical to honing your brand's reputation and getting employees to support the company's mission. These initiatives amplify and direct the voices of your team members so they become your brand's greatest champions, contributing to revenue growth rates more than twice the avarage.

In addition, companies with engaged workers have employees who are 57 percent more effective, 87 percent less likely to leave, and enjoy more than 20 percent annual growth as opposed to the 9 percent average, while employee disengagement can lead to around $300 billion losses in 1 year.

In the AI-enabled future, leaders who leverage AI will have a distinct advantage in productivity, efficiency, and decision-making. At the same time, leaders who exhibit more human-centered leadership will excel at attracting, retaining, developing, and motivating top talents. How do you figure out whether you should leverage AI or bring your human qualities to a situation—or utilize a combination of these resources? See the chart:[19]

AI Versus Human: A Matrix of Leadership Activities

A guide for leaders to assess where they should leverage AI versus where they should leverage being human.

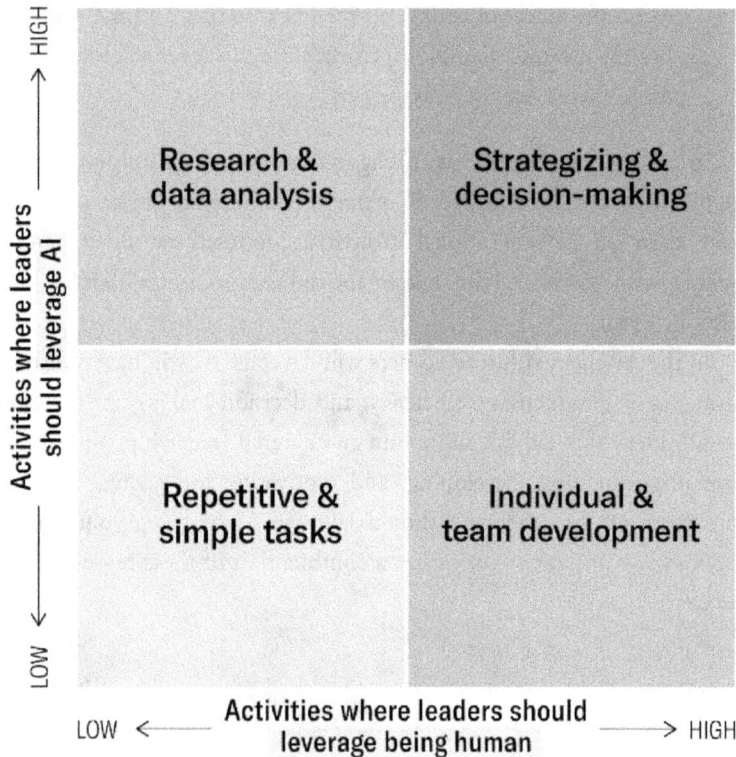

	Activities where leaders should leverage being human	
Activities where leaders should leverage AI (HIGH)	Research & data analysis	Strategizing & decision-making
(LOW)	Repetitive & simple tasks	Individual & team development
	LOW ←	→ HIGH

Source: Potential Project   ▽ HBR

AI versus human: A matrix of leadership activities

Today's best leaders are already engaged in understanding what AI can do and what it cannot do. At the very core of human leadership are three core qualities: awareness, compassion, and wisdom.

Awareness is the capacity of the mind to be cognizant of your mental state, thoughts, and emotions, as well as the world and people around you. With awareness, you gain greater self-mastery of your thoughts and emotions and are better able to lead others. With awareness, you also develop mental agility, the ability to alternate between zooming in on important priorities and tasks and zooming out on the bigger picture. In a fast-paced world, mental agility is foundational for getting important work done while making sure there is alignment between the bigger picture and the details of your task. Awareness is a uniquely human quality. AI is not (yet) self-aware and is not able to make independent choices based on nonlinear, noncomputable awareness.

Compassion is the capacity of the mind to care for oneself and others. Compassion begins with empathy as the spark but then adds action and an intention to benefit others. When you practice compassion, you develop caring courage—the ability to engage courageously in human dynamics and never shy away from difficult conversations. And you learn caring transparency—the ability to be upfront and honest so people know where they stand. Compassion is a uniquely human quality that fosters trust and enhances psychological safety, enabling greater performance in your people and teams. Although AI is becoming better at mimicking human emotions like empathy, compassion remains out of reach.

Wisdom is the capacity of the mind to discern and form sound judgment based on experience. Wisdom is about seeing things as they really are, free from the limitations of one's ego, and knowing the right thing to do for your people and your organization. A key component of wisdom is a beginner's mind, or the ability to stay radically open and not let experience overly influence you. When you practice wisdom, you also deepen your integrity, or the ability to act according to your conscience and morally guided values. Although AI can provide us with vast amounts of data and knowledge, it requires leaders' unique capacity for discernment and the ability to make wise decisions to be truly valuable.

The emergence of AI triggers collaboration among companies because no one knows exactly how AI will evolve: companies, clients, suppliers, and consultants are united in the same ignorance, because for now, everyone is learning by doing. Nevertheless, it is crucial to keep up with what is happening or your company might not be around a few years from now. Not all companies invest, develop, and use innovation the same way and at the same pace. There are differences across countries too. For example, in the 1990s, India had no internet and no cell phones. Today the country has the best IT engineers in the world and even the lowest-income families have one mobile device they can share. For example, Johnson & Johnson (J&J) has leveraged mobile phones to expand prenatal and early childhood care across the country. Working with the Mobile Alliance for Maternal Action, J&J launched a free program that leaves voice messages twice a week for pregnant women and new mothers. Since its launch, more than 700,000 women have learned more about how to make healthy choices that help get their children off to a good start in life.

AI and the Power of Inclusion

Humans have an innate drive to feel included in social settings.[20] According to the social identity theory,[21] an important component of the self-concept is derived from memberships in social groups and categories because human beings have a basic motivation to categorize the social world in terms of group membership and carry positive or negative values. They may perceptually accentuate their differences with out-group members and similarities with in-group members to facilitate the communication of desired social identities.[22, 23, 24] Moreover, they might favor in-group social identities over out-group identities because their self-concept is defined in terms of group membership and their self-enhancement with the group.[25, 26]

Therefore, when a consumer is included in a social group, their in-group social identity will be enhanced, and their propensity for compliance with the in-group members' choices might be increased by the acceptance of their teammates or coworkers. While technology enables inclusion in many ways giving access to free services such as free YouTube videos and tutorials, free knowledge with Wikipedia, free maps, translations, and information with Google, it also enables anyone to exclude others if they do not agree with the ideas and the, sometimes unstructured and implicit, norms ruling their virtual community.

Technology gives anyone the power to make others disappear, just like with magic. People are canceled and blocked so that others can no longer see, read, or hear them. It also gives companies the possibility of getting rid of negative reviews when the moderator decides that such reviews are detrimental to the brand even when they are not offensive. It should come off as a way of protecting the community from toxic ideas, yet sometimes the reviews are genuine and only describe a negative customer experience. While Google reviews were created to help consumers to make better-informed choices thanks to customer-to-customer communication, this moderation introduces a significant bias when information is filtered to yield room only to the positive ones.

The mainstream narrative tells you what you should do and what you should not do to save the planet. If you believe that this is true and possible, you will follow that narrative. Yet, your gratification, other than social, will be all but immediate. You will never experience the results of your good deeds, because what ecologists are aiming at will never happen during your lifetime. This is called the bandwagon effect, which refers to our tendency to come to conclusions and make decisions based on what is popular, even if we always find a way of persuading ourselves that we follow our own rational and well-weighted reasons. Our desire to be in control of our lives creates the illusion of control. Thanks to the confirmation bias, we tend to look only for information that confirms what seems to be our beliefs and our worldview and tend to reject, or cancel, all the opposed ones.[27]

An example of complying with trends is that, while looking for immediacy, consumers are now fond of Yoga, which is all but a fast-paced sport, but it is trendy and people look cool going around in their yoga pants and carrying their yoga mats. Yoga is not even a sport although it has been positioned as a fitness practice so that more people would join in. Originally, this older than 50,000 years Indian spiritual practice which brings together your spirit, mind, and body requires total concentration which is all the opposite of what consumers do today with access to so much information coming in simultaneously. Yoga is meant to intensify the power of the mind rather than of the muscles and invites peace and meditation. Meditation invites you to disconnect, to empty your mind for several minutes. Yet, there is always a smartphone on the yoga mats! Do we live in a paradoxical world or what?

Because consumers hear the same narrative every day several times a day some beliefs become universal and end up creating some degree of dependence. Consumers are told that they do not consume enough vitamins with food or have a lack of energy and focus. The belief in this narrative makes them dependent on daily doses of magical supplements such as vitamins for energy, Cannabidiol (CBD) for focus and diets (Atkin, Keto, vegan, etc.), in addition to their addiction to their devices, social media, and everything else that is home delivered. Yet, when they can hardly see tangible results for their efforts, they turn to magic because this is where their real beliefs rest. One thing is following a general trend and doing as others do socially, but beliefs are personal and they are what really rule peoples' lives when their social masks come off. Trends are ephemeral and do not need to be believed: social pressure is enough to make people adhere, but beliefs are culturally deep-rooted and long-lasting, that is why they are more credible. This is what makes the difference between conformity and uniqueness and humans juggle with both every day.

Embrace the Dark Mystery and Hunt As if It Was Clear

Availability, accessibility, and representativeness are the keywords associated with AI. More and more AI platforms will be available, and ChatGPT is now accessible to everyone. Representativeness is materialized by the fact that, already today, those who do not use AI are seen as dinosaurs. In a world of social pressure, being part of what some define as being unavoidable becomes vital, and most important decisions are left to someone or something else—a device that will write or draw or purchase on your behalf.

For example, in the Google's Gemini program mentioned earlier, the opinion or vision of reality of one person in power of programming AI can propagate fake information as being true to millions of people at once. While trying to change the past is delusional, the new generations having been exposed to that information will have a totally mistaken understanding of what history stands for. Although Google withdrew the software and claimed that the issue was caused by a malfunction, the reality is that the malfunction was the programmer's own ideology and vision of what the past should have been or what he would have liked it to be. His skewed vision of history had been viewed by millions of people worldwide, much many than those who complained and drew media attention to it. One might wonder what would have happened if no one had reported such historical extravagances and that millions of children and teenagers would have learned about history through that digital resource incorporating such historical and genetic inaccuracies.

This issue with Gemini is extremely important because it represents the opposite of everything that multiculturalism stands for. The beauty of multiculturalism is accepting people as they are, independent of sex, gender, race, or culture, never yielding to filters. History is the answer to *why*. If you know no history, you cannot explain what happens today, because today is an outcome of yesterday and tomorrow will be the result of what we do today. If you change the facts, you are choosing distraction over clarity. We should think more about inspiring people than not offending them. We learned enough from past events to know that no one has the right to decide that some cultures or races are better than others. Stating otherwise demonstrates either cultural ignorance or a deliberate attempt of manipulation and discrimination.

Companies dealing with AI should be committed to neutrality rather than conveying their own opinions, political stands, and personal preferences to millions of people. Otherwise, AI will turn into a tool for propaganda rather than for creativity and knowledge. Choice architects play a critical role in influencing peoples' opinion, purchases, and brand preferences. They are people who choose what you should know, where you should go, and what you should purchase. AI programmers are choice architects who create an information cascade for people to receive information from the choices of others. It is a big responsibility.

Beyond establishing guiding values, companies need to think about explicitly constraining the behavior of their AI. Practices such as privacy by design, safety by design, and the like can be useful in this effort. Anchored in principles and assessment tools, these practices embed the target value into an organization's culture and product development processes. The employees of companies that apply these practices are motivated to carefully evaluate and mitigate potential risks early in designing a new product; to build in feedback loops that customers can use to report issues; and to continually assess and analyze those reports.

Whereas people tend to take options that require the least time and effort, they enjoy the benefits of inertia and status quo. Then, when confronted with complex decision making situations, they gather help from others, including their own devices, because those are useful and reassuring, and one might thus question the *by default* decisions made by machine customers. Therefore, active choosing has the power of overcoming inertia, inattention, and procrastination. Active choosing can also lead to variety, because the machine will tend to renew what has already been done.

A machine customer is the material reflection of mental account-ing. It is a way of evaluating, regulating, and processing one's budget according to pre-established categories: food, travel, home appliances, devices, clothing, education, and so forth. The machine will always look for cost-efficiency as opposed to creativity and that is why they are perfect for routine tasks.

It Is All About Data

Traditionally, industrial manufacturers looked mostly at sales and marketing data. They analyzed it to spot the demographics having bought a particular product or which consumers would be willing to spend more money on a better product. Digital systems were not that important. Companies viewed them as a way to lower manufacturing costs or add features, such as Wi-Fi, to existing analog products. Today, however, industrial goods companies must also focus on what happens after the sale—on how combinations of digital and analog products enable positive outcomes for customers. Data on that must be gath-ered constantly, and insights from it applied in real-time to customers' problems.

Just like with the internet of things (IoT), fusion strategy involves a network of physical objects embedded with sensors, software, and connectivity. But fusion strategy goes beyond equipping an analog product so that you can monitor it and collect data from it over the internet. With fusion strategy, you completely reimagine how that analog product could be designed to function if it were built from scratch using every digital tool and functionality available.

Responsibility for fusion strategy is also handled differently in organizations. The IoT is owned at the functional level, and use cases are straightforward: managers in operations (such as supply chain coordinators and quality control executives) use the data from sensors to ensure that machinery-based processes adhere to specific industry standards and protocols. Designers build internet-enabled products that generate data that can be used in future iterations of those products. The separate functions do not really have to coordinate their efforts. Fusion strategy, in contrast, is cross-functional. It requires senior-level executives from different departments to work together to determine how sensor data can be harnessed to deliver value to existing customers and to create new products for future customers.

Fusion strategy also generates insights and benefits quicker than the IoT does. While the machinery behind the IoT ensures that data are recorded and logged, fusion strategy applies that data immediately, observing products' use across diverse settings and then leveraging information on it to offer automated, personalized recommendations or experiences to customers.[28]

Key Takeaways

- Data are critical but remember that they are meant to describe consumer behavior.
- AI is accessible to all marketers and thus cannot be seen as a competitive advantage *per se.*
- Reassure your team and prevent them from seeing AI as a threat.

Implications for Marketers

AI prompts are any type of text, data, or question that tells the AI the desired response you seek. These prompts can inspire and generate ideas for limitless content marketing concepts.

Before diving into AI-generated prompts, define your content marketing goals. As stated by Professor Tea-makorn, first know what you will use AI for. Are you aiming to educate your audience, generate leads, or increase brand visibility? By having clear objectives in mind, you can better tailor your AI prompts to deliver the desired outcomes. Use AI prompts effectively to pose thought-provoking questions about your industry.

These questions can be excellent starting points for blog posts, social media content, or videos: (https://searchengineland.com/ppc-chatgpt-disconfirming-questions-428377):

- Include relevant examples or desired output formats to guide the AI's understanding.
- Showcase the desired structure or style of the response to improve the AI's content generation capability.
- Creating thought-provoking prompts for marketers can help stimulate creativity, encourage critical thinking, and generate innovative ideas (https://metricool.com/).

Prompt ideas:

- How will advancements in technology shape the future of marketing?
- What role will AI play in marketing strategies?
- How will VR and AR impact consumer behavior and marketing tactics?
- In an increasingly digital world, what will be the future of traditional advertising media like print and television?
- How will privacy concerns and data protection regulations affect how marketers collect and utilize consumer information?
- What ethical considerations should marketers take into account when leveraging personal data for targeted advertising?
- Will influencer marketing continue to be an effective strategy or will it evolve into something else?
- How will changing demographics and cultural shifts influence marketing strategies and messaging in the future?

- What impact will voice search and smart assistants have on how consumers discover and engage with brands?

Your goal is to find a relevant audience, just as much as the algorithm's goal is to deliver relevant content. Therefore, you need to be making content that resonates with your audience. Consider creating a signature so you are instantly recognizable to your audience, even if they have never met you.

Basically, traditional AI is appropriate for utility and productivity at scale, like research, analysis, and marketing automation, and Gen AI models for creative and connective tasks involving complex and unstructured inputs or outputs. However, the main issues remain unresolved because AI's ethical use is difficult when technology outpaces regulations.

Conclusion

We should not lose sight of the fact that AI is not what we are but a reflection of us, just like a plane is a reflection of birds and boats of ducks, something similar or inspired of. It is just human behavior cloning/mimicking. It tries to speak like a human and say the same sentence in any language but can also come up with reasonable results to absurd inputs as stated by John Burkey. Humans should monitor the accuracy in the use of data, proceed with fact-checking and source reliability, and correct answers rather than building on them. AI needs human monitoring to follow the right path.

The main difficulty in concluding this book was knowing when to stop writing it. As I kept researching, the news about AI and its countless applications in all industries kept proliferating at high speed. We know that it will keep going even quicker, influencing our lives and changing marketing management's landscape. Marketers should consider upskilling and increasing awareness and versatility for themselves as well as for their teams. Their clairvoyance and their consciousness too, because their responsibility is engaged in much higher levels than with their products' safety only as it has once been. Today, they convey values and norms through their digital influencers and the responses from their bots. Interactions with consumers are more frequent and intense thanks to social media.

Unlike magic that survived across centuries, AI will become obsolete and be replaced by some other technology very shortly. But human nature will remain the same, that is why beliefs in magic persevere. Marketers and consumers alike should not get too attached to AI, because as with all the other innovations and tools, it will also complete its life cycle. We expect AI to adapt to ourselves, but we are the ones adapting and getting used to it. Humans are distinguished from machines, thanks to their ability to adapt themselves to multiple situations and for their consciousness.

Unlike marketing, AI evolves at a pace that is difficult to keep up with. Marketing is timeless and has remained fundamentally the same across eras with the only goal of satisfying consumers' needs. Yet, it seems that the fascination with new technological tools is taking over the essential role of marketing and the discernment among concepts, models, and tools. Marketers should ask themselves how will they make their offers stand out when everyone is using the same tools: social media, (digital) influencers, and AI? What will be their Unique Selling Proposition?

By constantly getting people confused, now marketers are getting confused too. Words have lost their meanings: *benchmark* is used as a synonym for competitive analysis, while they are two different practices. *Race* and *ethnicity* are used as synonyms, while they are totally different: race is biological, and ethnicity is a social construct. *Panel* is used to describe what is in reality a *sample*, and *paradigm* is used to describe behaviors, whereas it is a set of concepts or thought patterns, including theories, research methods, postulates, and standards for what constitute legitimate contributions to a field.

And now there is the expression *how to market your product*, as if the market was a verb. Marketers and some academics don't make the difference between creating, pricing, distributing, and promoting a product. Whatever they are talking about, they use *market* as an umbrella verb. You don't market a product; you address a target market with it. Of course, *target* market and *audience* have been used as synonyms too, while we know that they don't describe the same population. In addition, *rebranding* has been used to describe a brand's *repositioning*.

This is not just a matter of vocabulary, but a matter of semantics. Words have meanings and concepts have definitions. If words are used indistinctly, how will we know what exactly we are talking about? If you ask AI how to *market* your product, what kind of data should it consider? Product, price, distribution, promotion, positioning, targeting, and so on? If I ask the machine to show me the best benchmark for my product and it gives me information about my competitors, it will be useless—I already know what my competitors do. And what if I ask it to help me to rebrand (look for a new brand name) and it gives me information about how to reposition my current brand? Accuracy in wording has never been this critical. In a world where rationality, logic, and thus calculations are the only variables taken into account, the real meaning of words has been neglected and will end up leading to absurd decision making. Input your AI with the right concepts if you want useful outcomes. Inputting the wrong words can lead to unexpected or unplanned signaling of a company or brand to the eyes of its consumers.

We can only hope that with AI and the logic followed by machines, people will need to be more accurate with their inputs. I believe that if we want to take the best away from AI, we will need to be very rigorous. Because I had the privilege of learning from the best, I have the feeling that having anyone speaking about marketing online is creating considerable confusion and inaccuracies. It is up to the professionals and academic marketers to collaborate with AI with the goal of fixing these issues and ensuring accuracy if we want the human–machine collaboration to make sense in the field.

Marketing has never been this crucial to companies. Markets became homogenous because companies had access to the same tools and information at the same time. In addition, marketers are all formatted the same way, regardless of the industries they operate in. Standing out in markets that are saturated with exacerbated flows of information and products, where people don't pay undivided attention to anything and where all that counts is speed as opposed to depth, is a real challenge to marketers. The plethora of available alternatives made consumer volatility higher than ever. Marketers should not be blindsided by their fascination for new technologies and forget that in a world where everything is ephemeral, their consumers, as human beings, still need stability. That is why they turn to magic and superstition!

Appendix

Additional Information and Techniques

What Is E-E-A-T?

https://digitalmarketinginstitute.com/blog/a-guide-to-google-e-e-a-t?utm_source=Email&utm_medium=Email&utm_campaign=-free-members-weekly-tips&mkt_tok=NjI1LUdYSi0xODcAAAGSrpSk-FW6M0WCYZPlOCUurE2-CeAl_22AiMLNak7W3xC-hArDVDul-qYXgBfs8Fq79DPGQzrLc8EOSS4ysd6lWzstSvC6kGqtNR0YBniTxu_A1TEw.

Originally, Google's quality rating was expertise, authoritativeness, and trustworthiness (E-A-T). The extra E for *experience* was added in 2022 to include experience in ranking content.

Experience, expertise, authoritativeness, and trustworthiness (E-E-A-T) is part of Google's Search Quality Rater Guidelines. These are used by people called quality raters to evaluate content based on three factors: **page quality**, **understanding user needs**, and **meeting user needs**.

The feedback from raters helps the search engine measure the success of algorithm updates.

Let's look at each E-E-A-T element in more detail:

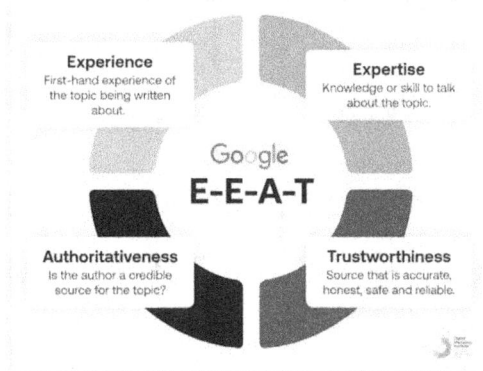

E—Experience

Does the content creator have first-hand or life experience on the topic they are writing about? For example, people are more likely to trust a review from someone who has used a product than someone who has not. Here's an example from Medium on the apps.

Apps I Use And Why You Should Too.

Gowtham Oleti · Follow
10 min read · Nov 14, 2023

21K   387

Let's skip past the usual suspects like YouTube, WhatsApp and Instagram. I want to share with you some less familiar apps that have become just as essential in my daily life. They may not be household names, but they're absolute game-changers for me.

PS: I'll be updating this list frequently with new apps, so I suggest you to save this article.

Artifact — News

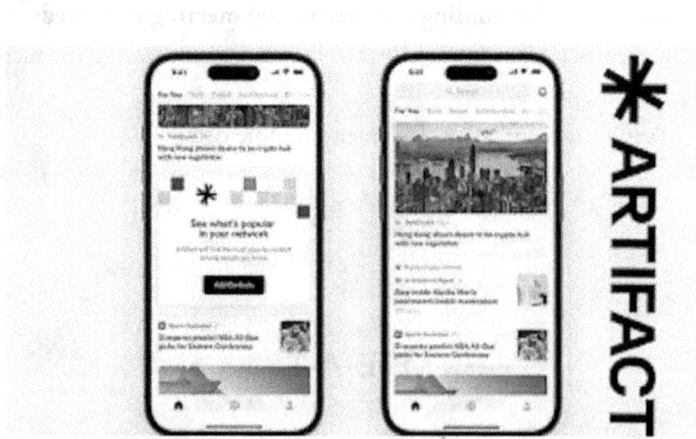

E—Expertise

Does the creator of the content have the knowledge or skill to talk about the topic? For example, when it comes to fixing a leak, people are more likely to trust content from a plumber than an enthusiast with little experience. Here's an example from a recent Digital Marketing Institute (DMI) podcast with marketing great Rand Fishkin that shows his level of expertise to talk about understanding an audience.

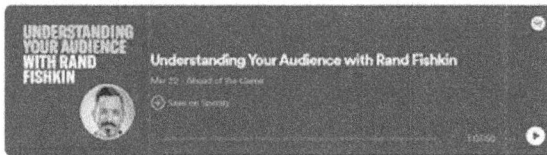

A—Authoritativeness

Is the website or page known as a go-to source for the topic? For example, if someone wants to find out about the latest fashion trends, a site like Vogue, as opposed to a blog from a fashion enthusiast, would be deemed an authority.

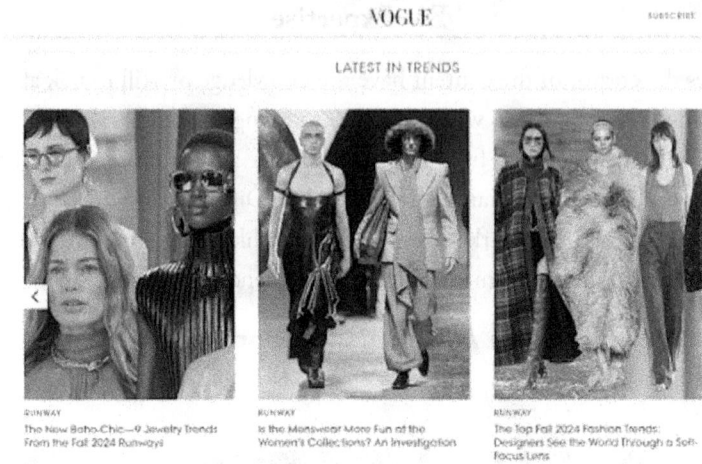

T—Trustworthiness

Trustworthiness is at the core of E-E-A-T and the most important factor to consider. In analyzing trustworthiness, quality raters look at the creator, content, and website. This is why it's so important for facts to be accurate, and for the author to be reputable and include trustworthy sources. (High-authority sites are a good place to start, such as the New York Times.)

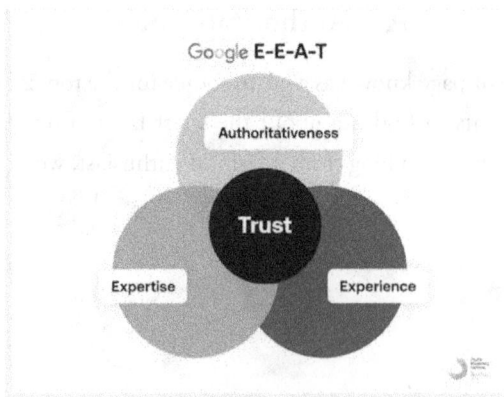

In addition, it's important for the site itself to be trustworthy, such as being secure for shopping or including data privacy guidelines. Here's an example of a privacy and cookie policy from the media site TechCrunch.

Why Is E-E-A-T Important?

Google and other search engines want to find content that people find valuable. They want to provide users with a good user experience that gives credible and useful answers to what they are searching for. These users are then more likely to use those search engines again.

This is evident in the regular algorithm updates, Google's new artificial intelligence (AI)-powered Search Generative Experience, and the inclusion of *experience* in E-E-A-T.

According to Google's guidelines, E-E-A-T are all important considerations in page quality rating. The most important member of the E-E-A-T family is trustworthiness.

The core of E-E-A-T is content that Google rates as trustworthy due to a combination of expertise, experience, and authority.

"Google added 'Experience' as another 'E' so they're clearly big on experience and reluctant to recommend rubbish websites in their search results as it rubs off on their reputation," said Luke O 'Leary, VP at Neil Patel Digital on a recent DMI podcast.

How Does Google Evaluate E-E-A-T?

Google's quality raters use levels to rank E-E-A-T. These are as follows:

- **Lowest**: These pages fall into three categories: harmful, untrustworthy, and spammy.
- **Lacking**: Pages in this category are seen as low quality as they lack expertise, experience, or authority for the topic or purpose of the page but are not harmful. For example, it could be a blog written about flying a plane but the writer has no experience in doing that.
- **High level:** These pages offer significant amounts of expertise, credibility, and trustworthiness to serve a purpose and achieve it well. Google looks at the level of effort, level of talent or skill, and originality, along with a positive reputation.
- **Very high level**: The highest ranking pages are those that show evidence of a high level of effort, originality, talent, or

skill. This would include people who demonstrate extensive hands-on knowledge of the topic they are writing about.

Below is an example with the highest quality justification listed in Google's guidelines as: "very positive website reputation for the topic of the page, very high E-E-A-T for the purpose of the page and YMYL topic."

What Is YMYL?

Another thing you should look at, alongside E-E-A-T, is "your money or your life" (YMYL).

Google classes web pages as YMYL when the content has the potential to impact a person's happiness, health, financial stability, or safety. This includes content that focuses on current events and news, finance, government and law, health and safety, and shopping. Examples of YMYL content could be: how to fill out a tax form, how to save for retirement, or how to treat bowel cancer.

This page from the Centers for Disease Control and Prevention about measles detection is a good YMYL example.

Google's quality raters have high page quality rating standards for YMYL pages because their content can affect the user.

What About E-E-A-T and AI-Generated Content?

Google does not currently label AI-generated content. However, it does recommend that content publishers label AI-generated images using IPTC image data metadata and adds that image AI companies will soon add the metadata automatically.

For text-based content, Google is leaving it up to publishers to decide whether they label AI content. But, at a recent conference, the search engine giant did say that its algorithms and signals are based on human content, so it will rank natural (or human-created) content at the top.

Note: This could change as Google looks to create an AI policy, so it's important to keep an eye on developments.

How Can You Improve E-E-A-T?

As you can see, improving your E-E-A-T can help optimize your content and boost your SEO efforts. It can also help you to create quality content that's relevant and useful to your target audience.

So how can you improve your E-E-A-T? Here are six tips.

Fill Knowledge Gaps

If you understand your audience, you should know what they are looking for online.

Once you've covered the core topics that relate to your product or service, what else can you write about?

That's where you need to be clever about your content marketing strategy and look for gaps that your competitors are not filling. Is there an in-house expert who has an interesting perspective on a popular topic? Or, have you come across customer feedback looking for information on a topic?

For example, let's say you work for a makeup company. You've probably already created content around the benefits of the products or advice on how to look after your skin. But what about content that maps out a beauty routine based on skin type? This could be an infographic or mini e-book that you can use for data capture.

You can come up with new content ideas through brainstorming or use a tool like Semrush's Topic Research Tool or AnswerThePublic.

Top tip: Gossip websites, fashion websites, and fan forums can show evidence of high E-E-A-T. In addition, some types of information are found almost exclusively on forums and discussions, where a community of experts can provide valuable perspectives on topics.

Add and Refresh Content

Google loves new content as it shows that your site is maintained regularly. The regularity of your content will depend on the type that you create.

If your company is known for big research publications, then your content schedule should reflect that. However, if you produce informative blogs or weekly webinars, then you should post more frequently to reflect that and keep your audience up to date.

Don't just leave your existing content untouched. Content can go out of date quickly, particularly if it's based on trends or uses statistics. You should conduct a content audit to see how existing content is performing. Following an audit, you should look to optimize top-performing content or content your audience finds valuable to give it a refresh. Google will see that you have updated the content and reward you for your efforts.

Work With Experts

It doesn't matter what size the company you work for is, it's always beneficial to work with experts to generate original content that feeds into E-E-A-T.

This could be in-house staff with in-depth knowledge of a particular area or an external expert who can provide a new perspective or angle on a topic relevant to your business.

At DMI, we regularly partner with many experts, including some from Neil Patel Digital on podcasts, blogs, and webinars. This provides our members and students with up-to-date and practical knowledge and also helps boost brand awareness and generate leads.

There are many content formats you can use to collaborate with experts, such as:

- A guest blog
- Webinar interview
- Podcast interview
- Quotes in a blog
- Whitepaper
- E-book or guide

However, it's important to choose an *expert* that Google will recognize. This can be done by looking at the expert's E-E-A-T signals, such as a social media profile, personal blog or site, author credentials (e.g., *New York Times* bestsellers), or online publications.

Top tip: You can also consider using influencers who are aligned with your brand and have a following that matches your target audience. If you pick the right influencer and develop the right content, you can get on the radar of high-intent customers and feed into E-E-A-T.

Use Links to Build Connections

If you produce a lot of content, you will find that you will write about a set of key topics that matter to your audience.

While it's important to have top-performing content pieces, it's also important to link them to other relevant content. This can be done strategically by using a hub-and-spoke (or content pillars) model.

This model means that you have *hub* topics (such as social media or SEO) that you link to a series of related posts, or *spokes* (that could be more in-depth pieces about social media or SEO).

For example, let's say you focus on social media as a topic. Your hub could be "What are the most popular social media channels?" From that, you could create several articles that focus on each social platform such as TikTok, Facebook, and so on. You could then add another layer that focuses on specialist topics such as social media algorithms or content creators. These other articles are the spokes that branch out from your hub article.

By using this model, you are developing authority on the topic. Including internal links from the hub to each spoke and amongst the spokes can help feed into E-E-A-T.

Top tip: Make sure you are using clear anchor text when linking your content to clarify exactly what other content a link is going to. You can check if your existing links use anchor text by using a site audit tool.

Manage and Monitor Brand Reputation

Trustworthiness is at the core of E-E-A-T, so it's important to have a positive reputation online. Conversely, if you have a negative reputation, you should do something about it because it will affect your credibility and SERP rankings.

You can monitor your brand reputation through Google or review sites like Trustpilot and Yelp. Forums, such as Reddit and Quora, can also be scanned for brand mentions, while social media platforms are commonly used for customers to air their views—positive and negative. The key to building a positive reputation is to respond to customers across channels.

- If it's a **positive review,** thank the person for leaving it and consider asking them for a testimonial you can use for social proof.
- If someone leaves a **negative review** or comment, respond and ask them what you can do to solve the issue, or apologize if it's a complaint about a product or service.

Top tip: Set up a Google Business Profile to give details about a business such as location, opening hours, and so on. There is also a review section you can manage and monitor.

Focus on Customer Experience (CX)

CX is crucial for Google. It's the bread and butter of its business because its goal is to feed into search intent to direct people to valuable and credible content that meets their needs.

A big part of that is the customer journey. On the DMI podcast, Luke O'Leary indicates that brands need to align with what users expect from clicking a search result. So if a user clicks on a link to a blog, they need to be led directly to that blog and see the content they expected based on the content in the SERP.

Top tip: Familiarize yourself with Core Web Vitals to understand how to optimize your website to deliver a better online experience.

Use SEO to Attract, Engage, and Convert

Creating content that matches search intent is crucial to getting seen online. Our certified Search Marketing course developed with Neil Patel will help you understand the fundamentals of search marketing. It explores SEO, paid search, analytics, demand generation, search strategy, and much more. Get started today!

AI stokes creativity by allowing a company to test ideas rapidly and to do more at scale. Furthermore, it learns from the past, across millions of data points, unlocking innovation quicker than a human could. But AI does not invent; it just predicts, on the basis of past patterns. Marketers invent, and the AI learns what works, for whom, when, and how. Invention requires a culture that values experimentation and risk-taking.

To drive competitive advantage with AI, you need to integrate your internal systems with external ones—first to collect accurate customer data and then to present the resulting insights as personalized offers. Both processes must be carried out with relentlessly expanding scale and scope, continually adding new variables and increasingly granular detail. For the executive who must begin thinking like a smart integrator, this approach calls for a new leadership model with new priorities to take advantage of the infinite possibilities. Getting integration right increasingly drives a superior CX, and it will be the decisive factor in how brand equity is built. *HBR* July/August 2023

*The Customer Journey Matrix*It includes four archetypes:

- A *routine* is effortless and predictable.
- A *joyride* is effortless and unpredictable.
- A *trek* is effortful and predictable.
- An *odyssey* is effortful and unpredictable.

The Routine

A routine is a simple procedure for completing a recurring task and typically involves a trigger for an activity that produces a reward. Routines are well suited for utilitarian products that make tasks incrementally easier and more predictable.

The Joyride

Joyrides are amusing journeys that allow people to escape the tedium of everyday routines. Effortless, unpredictable, and a lot of fun, joyrides work well for products that deliver an on-demand thrill, such as music-streaming platforms, sports media, and video games. Joyrides can also be used in brick-and-mortar settings such as fast-fashion stores with high product turnover, local cinemas with weekly releases, restaurants with rotating menus, and bars with happy-hour specials.

Just as it is for routines, streamlining is necessary for joyrides, though it isn't enough to create them. Streamlining only mitigates pain points; it doesn't induce pleasure. To facilitate joyrides, companies must also apply the design principle of *endless variation* across the customer journey to generate frequent moments of delight.

Consumer-generated content is another way to provide endless variation. On TikTok, new users are instantly immersed in a For You feed with trending videos they can swipe through. One video might feature a cat pouting while sad music plays; the next might show a cooking demonstration set to pop music. The staggering variety is part of the fun. Over time, users might like or comment on videos and discover creators they want to follow. TikTok's algorithms constantly process the engagement data and use that information to customize the feed.

The Trek

Treks are predictable journeys in which customers labor to achieve challenging long-term goals such as learning a language, recovering from surgery, and saving for retirement. Typically associated with personal service providers such as tutors, coaches, and financial advisers, treks are now increasingly facilitated by mobile apps and smart products.

The Odyssey

Odysseys are challenging, thrilling, and unpredictable adventures that are fueled by a customer's enthusiasm, determination, and sense of purpose. They tend to require great effort and generate a lot of excitement. Odysseys are perfect for products that facilitate passion projects that customers are already highly motivated to pursue, such as cultivating a social media following, playing a strategy game, learning a performance art, filming a documentary, and training for a fitness contest. They keep customers returning to a product because they want to learn and grow. Odysseys are particularly common in the recreation industry.

The Customer Journey Matrix

Customer journeys can be categorized into four distinct archetypes according to their level of effort and predictability.

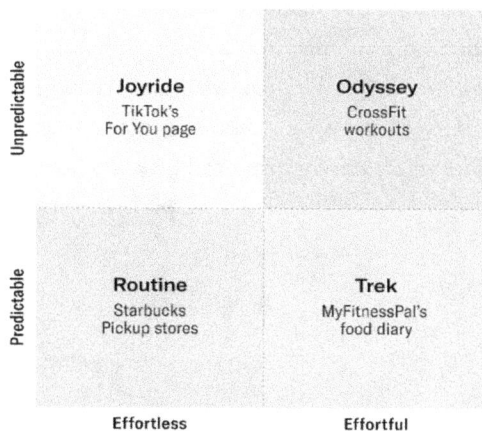

Unpredictable	**Joyride** TikTok's For You page	**Odyssey** CrossFit workouts
Predictable	**Routine** Starbucks Pickup stores	**Trek** MyFitnessPal's food diary
	Effortless	Effortful

© HBR

When companies have customers enrolled in multiple types of journeys, they're more likely to retain them. As some journeys lose their allure,
others might begin to gain momentum. The net effect is that customers
are continually engaged with the company's products on one journey or
another. *HBR* July/August 2022

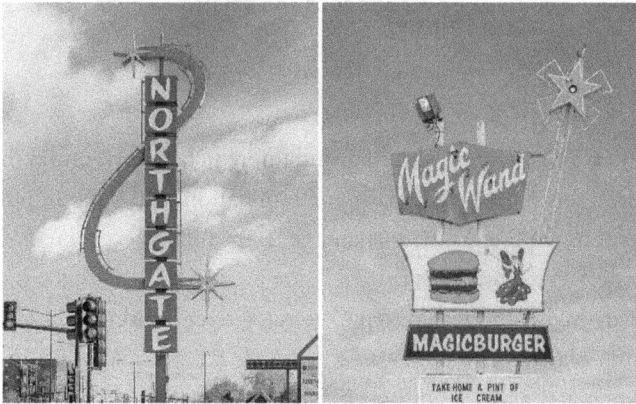

The battle has become tougher with the advent of online advertising and *performance marketing*—that is, spending to capture and convert potential demand that has already arrived (for whatever reason) at
the top of a brand's sales funnel. In other words, the advertiser pays for
clicks. However, in what is now called *brand advertising*—designed to
help establish awareness for a brand, a product, or a service to strengthen
identity and increase customer loyalty—the link between advertising
spending and positive financial outcomes is more tenuous.

Creating and executing on a customer promise is an act of strategy
making. It defines where the company will play and how it will win.

The Power of a Customer Promise

Ad campaigns rooted in making and fulfilling a customer promise may not always generate the most buzz, but they deliver on the dimensions that count. The World Advertising Research Centre uses six levels of performance to rate campaigns, shown here from least to most commercially successful. We studied WARC's data for more than 2,000 campaigns to compare their results.

PERFORMANCE LEVEL	CRITERION	DOES THE CAMPAIGN MAKE A PROMISE TO THE CONSUMER?
Influential idea	Overachieves on campaign metrics	NO 51% / YES 49
Behavior breakthrough	Changes consumer behavior	43 / 57
Sales spike	Leads to short-term growth	45 / 55
Brand builder	Improves brand health	41 / 59
Commercial triumph	Creates sustained sales success	38 / 62
Enduring icon	Results in long-term brand and sales growth	33 / 67

Source: World Advertising Research Centre   ♡HBR

What Does a Customer Promise Involve?

We began by looking at the kinds of promises made in our data set of 808 CP campaigns. The majority of promises fell into three types, and 89 percent of campaigns made at least one type. Some made more than one.

Emotional

Perhaps surprisingly, this was the biggest category, with 35 percent of the campaigns having made it their primary kind. It involves the emotional benefits a customer will receive from using a product or service. A classic example is the Mastercard *priceless* campaign: "There are some things money can't buy. For everything else, there's Mastercard." The promise is that Mastercard will take care of everything involving money, allowing you to focus on your treasured experiences. Another classic is *Have a Coke and a Smile*, which focused customers on the pleasure associated with drinking a Coke with someone else. And De Beers's famous *A diamond is forever* has since 1947 promised that the endurance of a diamond confers permanence on the emotions attached to it. More recently, Lysol's *Protect Like a Mother* makes the emotional promise that using the product will make you as protective as fierce mothers in the animal kingdom.

Functional.

In 32 percent of our sample, the primary promise was functional. For instance, Snickers's *You're not you when you're hungry* promises that customers will be able to operate at full capacity after consuming one of its candy bars. FedEx launched its "When it absolutely, positively has to be there overnight" campaign in 1978, and the promise was so powerful that it resulted in the creation of a new verb: to FedEx. Part of the campaign's success is that it conveys an emotional promise as well: You don't have to worry, because it's FedEx.

Enjoyable to Buy

A surprisingly large number of companies (22 percent) adopted as their primary promise the idea that customers would enjoy the process of purchasing. A good example is provided by the paint maker Sherwin-Williams, which won the 2022 B2B Grand Prix at Cannes for its campaign based on an AI tool that allows customers to create and choose a paint color by using voice to describe it (*a turquoise like the sea in the Maldives*, e.g.). Designers and architects loved it. The promise that Uber is *the smartest way to get around*, which focuses heavily on the ease of ordering and paying, is another example.

The remaining campaigns fell into three minor categories: *value for money* (5 percent), such as Geico's "15 minutes could save you 15 percent"; *sustainability* (4 percent), including Tide's *Turn to Cold* campaign, which promises that its new product is as effective in cold water as regular Tide is in hot; and *making amends* for prior failures (2 percent), with

Wells Fargo's *Earning back your trust* campaign in the wake of its fraudulent account-opening scandal being a prime example.

Having determined what kinds of promises companies make, we turned to look at what makes the promises attractive to customers. We found that successful campaigns share three features. They are shown as follows.

Memorable

In most cases, they run counter to expectations. Germany-based SIXT has quickly become the fourth-largest rental car company in Europe and is the fastest growing in the U.S. market. Its slogan is *Don't Rent a Car, Rent the Car*. Its promise is that SIXT won't disappoint you by foisting the only available vehicle on you when you arrive for pickup, as often happens to customers at other companies. You'll be given the car you originally chose.

Valuable

Customers must want what the promise offers. That's more likely if it diverges from a status quo they don't like. SIXT executives realized that customers willing to hire an expensive car actually cared about the make and model. That was less of an issue for bargain hunters—but they weren't SIXT's target market. Of course, other rental companies also offer premium cars, but in order to save costs, they don't always guarantee a specific car, giving SIXT an opportunity to differentiate itself from premium buyers.

Deliverable

Part of the value of any customer promise is precisely that it is a guarantee, which requires that the customer be able to determine that the promise was fulfilled. Making a promise involves risks. SIXT must deliver *the* car. Mastercard actually needs to take care of *everything else*. Coke has to be enjoyable (which is why its reputation suffered so much when people didn't like the taste of New Coke); Lysol must protect; Snickers must boost energy, and so on. Our assumption is that most of the 808 CP campaigns generally fulfilled their companies' promises; otherwise, they wouldn't have had disproportionally positive effects. But because customer promise has not been an explicit factor in previous surveys, the WARC data set includes no information about whether the companies making such promises actually fulfilled them. Our hypothesis is that had we been able to create a subsample of campaigns that definitively made good on their promises, we would have found that they scored even higher on the performance metrics. Of course, how a customer determines whether the promise has been kept may not be obvious, especially in emotional-value campaigns. But it clearly makes sense for companies to figure out exactly how to deliver on their promises.

Marketers always claim that their goal is to make campaign promises memorable, valuable, and deliverable. But as we've seen, their promises aren't always about the customer. The premier advertising event of the year is the Super Bowl, when many viewers pay more attention to the ads than to the game, and the 2023 Super Bowl was no exception. Most of the ads were feats of creative storytelling packed into a precious few seconds of very expensive airtime. They were memorable and often featured celebrities: The Hellman's mayonnaise ad depicted *Brie* Larson and Jon *Hamm* about to be eaten in a sandwich by Pete Davidson.

But our appraisal of the 51 commercials for the 2023 Super Bowl reveals that fewer than a third of them attempted to convey a specific promise of value to be delivered to the customer—a finding close to our results when we broke down the WARC campaigns. What most of those ads were aiming at was to enter the cultural conversation—advertising's equivalent of trying to be the most popular kid at the party. Only a handful actually made their tagline a memorable, valuable, and deliverable promise to the customer. Farmer's Dog, which promised *Real Food. Made Fresh. Delivered*, was one. *HBR* January/February 2024Most AI projects fail. Some estimates place the failure rate as high as 80 percent—almost double the rate of corporate IT project failures a decade ago.

AI is great at identifying patterns and providing predictions for well-formulated problems, but it fails to practice emotional intelligence and exercise moral or ethical judgment.

Understanding AI Workflows for Business

An AI workflow is a process that uses AI to perform productive tasks for you repeatedly. The AI workflow is meant to automate and streamline your work, saving you time and resources while improving efficiency.

AI workflows can handle many tasks, from simple automation to more complex business processes. If you can draw it on paper, you can probably build an AI to map that workflow, meaning you can tailor AI workflows to fit the specific needs of your business, regardless of your industry or company size.

For example, you could use AI workflow automation to analyze incoming emails, generate personalized responses, and follow up based on their content.

Implementing AI workflow automation for these repetitive manual tasks can improve customer service while freeing up time to focus on higher-level tasks.

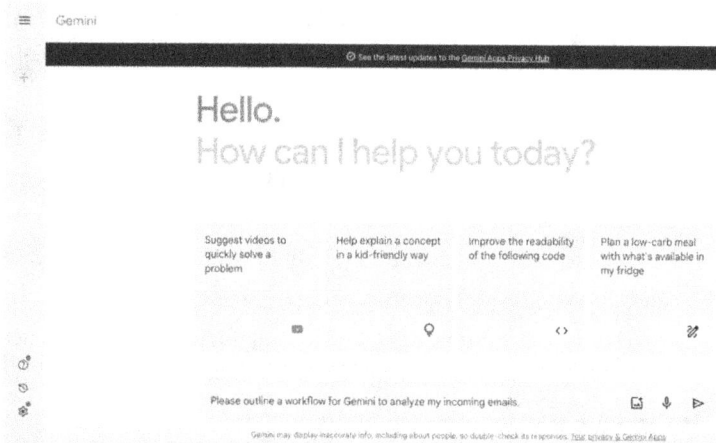

One key benefit of AI workflows is their ability to learn and improve over time. As the AI processes more data and receives user feedback, it can refine its algorithms and provide more accurate and relevant results. This continuous improvement ensures that your AI workflows remain effective and efficient even as your business evolves and grows.

Another advantage of AI workflows is their scalability. Unlike human workers, AI can handle vast amounts of data and perform tasks simultaneously without needing breaks or time off. This means you can scale your operations more efficiently without worrying about hiring and training additional staff.

#1: How to Identify Opportunities for AI Workflows in Your Business

To begin implementing AI workflows in your business, look for routine tasks you perform.

These could be processes that you or your team members do daily, weekly, or monthly. Some common examples of how AI workflows can automate repetitive tasks include:

Responding to leads generated from online forms: AI can analyze the information provided and generate personalized responses, increasing the likelihood of converting the lead into a customer. For instance, if someone fills out a form requesting information about your products or services, an AI workflow could automatically send them a tailored email with relevant details and a call to action based on their needs and interests.

Grading student essays and providing personalized feedback: For educators who handle large volumes of student essays, AI can grade the essays based on a predefined rubric and provide customized feedback to each student, saving significant time and effort. The AI can analyze the essay's content, structure, and language and provide suggestions for improvement, such as highlighting areas that need more development or pointing out grammatical errors.

Analyzing customer reviews and extracting actionable insights: AI can process thousands of customer reviews, identify common themes and sentiments, and provide insights to help improve your products or services. For example, if you have a lot of reviews for a particular product, an AI workflow could analyze the text and determine the most frequently mentioned positive and negative aspects and any recurring issues or suggestions for improvement. You can then use this information to make data-driven product development, marketing, and customer support decisions.

ChatGPT 4o ⌄

Create a workout   Study vocabulary   Python script for   Design a fun
plan   daily email reports   coding game

Please outline a workflow to use ChatGPT to analyze customer reviews, identify common themes and sentiments, and provide insights to help improve my salon services. For example, analyze the text and determine the most frequently mentioned positive and negative aspects and any recurring issues or suggestions for improvement. I will use this information to make data-driven product development, marketing, and customer support decisions.

ChatGPT can make mistakes. Check important info.

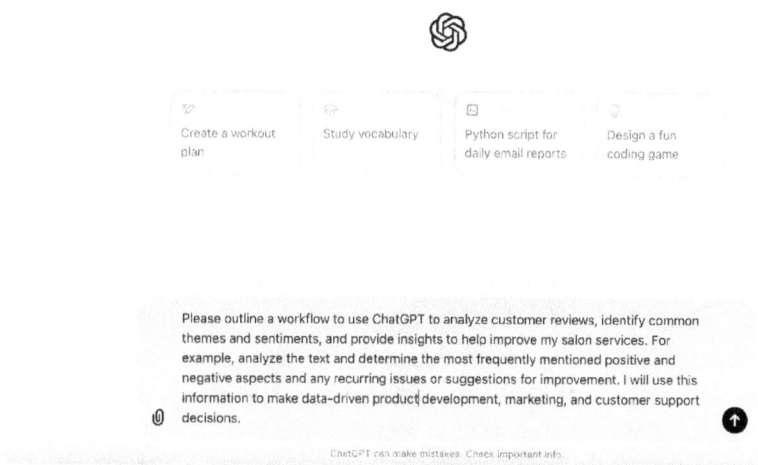

Offering personalized product recommendations on an e-commerce site: AI can generate tailored product recommendations by analyzing customer browsing and purchase history, enhancing the shopping experience, and increasing sales. For instance, if a customer has previously purchased a specific type of product, an AI workflow could recommend complementary items or new releases in the same category based on their preferences and behavior.

Handling routine customer support inquiries: AI-powered chatbots can handle common customer questions and concerns, providing quick and efficient support while freeing up your support team to focus on more complex tasks. You can train these chatbots to understand and respond to various inquiries, from basic product information to troubleshooting and account management. By providing instant, 24/7 support, AI chatbots can improve customer satisfaction and loyalty while reducing the workload on your human support staff.

Generating reports and data visualizations: AI can process large amounts of data and create informative reports and visualizations, helping you make data-driven decisions for your business. For example, if you have a large data set of sales figures, an AI workflow could automatically generate monthly or quarterly reports, complete with charts, graphs, and key performance indicators. You can customize these reports to highlight the most relevant information for stakeholders, such as executives, sales teams, or investors.

Two Real-World Examples of AI Workflows

In the education sector, imagine being able to take a picture of an essay with your phone, apply the rubric, grade it, and give your students personalized feedback on how to improve it. Some platforms allow this today.

In the e-commerce industry, imagine you run an e-commerce store and use an AI chatbot that acts as a recommendation chatbot that asks what customers are interested in and delivers recommendations based on their responses, your inventory, and any special offers.

#2: How to Choose AI Tools for Your Workflows

When searching for AI-powered workflow automation tools, focus on *low code, no code* solutions. These tools are designed to be user-friendly and accessible, even if you don't have extensive technical skills. Look for AI platforms that have a strong track record and are being used by reputable companies in various industries.

Rather than building your solutions from scratch using open source, focus on finding existing solutions that are available for a small monthly fee.

This advice is particularly relevant for small and medium-sized businesses that may not have the resources or expertise to develop their own AI solutions from scratch. By leveraging existing AI automation tools and platforms, these businesses can still reap the benefits of AI workflows without the need for significant upfront investment or technical know-how.

When evaluating AI tools, consider factors such as ease of use, scalability, and customer support. Look for tools offering intuitive interfaces, drag-and-drop functionality, and pre-built templates or workflows that you can easily customize.

Additionally, ensure that the tool can scale with your business as your needs grow and that adequate customer support is available to help you troubleshoot any issues or questions that may arise.

Another crucial factor to consider is how well the AI tool integrates with the other tools and systems you already use in your business. Ideally, you want an AI solution that seamlessly works with your existing data, whether you're storing it in Google Workspace, Office 365, or other platforms. This integration will make it easier to implement AI workflows without disrupting your current processes.

When you know what kinds of data your AI tool can work with, you can figure out the best ways to use it for your specific tasks and workflows.

For instance, you may want to prioritize AI tools specializing in natural language processing (NLP) and text analysis if you have a lot of customer support emails. On the other hand, if you're in the music industry, you may be more interested in AI tools that can generate and manipulate audio content.

This framework can help you find the best AI solution for your business:

Words: AI can process and analyze text data, such as emails, reviews, and documents. For example, an AI tool specializing in NLP can help you automate sentiment analysis, content categorization, and text summarization tasks.

Images: AI can interpret and generate visual content, such as photos and illustrations. AI tools with computer vision capabilities can assist with image recognition, object detection, and visual search tasks.

Numbers: AI can analyze numerical data, such as spreadsheets and financial reports. AI tools with machine learning algorithms can help you forecast sales, detect anomalies, and optimize pricing strategies.

Sounds: AI can process and generate audio data, such as music and voice recordings. AI tools with speech recognition and synthesis capabilities can enable tasks such as voice-based customer support, transcription, and audio content creation.

#3: 5 Steps to Implement AI Workflows in Your Business

To start implementing AI workflows in your business, use the following steps:

Step 1: Identify a specific task you perform repeatedly that AI could automate. For example, if you spend significant time responding to customer inquiries via email, consider automating this process with an AI-powered email response system. Start by mapping out the current process, including the inputs (e.g., customer emails), outputs (e.g., personalized responses), and any decision points or rules that need to be followed. This will help you determine the scope and requirements of your AI workflow.

Step 2: Research and select an AI tool that can handle that task and integrates well with your existing systems. Look for tools successfully implemented by other businesses in your industry that offer robust integration options. Read reviews, case studies, and testimonials to understand the tool's capabilities, limitations, and customer satisfaction. Take advantage of free trials or demos to test the tool's functionality and ease of use before committing.

Step 3: Start with a small-scale pilot project to test the AI tool and evaluate its effectiveness and value for your business. This will allow you to identify potential issues or limitations before committing to a full-scale implementation. Define clear goals and metrics for your pilot project, such as time saved, accuracy of responses, or customer satisfaction. Involve a small group of users or customers in the pilot and gather their feedback to refine and improve the AI workflow.

Step 4: If the pilot project yields positive results, consider expanding your use of AI workflows to other areas of your business. Gradually incorporating AI into your workflows will help you and your team adjust to the new technology and ensure a smooth transition. Develop a roadmap for AI implementation, prioritizing the workflows with the greatest impact and ROI potential. Provide training and support for your team members to help them effectively understand and leverage the AI tools.

Step 5: Develop an AI policy for your company that outlines guidelines and best practices for using AI tools responsibly and ethically. This policy should address issues like data privacy, security, and the potential impact on your workforce. Ensure your AI workflows comply with relevant laws and regulations, such as GDPR or HIPAA. Communicate the policy clearly to all stakeholders and provide ongoing education and guidance to ensure consistent and responsible use of AI across your organization.

Christopher Brock, founder of ChatGPT for Business & Life, emphasizes the importance of starting small and gradually expanding your use of AI workflows: "Try to think of things that are you're doing all the time repetitively. And you could draw a diagram from the beginning to the end. And if you can draw it on paper, you can probably build an AI to map that workflow."

This iterative approach allows you to validate the effectiveness of AI workflows in your specific business context while minimizing risk and disruption. By starting with a small, well-defined use case, you can demonstrate the value of AI and build momentum for broader adoption across your organization.

As you explore AI workflows, it's crucial to prioritize security and privacy. Ensure you thoroughly understand how the AI tool collects, uses, and protects your data. Develop clear policies and guidelines for your team to follow when using AI tools to ensure that sensitive information remains secure.

Christopher advises, "If you're paying for it, you sort of get at least one step of security that you're probably paying for your own secured space."

However, he also notes that it's essential to balance security with competitive advantage:

Right now, I think it's definitely a balance for privacy, but make sure that you're not valuing security over competitive advantage in that landscape. Because right now there's companies that will not have the same security hangups and they will move quicker, faster, and more efficiently than your business.

While security and privacy are important considerations, they should not paralyze your AI adoption efforts. By implementing appropriate safeguards and protocols, you can mitigate risks while still leveraging AI's power to drive your business forward. www.socialmediaexaminer.com/ai-workflows-how-to-get-started/?utm_medium=email&utm_source=rasa_io&utm_campaign=newsletter.

Generative AI Enhancing Efficiency in Marketing

Generative Marketing Efficiency

www.dmnews.com/generative-ai-enhancing-efficiency-in-marketing/?utm_medium=email&utm_source=rasa_io&utm_campaign=newsletter.

Generative AI is proving to be a major boon across various sectors. Its applications range from creating animations, composing music, to writing complex literary pieces. Recent advancements have also facilitated the use of generative AI in areas such as fashion designing, video game development, and 3D modeling, showcasing the extraordinary potential of AI in content creation.

In the marketing industry, generative AI holds a particularly exciting prospect. Given the creative, adaptive, and continuous nature of marketing, generative AI can substantially enhance engagement and conversion rates for businesses. Generative AI tools have the ability to understand customer behavior, predict trends, and personalize campaigns precisely.

With a continually evolving digital sphere, the task of engaging customers across multiple platforms has become increasingly challenging for marketers. This challenge is something that generative AI can meet head-on.

Impact of Generative AI on Marketing Strategies

It has the ability to deliver personalized messages that resonate with individual consumers, thereby making marketing tasks more efficient and impactful.

Generative AI has had a significant impact on industries such as health care and automotive by contributing to personalized treatment plans for patients and generating unique car designs. As a result, increased cost-effectiveness and higher efficiency with the use of generative AI is evident.

The future of generative AI in marketing may include marketing copilots, marketing agents, and independent marketing teams. Currently, marketers are starting to use generative AI for creating initial drafts to focus on strategic tasks. We may witness the rise of fully independent marketing teams managed solely by AI in the future.

Projections suggest that these marketing copilots will process data from various sources to create brand-focused assets and assist with tasks that include audience segmentation and planning. As machine learning and AI technologies continue to advance, their abilities to predict trends and consumer responses will become more vital.

Generative AI is poised to become a crucial part of future marketing strategies. It will fundamentally change the perception and utilization of marketing automation, introducing a new paradigm of data-driven decision making. The potential of AI to predict customer behavior and identify market trends can help businesses position their products innovatively and competitively, paving the way for unprecedented growth opportunities.

How to Use AI to Market Your Small Business [+ My Favorite AI Tools]

https://blog.hubspot.com/marketing/ai-small-business-marketing?utm_medium=email&utm_source=rasa_io&utm_campaign=newsletter.

Being a small business is both easier and harder than ever. Yes, the competition is tough, but there have never been more AI tools that can help you in almost every segment of your business.

For example, I'd long wanted to sell merchandise with my designs. However, the thought of getting started and thinking about the initial steps felt overwhelming.

Turns out, I was wrong. With the help of AI tools, I got the name, slogan, and brand color suggestions in just a few minutes, and they were all stunning (more on this later).

So, in this piece, I'll show you how AI can benefit your small business, going far beyond just communication and content creation. Let's dive in.

How AI Can Level Up Your Marketing

There are so many different ways that AI can improve your marketing, and the list could probably include more than 100 ways, but I'll show you the 12 greatest.

How to Use ChatGPT at Work

Speeding Up Content Writing

In all, 79 percent of marketers believe that AI improves the quality of the content they create. And I totally agree. AI has changed content marketing in a very positive way (of course, only for those who know how to use it properly).

Struggling with writer's block? AI can analyze trends and suggest engaging content ideas which is the top reason why many marketers use AI, according to our study.

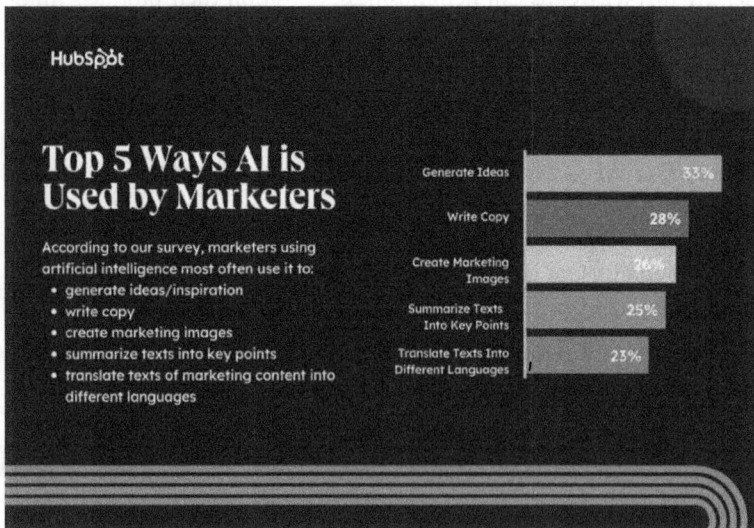

HubSpot

Top 5 Ways AI is Used by Marketers

According to our survey, marketers using artificial intelligence most often use it to:
- generate ideas/inspiration
- write copy
- create marketing images
- summarize texts into key points
- translate texts of marketing content into different languages

Generate Ideas	33%
Write Copy	28%
Create Marketing Images	26%
Summarize Texts Into Key Points	25%
Translate Texts Into Different Languages	23%

It can also automate repetitive tasks such as generating SEO descriptions and social media posts.

Additionally, AI can improve content by checking grammar, spelling, and sentence structure to ensure clarity and professionalism. Some AI assistants, like Jasper, can even adapt their writing style to match your desired tone.

But remember, none of these tools are plug-and-play solutions. You still need creativity and solid writing skills. Otherwise, the content might sound off, and readers will notice it's AI-generated. So, be ready to tweak and refine.

Pro tip: We have a free content assistant ChatSpot, which combines the power of ChatGPT with unique data sources like HubSpot CRM to streamline your working day.

Automating Personalized Offers

Personalization isn't just about sending generic birthday coupons anymore.

You need to understand each customer's preferences and then craft special offers just for them. Even though it may seem like a mountain of work, AI can swoop in to save you.

Based on customer data, AI can personalize your marketing content, recommendations, and offers for each individual customer.

This can significantly improve Click Through Rate (CTRs), conversion rates, and, most importantly, customer satisfaction. To prove how AI can help with personalization, I explored a bit and found a great case study.

U.S. Beauty retailer Ulta Beauty benefited from SAS Customer Intelligence 360, which combined all their data and sent personalized messages and recommendations to each customer.

The outcome? A massive win. Ulta Beauty's sales went through the roof—an incredible **95 percent of their sales were influenced by their personalized marketing efforts.**

Pro tip: Always analyze customer sentiment during the checkout process. If you notice they're hesitant, let your AI suggest a less pushy and more intriguing Call To Action (CTA) like *Are you sure you need me? Let's find out* instead of *Buy Now*. This subtle shift can address purchase anxieties and improve conversion rates.

Analyzing Customer Behavior

AI is seriously good at sifting through massive amounts of customer data—website visits, app interactions, social media activity, purchase history, email clicks, and more.

It can map out the different touchpoints customers interact with on their way to making a purchase, so you can identify any roadblocks or friction points in the customer journey.

It can also analyze customer purchase history to identify products that customers are likely to buy together. You can use this information to create targeted upsell and cross-sell campaigns that increase the average order value.

One pretty good tool for this purpose is Adobe Customer Journey Analytics, which provides insights into customers' journeys across channels—online and offline. It offers connected data and unlimited customer data collection. And you can get contextual insights instantly, which is a huge plus.

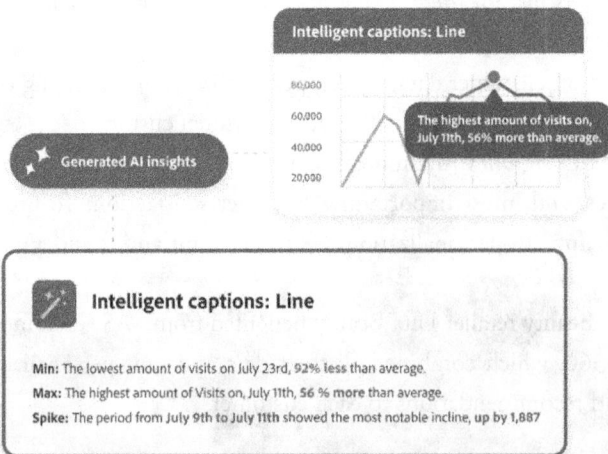

Intelligent captions: Line

80,000
60,000
40,000
20,000

The highest amount of visits on, July 11th, 56% more than average.

Generated AI insights

Intelligent captions: Line

Min: The lowest amount of visits on July 23rd, 92% less than average.
Max: The highest amount of Visits on, July 11th, 56 % more than average.
Spike: The period from July 9th to July 11th showed the most notable incline, up by 1,887

Pro tip: Give a try to HubSpot's Behavioral Targeting tool to create segmented lists based on personas and engagement levels. Plus, the tool helps identify and respond to high-intent behaviors like website visits, email interactions, and form submissions.

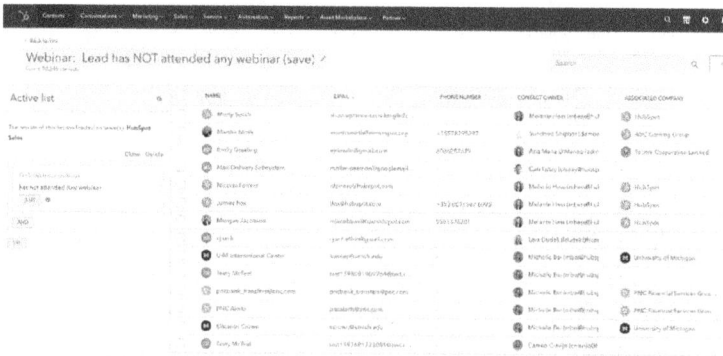

Predicting Audience Behavior

One of the best things about AI is its ability to predict audience behavior and pinpoint customers who are super interested in taking some action or those who are at risk of churning (canceling a subscription or stopping using your service).

For instance, Google Analytics and its Predictive audiences are great for this purpose. Predictive audiences help target users likely to take specific actions, like making a purchase soon.

It includes users with high probabilities of performing specific actions. For instance, *Likely 7-day purchasers* include those with high purchase probabilities. Adding extra conditions can refine the audience even further.

Configure prediction

User range ⑦

○ Most likely to churn
  Top 20% of users

○ Least likely to churn
  Bottom 20% of users

◉ Custom
  Customize user range

  [40] to [100] percentile

Prediction window ⑦

In the next 7 days

Prediction summary

This summary only considers the predictive metric. Any additional condition filters will also impact the audience size.

Churn probability over user percentile

CHURN PROBABILITY

Average probability ⑦
0.55

1

0.5

0

0th   20th   40th   60th   80th   100th
USER PERCENTILE

[40th]   [100th]

Users in selected range ⑦	Users expected to churn ⑦
3,133,909	1,715,533
96% of all users active in last 7 days	100% of all users expected to churn

Cancel   Apply

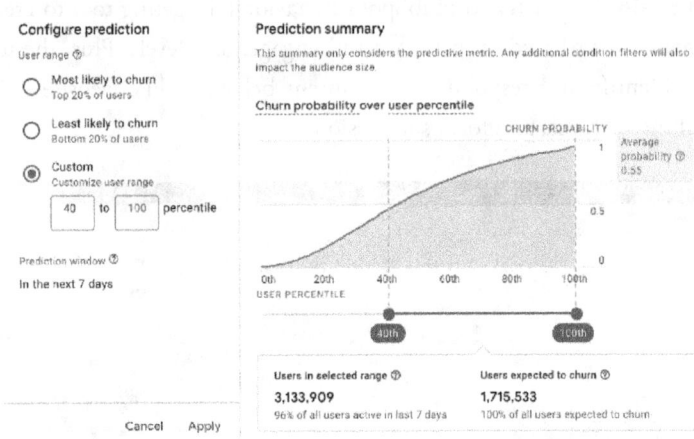

Pro tip: Partner with industry experts and trend forecasters to develop *what-if* scenarios for your customer journey. Explore potential disruptions, changing customer expectations, or even the impact of new technologies.

Automating Email Campaigns

Email marketing automation has been around for a while, but new AI tools are making it even better.

They can help you write more interesting emails and understand what your subscribers like. This lets you spend less time planning and more time running successful campaigns.

Here's how AI can help you with emails:

- Analyzes user data to send targeted messages that resonate, boosting open rates and clicks.
- Checks historical data and subscriber behavior to predict the optimal send time, so your emails land in inboxes when recipients are most likely to open and engage.
- Automates A/B testing of various email elements like subject lines, CTAs, and design layouts to identify the best versions for future campaign.
- Analyzes your email content and flag potential spam triggers, so you can avoid landing in the dreaded junk folder.

- Identifies subscribers at risk of unsubscribing and creates personalized re-engagement campaigns to win them back.

Pro tip: HubSpot's AI assistant can create an email that grabs attention and gets your subscribers clicking through to your content. It crafts catchy subject lines, product descriptions, and even whole email drafts.

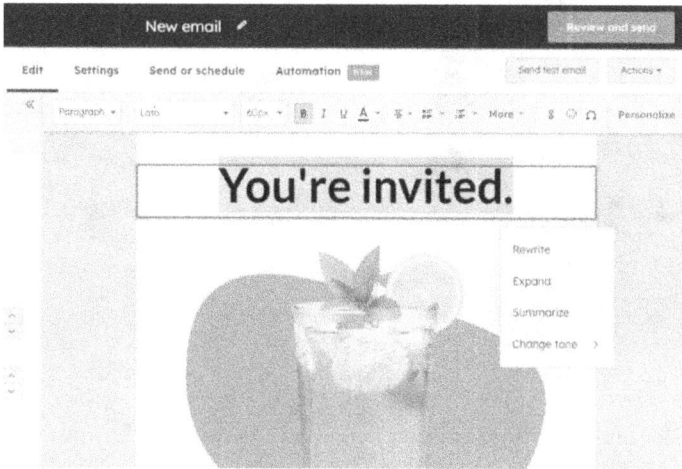

Conducting Research

Market research can be time-consuming and labor-intensive. That's why 48 percent of marketers use generative AI for research. Here›s how:

- **No more legwork.** AI automates boring tasks like sending surveys and sorting piles of responses.
- **Mind reading (almost).** AI can analyze social media posts, reviews, and surveys to understand the emotions and opinions hidden behind the words.
- **Spotting hidden clues.** AI can scan massive amounts of data to find trends and patterns that you might miss on your own.
- **Seeing into the future (sort of).** AI can analyze data to predict how customers might behave and what trends might emerge. This lets you make smarter decisions about products, campaigns, and where to invest your resources.

- **Tailored questions for tailored answers.** AI can personalize surveys and automatically create questions for different customer groups, which saves a lot of time.

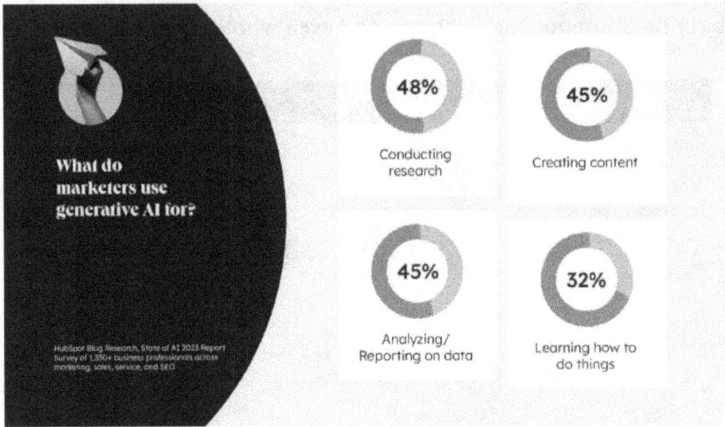

Image Source

Pro tip: HubSpot Service Hub offers access to awesome Customer Feedback Software, which helps you run surveys and gain insights into your customers' shopping habits. Plus, there are tons of ready-to-go survey templates, so you can quickly learn about your customers' habits and preferences.

Transcription and Summarization

After having a brainstorming session with your marketing team, you definitely don't want to spend time sifting through hours of recordings.

You need someone, or even better—something—to do it for you. That's where AI transcription tools take the stage.

Actually, 63 percent of marketers use AI tools to take notes and summarize meetings.

Before adding such software to my toolkit (Notta is currently my fav), I was constantly scrambling to take notes, worried about missing something crucial.

This left me feeling overwhelmed, and frankly, I hated meetings altogether. Emails were my haven—clear, written communication where I could keep track of everything.

Now, I can be fully present in the discussion while, after the meeting, sorting all transcripts into clear text and bullet points.

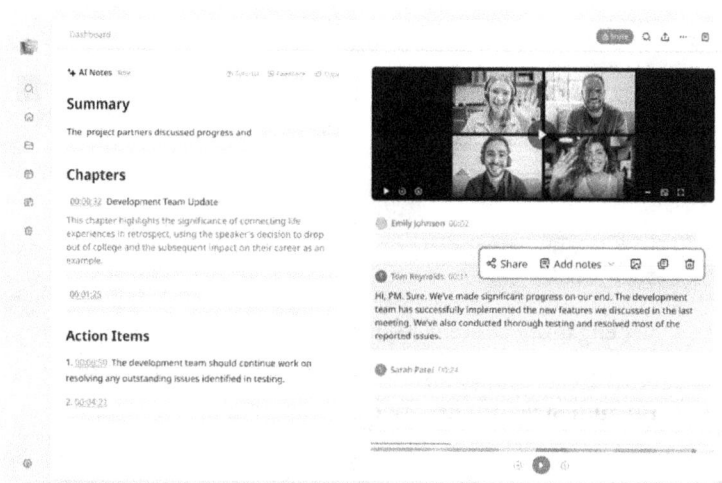

Image Source

Pro tip: Most AI transcription tools have the ability to summarize the entire transcript into bullet points to make it clearer and more organized. Also, if you need a specific word, you can simply find it by typing it in the search bar.

Automating Social Media Management

To market your small business, you need to be active on social media and keep regular track of what's going on there, which can be overwhelming.

That's why you need AI-powered social media tools that offer a range of features to help you:

- **Schedule posts efficiently.** Plan your content calendar in advance and publish across all your social media platforms at optimal times.

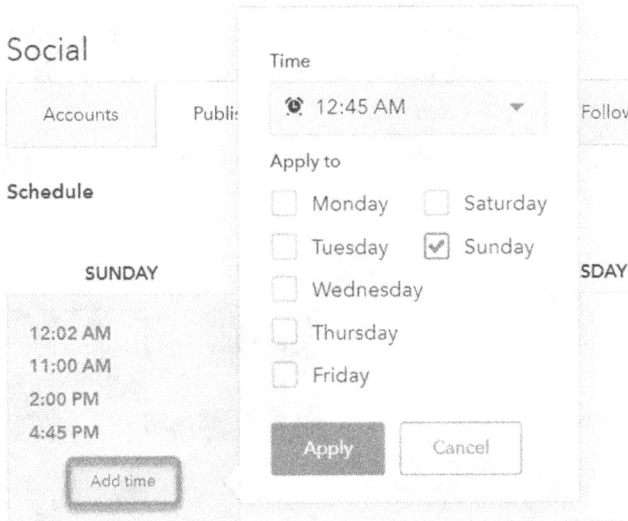

- **Craft engaging content.** Generate content ideas, write attractive captions, and personalize posts for each platform.
- **Gain audience insights.** Track brand mentions, analyze customer sentiment, and identify trends to understand your audience better.
- **Optimize ads.** Improve your advertising efforts and identify relevant influencers for marketing campaigns.

Pro tip: HubSpot AI Social Media Post Generator refines post ideas, adjusts tone to match your brand, and helps create better posts in less time. You can also repurpose posts by channel and track the Return on Investment (ROI) of Social Media (SM) accounts.

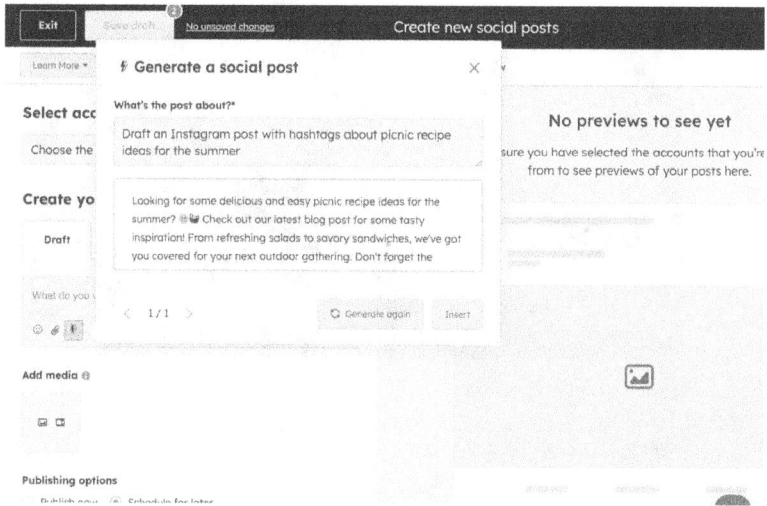

Faster Video Creation

Out of 701 people we asked about their favorite content types, 45 percent said they like short videos like TikToks, while 24 percent prefer longer videos.

So, it's clear—if you want your business to stand out, you need video content. But, for small business owners and startups, hiring professional videographers and editors can be a budget-breaker.

Luckily, AI tools for video creation are incredibly good.

They allow you to script, generate, and even edit videos without needing pro equipment or expertise. These tools turn your ideas into engaging visuals with features like text-to-video conversion and footage libraries.

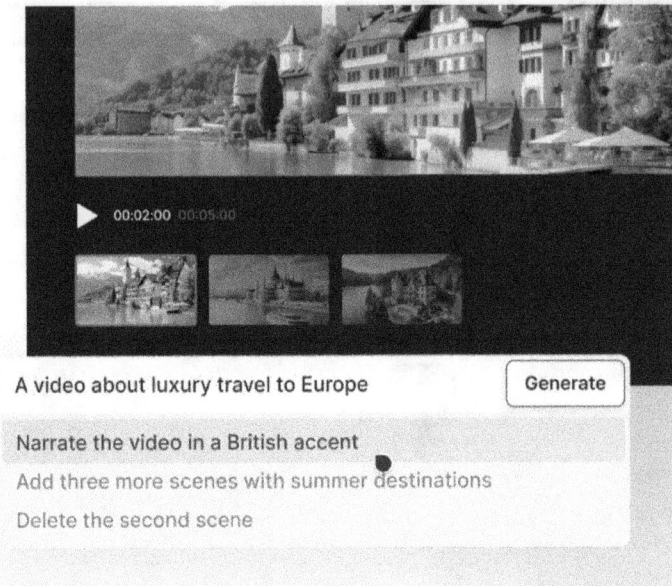

Some popular options are InVideo, Lumen5, and Kapwing, all offering user-friendly interfaces and budget-friendly plans.

Pro tip: Avoid stock footage that screams *fake* and *boring*. Always film some of your content with a phone (it doesn't have to be a pro camera), upload your clips, and then let the AI tool do its part of the work.

24/7 Customer Support

Unlike human reps who need breaks and work limited hours, AI chatbots are tireless. They can answer customer queries and provide basic support anytime, day or night.

This is especially good for small businesses with limited staff or operating in global markets with different time zones.

We surveyed people to see how they feel about using AI chat for customer support on websites. It turns out that 25 percent always turn to web chat for help, while only 15 percent prefer sending direct messages.

The good thing about AI chatbots is that they're trained to handle various FAQs and common issues.

For instance, a clothing store chatbot could answer questions about sizing, return policies, or order tracking.

AI bot will have all answers to these questions because they're general and repetitive, so human reps can focus on more complex problems that require a personal touch.

Pro tip: You can build your AI chatbot using HubSpot's Free AI Chatbot Builder. Sweet spot? No coding skills are required. Your chatbot will qualify leads, schedule meetings, and offer customer support round-the-clock. The best part? **You can customize it to perfectly match your brand.**

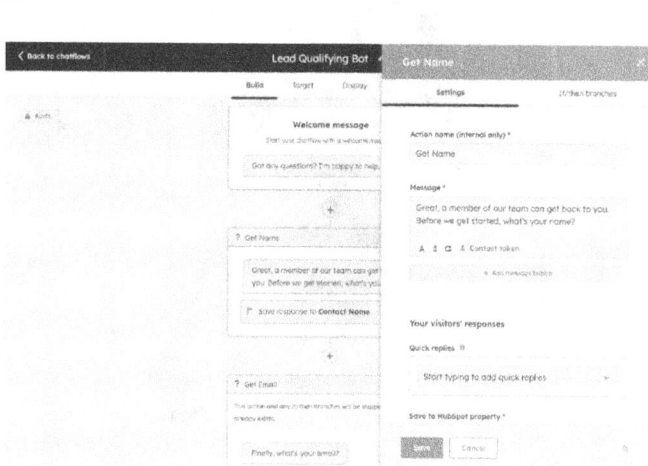

Intelligent Advertising

As a small business owner, the last thing you want is to throw money on ads that bring nothing. That's why you should think about incorporating AI advertising tools. AI digs through information about past customers and website visitors.

It analyzes things like demographics (age, location) and browsing habits to understand who your ideal customer is.

With this customer profile in hand, it finds similar people on the Web and personalizes your ads accordingly. Another way to use AI tools in advertising is for designing.

Kipp Bodnar, HubSpot's CMO, shared that using AI to design ads for subscriber growth slashed contact acquisition costs by 300 percent.

A great AI advertising tool is AdCreative.ai, which helps generate high-performing ad creatives quickly. It provides insights, generates text and headlines, creates social media post creatives, and even produces superquality videos for ads.

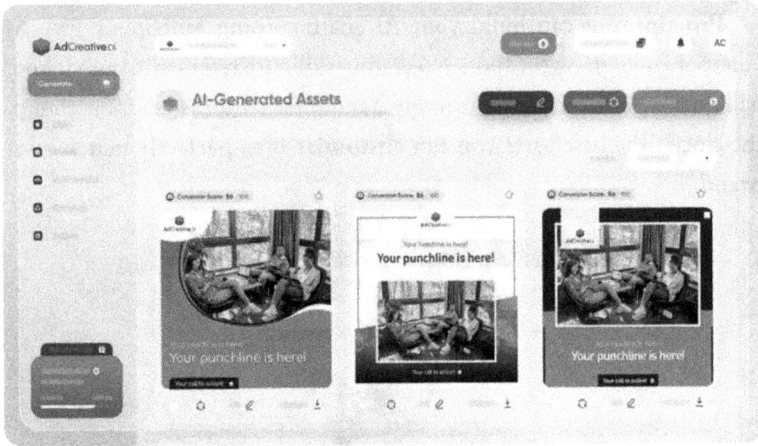

Image Source

Pro tip: Involve consumers in your AI-powered advertising to ditch the cold, *robotic* feel. Encourage User Generated Content (UGC) through contests or challenges. Then feed the customer-created pics/videos to AI tools and watch the magic happen.

Search Engine Optimization

Last but not least, AI tools can help with SEO—not only for SEO content creation but also for keyword research, competitor analysis, and overall optimization.

For instance, here's how HubSpot SEO tools can make *ranking climbing* easier:

- Get keyword recommendations to optimize your website content.
- Plan your content strategy by discovering relevant topics to target—those that resonate with your audience and boost search authority.
- Generate content ideas based on search popularity and competition.

- Track your website's SEO performance with detailed reports.
- Integrate with Google Search Console for even deeper insights.
- Scan your website with an SEO recommendations tool that shows improvement opportunities automatically.
- Use AI Blog Writer to generate engaging SEO posts from outlines or bullet points.

Pro tip: Use AI Paragraph Rewriter to refresh existing content for relevance and engagement, extending its reach and effectiveness.

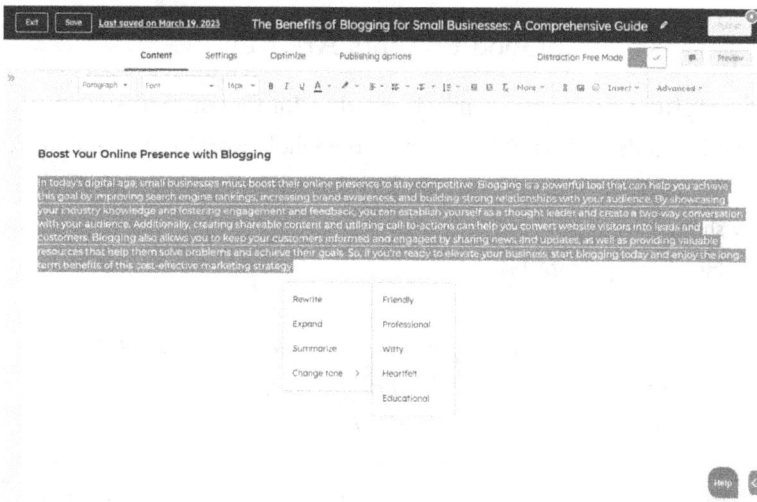

My Favorite AI Marketing Tools

I love AI marketing tools, and I'm often impressed by them. I've tried so many different ones. And of those tools, here are my four favorites.

ChatGPT Plus

My forever favorite is undoubtedly ChatGPT, especially its Plus version, which I can access even during peak times and get faster responses.

I always say that ChatGPT is the most versatile tool ever. I use it for all kinds of my projects.

- Need to sort out the messy data order? ChatGPT helps.
- Need to create an article outline? ChatGPT helps.
- Need to understand the overly complicated law? ChatGPT helps again.
- Need to proofread, reword, and find a creative angle? ChatGPT 4 helps here.

The most important thing to get the most out of ChatGPT is to give it the clearest possible directions so it can understand you and adapt to your writing style, tone of voice, or task.

Good Prompts Are Key

If you give it a good command, it will do a lot for you, and you'll avoid generic words such as *unleash*, which the whole world is making a joke of. For instance, let me show you how I used it to invent the name for my shop.

Here's the prompt I sent:

> *I need some ideas for a unique name for my new merch brand. I'll sell clothes featuring personalized prints, capturing moments with family and friends that hold sentimental value. I want the name to be cute, maybe with 'charm' in it. But here's something important: it has to be totally made up, invented, fictional, easy to remember, and sound nice. Give me some good words with all these qualities, please.*

Post-SEO Content and Influencer Trends

https://blog.hubspot.com/marketing/post-seo-marketing?utm_medium=email&utm_source=rasa_io&utm_campaign=newsletter.

B2B Creators and Creator Channels

Even before the algorithm updates, marketing channels like Google search and paid ads were becoming less effective at driving exponential growth in traffic. Meanwhile, platforms favoring creators and indirect conversions, such as podcasts, TikTok, Instagram, and YouTube, are gaining traction. Why? *Because B2B is having its creator moment*, says Kieran.

Creator-focused channels prioritize personalities over brands, fostering person-to-person connections between customers and products or services. Particularly for B2B companies, integrating creator-led strategies—whether through influencer partnerships or hiring creators in-house—is now crucial.

Outbound Marketing and AI

We're seeing a significant boom in outbound marketing and sales, which I believe will continue for the next three to five years while the internet recalibrates after the recent algorithm changes and new inbound channels emerge.

Therefore, to stay ahead, it's becoming even more important to **sharpen your sales and marketing team's proficiency with "AI tools**." For example, AI can streamline prospecting efforts and personalize outreach, making it easier to identify and engage potential leads.

Video Content

"I see a world where YouTube maybe becomes Google's core business long term,» says Kieran. And I absolutely agree, as video content is far harder to replicate and much more defensible from AI.

Kieran goes on to emphasize that pivoting toward *more difficult* content like video can offer marketing teams significant leverage. Why? **Easier content strategies become less effective quickly because** *everyone* **adopts them.** So while pivoting your strategy to invest in platforms like YouTube and partnerships with video creators may require more time and effort upfront, it can lead to lower costs per lead and higher engagement in the long run.

Product Differentiation

Adopting a strategy of being *different in every way* like James Dyson's approach—which we discuss in further detail on the podcast—ensures that your product stands out. Differentiation is essential, especially as markets become more saturated and traditional strategies become commoditized.

I believe a product needs to be at least ten times more differentiated to succeed. Taking **product differentiation to another level will be a core trademark of successful companies over the next 5 to 10 years**.

Community-Driven Platforms

Another significant result of the algorithm update is that **community-driven sites like Reddit and Quora can have "preferential search engine ranking"** over traditional informational articles, as these platforms are also difficult to replicate with large language models and AI.

For marketers, this means that previously high-ranking content may be outranked by a rich Reddit or Quora thread on the same topic. As a result, it's becoming increasingly important for businesses to establish a presence on these community-aggregated sites to stay connected to users.

Founders as Creators

This last trend is a controversial take but I believe that **if you are considering starting a company, you need to be a creator in that market** for six to 18 months before starting that company.

Founders who build an audience using media channels such as YouTube, newsletters, and podcasts can create significant authority and trust within their industry. Building a strong personal brand early on helps founders get to know and engage their audience, fostering loyalty and trust even before the product hits the market.

Notes

Foreword

1. Gardener, *The Meaning of Witchcraft.*
2. Karsaklian, E. 2023. *Multicultural Marketing Is Your Story.*
3. Rapaille, *The Culture Code: An Ingenious Way to Understand Why People Around the World Live and Buy as They Do.*

Introduction

1. Kahneman, *Thinking Fast and Slow.*
2. Schaefer, Businessesgrow.com.
3. Cannon, Perreault, and McCarthy, *Essentials of Marketing.*
4. Harvard Business Review (2024).
5. Valenzuela et al., "How Artificial Intelligence Constrains the Human Experience," 241–256.
6. Kim and Lehmann, "The Effect of Variety in Past Consumption on Openness to Personalized Recommendation Services," 297–305.
7. Usman et al., "The Persuasive Power of AI Ingratiation: A Persuasion Knowledge Theory Perspective," 319–331.
8. Maslow, "A Theory of Human Motivation," 370–396.
9. Allport, *Pattern and Growth in Personality.*
10. Harvard Business Review (2024).
11. Zedelius, Müller, and Schooler, *The Science of Lay Theories How Beliefs Shape Our Cognition, Behavior, and Health.*

Chapter 1

1. Crowley, *Magic in Theory and Practice.*
2. Schaefer, *Belonging to the Brand. Why Community Is the Last Great Marketing Strategy.*
3. Tylor, *Primitive Culture.*

4. Durkheim, *The Elementary Forms of Religious Life.*

5. Bailey, *The Meanings of Magic. Magic, Ritual, and Witchcraft,* 1–23.

6. Ball, *The Book of Practical Witchcraft. A Compendium of Spells, Rituals and Occult Knowledge.*

7. Pradel and Casgha, *Haiti, la republique des morts vivants.*

8. Kotler, Kartajaya, and Setiawan, *Marketing 3.0. From Products to Customers, to the Human Spirit.*

9. Harris, "Embracing Make Believe Play and Theories of Childhood: Understanding Children's Spirituality and the Spiritual Essence of a Young Child," 12–21.

10. Subbotsky and Quinteros, "Do Cultural factors affect causal beliefs? Rational and magical thinking in Britain and Mexico," 519–543.

Chapter 2

1. Shermer, *Why People Believe Weird Things: Pseudoscience, Superstition, and Other Confusions of Our Time.*

2. Vyse, *Believing in Magic: The Psychology of Superstition.*

3. Wheen, *How Mumbo–Jumbo Conquered the World.*

4. Scheibe and Sarbin, "Towards a Theoretical Conceptualisation of Superstition," 143–158.

5. Devenport, "Superstitious Bar Pressing in Hippocampal and Septal Rats," 721–723.

6. Brugger, Dowdy, and Graves, "From Superstitious Behavior to Delusional Thinking: The Role of the Hippocampus in Misattributions of Causality, 397–402.

7. Shaner, "Delusions, Superstitious Conditioning and Chaotic Dopamine Neurodynamics, 119–123.

8. Nayha, "Traffic Deaths and Superstition on Friday the 13th," 2110–2111.

9. Hira, et al., "Influence of Superstition on the Date of Hospital Discharge and Medical Cost in Japan: Retrospective and Descriptive Study," 1680–1683.

10. Diamond, *Snake Oil and Other Preoccupations.*

11. Shermer, M. (1998). *Why people believe weird things: pseudoscience, superstition, and other confusions of our time*. New York, NY: W. H. Freeman & Co.

12. Tinbergen, "On Aims and Methods of Ethology," 410–433.

13. West, Griffin, and Gardner. "2007 Social Semantics: Altruism, Cooperation, Mutualism, Strong Reciprocity and Group Selection," 415–432.

14. Vyse, *Believing in Magic: The Psychology of Superstition*.

15. Keinan, "The Effects of Stress and Desire for Control on Superstitious Behavior," 102–108.

16. Malinowski, *Magic, Science, and Religion*.

17. Dudley, "The Effect of Superstitious Belief on Performance Following an Unsolvable Problem," 1057–1064.

18. Taylor, Harris Interactive.

19. Harvard Business Review (2023).

20. Roach, "Friday the 13th Phobia Rooted in Ancient History."

21. Dagnall, Parker, and Munley, "Assessing Superstitious Belief," 347—454.

22. Matute, Yarritu, and Vadillo, "Illusions of Causality at the Heart of Pseudoscience," 392–405.

23. Vyse, *Believing in Magic: The Psychology of Superstition*.

24. Albas and Albas, "Modern Magic: The Case of Examinations," 603–613.

25. Matute, Yarritu, and Vadillo, "Illusions of Causality at the Heart of Pseudoscience," 392–405.

26. Kramer and Block, "Conscious and Nonconscious Components of Superstitious Beliefs in Judgment and Decision Making, 783—793.

27. Harvard Business Review—The Failure Issue—April 2011.

28. Andrews, Nimanandh, Htun, and Santidhirakul, "MNC Response to Superstitious Practice in Myanmar IJVs, 1178—1201.

29. Harvard Business Review (2024).

30. Schaefer, Businessesgrow.com.

31. Bush, *Designing the Mind. The principles of Psychitecture*.

32. Sutherland, *Alchemy. The Dark Art and Curious Science of Creating Magic in Brands, Business and Life*, 136137.

33. Karsaklian, *Multicultural Marketing Is Your Story*.

Chapter 3

1. Twenge, Baumeister, Dewall, Ciarocco, and Bartels, "Social Exclusion Decreases Prosocial Behavior," 56–66.
2. Wang, Zhu, and Shiv, "The Lonely Consumer: Loner or Conformer?" 1116–1128.
3. Kuhn, Amlani, and Rensink, "Towards a Science of Magic," 349–354.
4. Verdet, *The Sky. Order and Chaos.*
5. Kuhn, *The Structure of Scientific Revolutions.*
6. Rensink, and Kuhn, "The Possibility of a Science of Magic, 1576.
7. Feyerabend, *Against Method.*
8. Harvard Business Review (2024).
9. Allport, *Pattern and Growth in Personality.*
10. Laz, *The alchemy of Your Dreams.*

Chapter 4

1. John, Pechmann and Chaplin, "Understanding the Past and Preparing for Tomorrow: Children and Adolescent Consumer Behavior Insights From Research in Our Field," 107–118.
2. Twenge, et al., "Worldwide Increases in Adolescent Loneliness," 257–269.
3. Ranganath, *Why We Remember. Unlocking Memory's Power to Hold on to What Matters,* p.27.
4. Scheibenreif and Raskino, *When Machines Become Customers.*

Chapter 5

1. Duani, Barash, and Morwitz, "Demographic Pricing in the Digital Age: Assessing Fairness Perceptions n Algorithmic versus Human-Based Price Discrimination, 257–268.
2. Scheibenreif and Raskino, *When Machines Become Customers.*
3. Harvard Business Review (2023).

Chapter 7

1. Thaler and Sunstein, *Nudge*.
2. Partridge, *The Power of Community*.
3. Harvard Business Review (2024).

Chapter 8

1. Singh, "Magic, Explanations, and Evil the Origins and Design of Witches and Sorcerers.
2. Wiseman and Watt, "Measuring Superstitious Belief: Why Lucky Charms Matter."
3. Jahoda, *The Psychology of Superstition*.
4. Newport and Strausberg, *Americans. Belief in Psychic and Paranormal Phenomena Is up Over Last Decade.*
5. Frazer, *The Golden Bough*.
6. Malinowski, *Magic, Science, and Religion*.
7. Vyse, *Believing in Magic*.
8. Hadjichristidis, Geipel, and Surian, "Breaking Magic: Foreign Language Suppresses Superstition, 18–28.
9. Shoda, Cervone, and Downey, *Persons in Context. Building a Science of the Individual.*
10. Kopalle and Lehmann, "Setting Quality Expectations When Entering a Market: What Should the Promise Be?" 8–24.
11. Oliver, "A Cognitive Model of the Antecedents and Consequences of Satisfaction Decisions, 460–469.
12. Oliver and Bearden, "Disconfirmation Processes and Consumer Evaluations in Product Usage, 235–246.
13. Kopalle and Lehmann, "The Effects of Advertised and Observed Quality on Expectations About New Product Quality," 280–290.
14. Goering, "Effects of Product Trial on Consumer Expectations, Demand, and Prices," 74–82.
15. Zeithaml, Berry, and Parasuraman, "Communication and Control Processes in the Delivery of Service Quality, 35–48.
16. Vyse, *Believing in Magic: The Psychology of Superstition*.
17. Case, Fitness, Cairns, and Stevenson, "Coping With Uncertainty: Superstitious Strategies and Secondary Control, 848–871.

18. Keinan, "The Effects of Stress and Desire for Control on Superstitious Behavior," 102–108.

19. Malinowski, *Magic, Science, and Religion*.

20. Kramer and Block, "Conscious and Nonconscious Components of Superstitious Beliefs in Judgment and Decision Making," 783–793.

21. Block and Kramer, "The Effect of Superstitious Beliefs on Performance Expectations," 161–169.

22. Moran, Weddingbells.ca.

23. Areddy, J.T. (2007). Chinese investors crunching numbers are glad to see 8s. *Wall Street Journal*, A1.

24. Kramer and Block, "Conscious and Nonconscious Components of Superstitious Beliefs in Judgment and Decision Making, 783–793.

25. Munoz, "When It Takes a Miracle to Sell Your House."

26. Andrews et al., "MNC Response to Superstitious Practice in Myanmar IJVs, 1178–1201.

27. Kristof-Brown, Schneider and Su, "Person-Organization Fit Theory and Research, 375–412.

28. Johnson, *God Is Watching You*.

29. Norenzayan, et al., "The Cultural Evolution of Prosocial Religions."

30. Purzycki et al., "What Does God know? Supernatural Agents' Access to Socially Strategic and Non-Strategic Information," 846–869.

31. Purzycki et al., "Moralistic Gods, Supernatural Punishment and the Expansion of Human Sociality," 327–330.

32. White et al., "Supernatural Norm Enforcement."

33. Norenzayan et al., "The Cultural Evolution of Prosocial Religions."

34. Watts et al., "Broad Supernatural Punishment But Not Moralizing High Gods Precede the Evolution of Political Complexity in Austronesia, 20142556.

35. Shariff et al., "Religious Priming," 27–48.

36. Yilmaz and Bahcekapili, "Supernatural and Secular Monitors Promote Human Cooperation Only If They Remind of Punishment," 79–84.

37. Purzycki et al., "Moralistic Gods, Supernatural Punishment and the Expansion of Human Sociality, 327–330.

38. Shariff and Norenzayan, "Mean Gods Make Good People," 85–96.

39. Karsaklian, E. 2023. *Multicultural Marketing Is Your Story*.

Chapter 9

1. Sutherland, *Alchemy: The Dark Art and Curious Science of Creating Magic in Brands, Business and Life.*

2. Ibid.

3. Maffesoli, *L'ombre de Dyonisos.*

4. Sutherland, *Alchemy: The Dark Art and Curious Science of Creating Magic in Brands, Business and Life*, 69.

5. Sutherland, *Alchemy: The Dark Art and Curious Science of Creating Magic in Brands, Business and Life.*

6. Ibid.

7. Sutherland, *Alchemy: The Dark Art and Curious Science of Creating Magic in Brands, Business and Life,*.113.

8. Maffesoli, *L'ombre de Dyonisos.*

9. Harvard Business Review, "The Year in Tech 2024."

10. Harvard Business Review, May/June 2024.

11. Bluvstein et al., "Imperfectly Human: The Humanizing Potential of (Corrected) Errors in Text-Based Communication," 3.

12. Harvard Business Review, March/April 2024.

13. Harvard Business Review, November/December 2023.

14. Wilde, *The Picture of Dorian Gray.*

15. Ranganath, *Why We Remember. Unlocking Memory's Power to Hold on to What Matters.*

16. Ruiz, *The Four Agreements*, 26.

17. Ruiz, *The Four Agreements,* 38.

18. Harvard Business Review, May/June 2024.

19. Ibid.

20. Mead et al., "Social Exclusion Causes People to Spend and Consume Strategically in the Service of Affiliation," 902–919.

21. Tajfel, "Social Identity and Intergroup Behavior," 65–93.

22. Berger et al., "Where Consumers Diverge From Others: Identity Signaling and Product Domains," 121–134.

23. Chan et al., "Identifiable but not Identical: Combining Social Identity and Uniqueness Motives in Choice," 561–573.

24. Escalas et al., "Self-Construal, Reference Groups, and Brand Meaning," 378–389.

25. Cialdini et al., "Social Influence: Compliance and Conformity," 591–621.

26. Terry et al., "The Theory of Planned Behaviour: Self-Identity, Social Identity and Group Norms," 225–244.

27. Bush, *Designing the Mind: The principles of Psychitecture*.

28. Harvard Business Review, March/April 2024.

References

Albas, D. and C. Albas. 1989. "Modern Magic: The Case of Examinations." *Sociological Quarterly* 30: 603–613. doi:10.1111/j.1533-8525.1989. tb01537.x.

Allport GW. 1961. *Pattern and Growth in Personality*. NY, New York: Holt, Rinehart and Winston.

Andrews, T.G., K. Nimanandh, K.T. Htun, and O. Santidhirakul. 2022. "MNC Response to Superstitious Practice in Myanmar Ijvs: Understanding Contested Legitimacy, Formal-Informal Legitimacy Thresholds and Institutional Disguise." *Journal of International Business Studies* 53: 1178–1201.

Areddy, J.T. 2007. "Chinese Investors Crunching Numbers Are Glad to See 8s." *Wall Street Journal*, A1.

Bailey, M.D. 2006. "The Meanings of Magic. Magic, Ritual, and Witchcraft." 1(1): 1–23. *DOI: 10.1353/mrw.0.0052.*

Ball, P. (2022). *The Book of Practical Witchcraft. A compendium of spells, rituals and occult knowledge*. Arcturus.

Berger, J., and Heath, C. (2007). Where consumers diverge from others: Identity signaling and product domains. *Journal of Consumer Research*, 34(2), 121–134.

Block, L and Kramer, T. (2009). The effect of superstitious beliefs on performance expectations. *Journal of the Academy of Marketing Science*. (2009) 37:161–169 DOI 10.1007/s11747-008-0116-y

Brugger, P., M.A. Dowdy, and R.E. Graves. 1994. "From Superstitious Behavior to Delusional Thinking: The Role of the Hippocampus in Misattributions of Causality." *Medical Hypotheses* 43: 397–402. doi:10.1016/0306-9877(94)90015-9.Bush, R.A. 2021. *Designing the Mind. The principles of Psychitecture*. DTM

Cannon, J.P., W.D. Perreault, and E.J. McCarthy. 2024. *Essentials of Marketing*, McGraw-Hill.

Case, T.I., J. Fitness, D.R. Cairns, and R.J. Stevenson. 2004. "Coping With Uncertainty: Superstitious Strategies and Secondary Control." *Journal of Applied Social Psychology* 34(4): 848–871. doi:10.1111/j.1559-1816.2004. tb02574.x.

Chan, C., J. Berger, and L. Van Boven. 2012. "Identifiable But Not Identical: Combining Social Identity and Uniqueness Motives in Choice." *Journal of Consumer Research* 39(3): 561–573.

Cialdini, R.B. and N.J. Goldstein. 2004. "Social Influence: Compliance and Conformity." *Annual Review of Psychology* 55: 591–621.

Crowley, A. 1936. *Magic in Theory and Practice*. Paris: Lecram Press

Dagnall, N, A. Parker, and G. Munley. 2009. "Assessing Superstitious Belief." *Psychological Reports* 104: 347–454.

Devenport, L.D. 1979. "Superstitious Bar Pressing in Hippocampal and Septal Rats." *Science* 205: 721–723. doi:10.1126/science.462183.

Diamond, J. 2001. *Snake Oil and Other Preoccupations*. London, UK: Vintage.

Duani, N., A. Barash, and V. Morwitz. 2024. "Demographic Pricing in the Digital Age: Assessing Fairness Perceptions in Algorithmic Versus Human-Based Price Discrimination." *JACR*, 9(3), pp. 257-268.

Dudley, R.T. 1998. "The Effect of Superstitious Belief on Performance Following an Unsolvable Problem." *Personality and Individual Differences* 26: 1057–1064. doi:10.1016/S0191-8869(98)00209-8.

Durkheim, E. 1995. *The Elementary Forms of Religious Life*. New York, NY: Free Press.

Escalas, J.E. and J.R. Bettman. 2005. "Self-Construal, Reference Groups, and Brand Meaning." *Journal of Consumer Research* 32(3): 378–389.

Feyerabend, P. 2010. *Against Method*. Verso.

Foster, K.R. and H. Kokko. 2009. "The Evolution of Superstitious and Superstition-Like Behavior." *Proceedings of the Royal Society* 276: 31–37.

Frazer, J.G. 1922. *The Golden Bough*. London: Macmillan.

Gardener, G. 2022. *The Meaning of Witchcraft*. Weiser Classics.

Goering, P.A. 1985. "Effects of Product Trial on Consumer Expectations, Demand, and Prices." The *Journal of Consumer Research* 12(1): 74–82. doi:10.1086/209036.

Hadjichristidis, C, J. Geipel, and L. Surian. 2019. "Breaking Magic: Foreign Language Suppresses Superstition." *Quarterly Journal of Experimental Psychology* 72(1): 18–28.

Harris, K.I. 2014. "Embracing Make Believe Play and Theories of Childhood: Understanding Children's Spirituality and the Spiritual Essence of a Young Child." *International Journal of Integrative Pediatrics and Environmental Medicine* 12–21.

Harvard Business Review—The Failure Issue—April 2011.

Harvard Business Review, Vol. 101, Issue 1—January/February 2023.

Harvard Business Review, Vol. 101, Issue 6—November/December 2023.

Harvard Business Review, Vol. 102, Issue 1—January/February 2024.

Harvard Business Review, Vol. 102, Issue 2—March/April 2024.

Harvard Business Review—The Year in Tech 2024—March 2024.

Harvard Business Review, Vol. 102, Issue 3—May/June 2024.

Hira, K., T. Fukui, A. Endoh, M. Rahman, and M. Maekawa. 1998. "Influence of Superstition on the Date of Hospital Discharge and Medical Cost in Japan: Retrospective and Descriptive Study." *British Medical Journal* 317, 1680–1683.

Jahoda, G. 1969. *The Psychology of Superstition*. Harmondsworth, England: Penguin.

John, D.B., C. Pechmann and L.N. Chaplin. 2024. "Understanding the Past and Preparing for Tomorrow: Children and Adolescent Consumer Behavior Insights From Research in Our Field." *Journal of the Academy of Consumer Research* 9(2): pp 107–118.

Johnson, D. 2015. *God Is Watching You: How the Fear of God Makes us Human.* New York, NY: Oxford University Press.

Kahneman, D. 2011. *Thinking Fast and Slow*. Penguin.

Karsaklian, E. 2023. *Multicultural Marketing Is Your Story*. Business Expert Press.

Keinan, G. 2002. "The Effects of Stress and Desire for Control on Superstitious Behavior." *Personality and Social Psychology Bulletin* 28(1): 102–108. doi:10.1177/0146167202281009.

Kim, S.S-E and D.R. Lehmann. 2024. "The Effect of Variety in Past Consumption on Openness to Personalized Recommendation Services." *JACR* 9(3): 297–305.

Kopalle, P.K. and D.R. Lehmann. 1995. "The Effects of Advertised and Observed Quality on Expectations About New Product Quality." *Journal of Marketing Research* 32(3): 280–290. doi:10.2307/3151981.

Kopalle, P.K. and D.R. Lehmann. 2006. "Setting Quality Expectations When Entering a Market: What Should the Promise Be?" *Marketing Science* 25(1): 8–24. doi:10.1287/mksc.1050.0122.

Kotler, P., H. Kartajaya, and I. Setiawan. 2010. *Marketing 3.0. From Products to Customers, to the Human Spirit*. Wiley.

Kramer, T. and L. Block. 2007. "Conscious and Nonconscious Components of Superstitious Beliefs in Judgment and Decision Making." *Journal of Consumer Research* 34: 783–793.

Kristof-Brown, A., B. Schneider, and R. Su. 2023. "Person-Organization Fit Theory and Research: Conundrums, Conclusions, and Calls to Action." *Personnel Psychology* 76(2): 375–412. https://doi.org/10.1111/peps.12581.

Kuhn, T.S. 1970. *The Structure of Scientific Revolutions,* 2nd ed. Chicago, IL: University of Chicago Press.

Kuhn, G., A.A. Amlani, and R.A. Rensink. 2008. "Towards a Science of Magic." *Trends Cognitive Science* 12: 349–354. doi:10.1016/j.tics.2008.05.008.

Laz, A. 2021. *The Alchemy of Your Dreams. A Modern Guide to the Ancient Art of Lucid Dreaming and Interpretation*. Penguin Random House.

Maffesoli, M. 2022. *L'ombre de Dyonisos*. Les Editions du Cerf.

Malinowski, B. 1954. *Magic, Science, and Religion*. Garden City, New York, NY: Doubleday.

Maslow, A.H. 1943. "A Theory of Human Motivation." *Psychological Review* 50(4): 370–396. https://doi.org/10.1037/h0054346.

Matute, H., I. Yarritu, and M. Vadillo. 2011. "Illusions of Causality at the Heart of Pseudoscience." *British Journal of Psychology* 102: 392–405. doi:10.1348/000712610X532210.

Mead, N.L., R.F. Baumeister, T.F. Stillman, C.D. Rawn, and K.D. Vohs. 2011. "Social Exclusion Causes People to Spend and Consume Strategically in the Service of Affiliation." *Journal of Consumer Research* 37(5): 902–919.

Moran, J. 2007. Weddingbells.ca. "Lucky Number Seven." www.weddingbells. ca/articles/article/lucky-number-seven.

Munoz, S.S. 2007. "When It Takes a Miracle to Sell Your House." *Wall Street Journal*. http://online.wsj.com/article_print/SB119370066239175607.

Nayha, S. 2002. "Traffic Deaths and Superstition on Friday the 13th." *American Journal of Psychiatry* 159: 2110–2111. doi:10.1176/ appi.ajp.159.12.2110.

Newport, F. and M. Strausberg. 2001. *Americans. Belief in Psychic and Paranormal Phenomena Is up Over Last Decade*. Princeton: Gallup News Service.

Norenzayan, A., A.F. Shariff, W.M. Gervais, A.K. Willard, R.A. McNamara, E. Slingerland, and J. Henrich. 2016. "The Cultural Evolution of Prosocial Religions." *Behavioral and Brain Sciences* 39: e1. doi: 10.1017/ S0140525X14001356.

Oliver, R.L. November 1980. "A Cognitive Model of the Antecedents and Consequences of Satisfaction Decisions." *Journal of Marketing Research* 17, 460–469. doi:10.2307/3150499.

Oliver, R.L. and W.O. Bearden. 1985. "Disconfirmation Processes and Consumer Evaluations in Product Usage." *Journal of Business Research* 13: 235–246. doi:10.1016/0148-2963(85)90029-3.

Partridge, H. 2018. *The Power of Community*. McGraw-Hill

Pradel, J. and J-Y. Casgha. 1983. *Haiti, la republique des morts vivants*. Rocher.

Purzycki, B.G., D.N. Finkel, J. Shaver, N. Wales, A.B. Cohen, and R. Sosis. 2012. "What Does God Know? Supernatural Agents' Access to Socially Strategic and Non-Strategic Information." *Cognitive Science* 36: 846–869. doi: 10.1111/j.1551-6709.2012.01242.x.

Purzycki, B.G., C. Apicella, Q.D. Atkinson, E. Cohen, R.A. McNamara, A.K. Willard, and J. Henrich. 2016. "Moralistic Gods, Supernatural Punishment and the Expansion of Human Sociality." *Nature* 530, 327–330. doi: 10.1038/ nature16980.

Purzycki, B.G. 2016. "The Evolution of Gods' Minds in the Tyva Republic." *Current Anthropology* 57, S88–S104. doi: 10.1086/685729.

Ranganath, C. 2024. *Why We Remember. Unlocking Memory's Power to Hold on to What Matters.* Doubleday.

Rapaille. C. 2006. *The Culture Code: An Ingenious Way to Understand Why People Around the World Live and Buy as They Do.* New York, NY: Broadway Books.

Rensink, R.A. and G. Kuhn. 2015. "The Possibility of a Science of Magic." *Frontiers in Psychology* 6:1576. doi: 10.3389/fpsyg.2015.01576.

Roach, J. 2004. "Friday the 13th Phobia Rooted in Ancient History." *National Geographic News.* http://news.nationalgeographic.com/news/2004/02/0212_040212_friday13.html.

Ruiz, D.M. 1997. *The Four Agreements.* Amber-Allen Publishing Inc.

Schaefer, M. 2023. *Belonging to the brand: Why Community is the Last Great Marketing Strategy.* US: Schaefer Marketing Solutions. Kindle.

Scheibe, K.E. and T.R. Sarbin. 1965. "Towards a Theoretical Conceptualisation of Superstition." *British Journal of Philosophical Science* 16: 143–158. doi:10.1093/bjps/XVI.62.143.

Scheibenreif, D. and M. Raskino. 2023. *When Machines Become Customers.* Gartner Inc.

Shaner, A. 1999. "Delusions, Superstitious Conditioning and Chaotic Dopamine Neurodynamics." *Medical Hypotheses* 52: 119–123. doi:10.1054/mehy.1997.0656.

Shariff, A.F. and A. Norenzayan. 2011. "Mean Gods Make Good People: Different Views of God Predict Cheating Behavior." *The International Journal for the Psychology of Religion* 21: 85–96. doi: 10.1080/10508619.2011.556990.

Shariff, A.F., A.K. Willard, T. Andersen, and A. Norenzayan. 2016. "Religious Priming: A Meta-Analysis With a Focus on Prosociality." *Personality and Social Psychology Review* 20 27–48. doi: 10.1177/1088868314568811.

Shermer, M. 1998. *Why People Believe Weird Things: Pseudoscience, Superstition, and Other Confusions of Our Time.* New York, NY: W.H. Freeman and Co.

Shoda, Y., D. Cervone, and G. Downey. 2007. *Persons in Context. Building a Science of the Individual.* Guilford.

Singh, M. 2021. "Magic, Explanations, and Evil the Origins and Design of Witches and Sorcerers." *Current Anthropology* 62(1). DOI: 10.1086/713111.

Subbotsky, E. and G. Quinteros. 2002. "Do Cultural Factors Affect Causal Beliefs? Rational and Magical Thinking in Britain and Mexico." *British Journal of Psychology* 83: 519–543. doi:10.1348/000712602761381385.

Sutherland, R. 2019. *Alchemy. The Dark Art and Curious Science of Creating Magic in Brands, Business and Life.* Custom House.

Tajfel, H. 1974. "Social Identity and Intergroup Behavior." *Society of Scientific Information* 13(2): 65–93.

Taylor, H. 26 February. 2003. "The Religious and Other Beliefs of Americans 2003." Harris Interactive. Harris Poll #11. Accessed July 14, 2008. www. harrisinteractive.com/ harris_poll/index.asp?PID_359.

Terry, D.J., M.A. Hogg, and K.M. White. 1999. "The Theory of Planned Behaviour: Self-Identity, Social Identity and Group Norms." *British Journal of Social Psychology* 38(3): 225–244.

Tinbergen, N. 1963. "On Aims and Methods of Ethology." *Journal—Z Tierpsychol* 20: 410–433.

Thaler, R.H. and C.R. Sunstein. 2021. *Nudge*. Penguin.

Twenge, J.M., R.F. Baumeister, N.C. Dewall, N.J. Ciarocco, and M.J. Bartels. 2007. "Social Exclusion Decreases Prosocial Behavior." *Journal of Personality and Social Psychology* 92(1): 56–66.

Twenge, J.M., J. Haidt, A.B. Blake, C. McAllister, H. Lemon, and A. Le Roy. 2021. "Worldwide Increases in Adolescent Loneliness." *Journal of Adolescence* 93: 257–269.

Tylor, E.B. 1958. *Primitive Culture*. New York, NY: Harper.

Usman, U., T. Kim, A. Garvey, and A. Duhachek. 2024. "The Persuasive Power of AI Ingratiation: A Persuasion Knowledge Theory Perspective." *JACR* 9(3): 319–331.

Valenzuela, A., S. Puntoni, D. Hoffman, N. Castelo, J. De Freitas, B. Dietvorst, C. Hildebrand, et al. "How Artificial Intelligence Constrains the Human Experience." *JACR* 9(3): 241–256.

Verdet, J-P. 1987. *The Sky. Order and Chaos*. New Horizons. Thames and Hudson.

Vyse, S.A. 2000. *Believing in Magic: The Psychology of Superstition*. Oxford, England: Oxford University Press.

Vyse, S.A. 1997. *Believing in Magic: The Psychology of Superstition*. Oxford University Press.

Watts, J., S.J. Greenhill, Q.D. Atkinson, T.E. Currie, J. Bulbulia, and R.D. Gray. 2015. "Broad Supernatural Punishment but Not Moralizing High Gods Precede the Evolution of Political Complexity in Austronesia." *Proceedings of the Royal Society B: Biological Sciences* 282: 20142556. doi:10.1098/ rspb.2014.2556.

Wang, J., R.J. Zhu, and B. Shiv. 2012. "The Lonely Consumer: Loner or Conformer?" *Journal of Consumer Research* 38(6): 1116–1128.

West, S.A., A.S. Griffin, and A. Gardner. 2007. "Social Semantics: Altruism, Cooperation, Mutualism, Strong Reciprocity and Group Selection." *Journal of Evolutionary Biology* 20: 415–432. doi:10.1111/ j.1420-9101.2006.01258.x.

Wheen, F. 2004. *How Mumbo–Jumbo Conquered the World*. New York, NY: Harper Perennial.

White, C.J.M., J.M. Kelly, A.F. Shariff, and A. Norenzayan. 2019. "Supernatural Norm Enforcement: Thinking About Karma and God Reduces Selfishness Among Believers." *Journal of Experimental Social Psychology.* https://doi.org/10.1016/j.jesp.

Wiseman, R. and C. Watt. 2004. "Measuring Superstitious Belief: Why Lucky Charms Matter." *The Parapsychological Association Convention.*

Wilde, O. 1992. *The Picture of Dorian Gray.* Wordsworth Classics.

Yilmaz, O. and H.G. Bahcekapili. 2016. "Supernatural and Secular Monitors Promote Human Cooperation Only If They Remind of Punishment." *Evolution and Human Behavior* 37, 79–84. doi: 10.1016/j.evolhumbehav.2015.09.005.

Zedelius, C.M., B.C.N. Müller, J.W. Schooler. 2017. *The Science of Lay Theories How Beliefs Shape Our Cognition, Behavior, and Health.* Springer

Zeithaml, V.A., L.L. Berry, and A. Parasuraman. 1988. "Communication and Control Processes in the Delivery of Service Quality." *Journal of Marketing* 52(2): 35–48. doi:10.2307/1251263.

About the Author

Eliane Karsaklian, PhD, HDR, is an unusual combination of big-picture thinker, academic, and practical businessperson. She has lived and worked in a number of countries during her career and has published several books about international marketing and international negotiation. Her last book *Multicultural Marketing is Your Story* describes the importance and impact of cultural communities in our lives and marketing. As an internationally known speaker and award-winning researcher, Dr. Karsaklian is currently a clinical professor at the University of Illinois Chicago. www.LinkedIn.com/in/ElianeKarsaklian

Index

www.ingramcontent.com/pod-product-compliance
Lightning Source LLC
Chambersburg PA
CBHW061149220326
41599CB00025B/4415